THE LIES WE WERE TOLD

Politics, Economics, Austerity and Brexit

Simon Wren-Lewis

BRISTOL
UNIVERSITY
PRESS

First published in Great Britain in 2018 by

Bristol University Press
1-9 Old Park Hill
BS2 8BB
UK
t: +44 (0)117 954 5940
www.bristoluniversitypress.co.uk

North America office:
Bristol University Press
c/o The University of Chicago Press
1427 East 60th Street
Chicago, IL 60637,
USA
t: +1 773 702 7700
f: +1 773-702-9756
sales@press.uchicago.edu
www.press.uchicago.edu

© Bristol University Press 2018

British Library Cataloguing in Publication Data
A catalogue record for this book is available from the British Library

Library of Congress Cataloging-in-Publication Data
A catalog record for this book has been requested

ISBN 978-1-5292-0213-7 paperback
ISBN 978-1-5292-0214-4 ePub
ISBN 978-1-5292-0215-1 Mobi
ISBN 978-1-5292-0553-4 ePdf

The right of Simon Wren-Lewis to be identified as author of this work has been asserted by him in accordance with the Copyright, Designs and Patents Act 1988.

The statements and opinions contained within this publication are solely those of the author and not of the University of Bristol or Bristol University Press. The University of Bristol and Bristol University Press disclaim responsibility for any injury to persons or property resulting from any material published in this publication.

Bristol University Press works to counter discrimination on grounds of gender, race, disability, age and sexuality.

Cover design by Liron Gilenberg
Front cover image: Getty
Printed and bound in Great Britain by TJ International, Padstow
Policy Press uses environmentally responsible print partners

MIX
Paper from
responsible sources
FSC® C013056

CONTENTS

LIST OF FIGURES AND TABLES

Figures

Tables

ACKNOWLEDGEMENTS

I should like to thank Chris Dillow, Mark Thoma and Paul Krugman for noticing what I was doing, and therefore encouraging me to continue, to my wife Jo who showed great tolerance of my oft-repeated phase 'I just need to finish this blog', and to Paul Stevens for many helpful conversations about this book.

PREFACE

In the years since the financial crisis, Simon Wren-Lewis has arguably been Britain's leading economic Cassandra. And I say this both in praise and in sorrow.

In the original Greek myth, after all, Apollo gave Cassandra the gift of true prophecy, but then cursed her by ensuring that nobody would ever believe her dire warnings. And so it has been with macroeconomics.

It's not widely appreciated, but basic, textbook macroeconomics – the kind of economics Wren-Lewis has been applying and trying to explain – has worked remarkably well since the crisis.

Thus, where many people were warning that central banks like the Bank of England or the Fed were courting runaway inflation by 'printing money', economists argued that this was no danger in a depressed economy; they were right. When many pundits warned that debt and deficits would send interest rates skyrocketing, economists argued that this wouldn't happen; they were right. And when politicians called for fiscal austerity to increase 'confidence', economists warned that this would deepen and prolong the slump; yet again, they were right.

And nobody would believe them.

On both sides of the Atlantic, the torch of economic truth was largely held aloft not by regular journalists – although there were a few, like Martin Wolf and, I hope, yours truly – but by economics bloggers. In America that meant people like Berkeley's Brad DeLong. In the UK it meant, above all, Wren-Lewis and his blog, *mainly macro*.

I've been following Simon's blog faithfully since he started it in 2012, both because of the depth and clarity of his analysis and because economic debate in the UK has provided an illuminating counterpoint to debate in the US. We had a broadly sensible administration hamstrung by divided government and a bizarre Beltway consensus that deficits were a more important problem than mass unemployment; you had unified government committed to bad ideas, cheered on by what Simon calls 'mediamacro'. Media malfeasance helped us stumble into the nightmare of Trump; it helped you stumble out of the European Union.

In this book Wren-Lewis collects a number of his plain-English blog posts in which he tried to debunk the myths driving UK economic policy – like the pervasive, utterly false myth that Labour profligacy made austerity necessary and inevitable. And he also collects a number of pieces in which he tried to understand why bad ideas persisted and all too often prevailed.

Reading these posts now is both an exalting and frustrating experience – exalting because they show just how good a good economist can be; frustrating because his warnings were ignored. In any case, this is a book you should read, for understanding what went wrong in the past is our only hope of doing better in the future.

Paul Krugman

TIMELINE

2007   June   Gordon Brown becomes UK Prime Minister after being Chancellor since 1997.

2009   Feb   President Obama signs American Recovery and Reinvestment Act, providing a large fiscal stimulus for US.

        April   Labour government's Budget shows the impact of the global financial crisis on the UK government's deficit.

2010   Jan   The European Commission condemns Greece for giving false data on its finances.

        Feb   First of many austerity packages to reduce Greek deficit.

        May   Eurozone members agree a bailout package for Greece.
UK general election leads to talks between Conservatives and Liberal Democrats, who then form a coalition government that includes more austerity than the Liberal Democrats campaigned for.

        Nov   The EU and Ireland agree to a bailout package to the Irish Republic.

2011   May   The Eurozone and the IMF approve a bailout package for Portugal.

        July   Second Eurozone and IMF bailout package for Greece.

	Dec	First post of mainly macro blog.
2012	Sept	ECB announces introduction of Outright Monetary Transactions (OMT).
2013	Jan	UK Prime Minister David Cameron announces that a future Conservative government would hold a referendum on EU membership.
	Feb	Moody's credit rating for UK government debt downgraded from AAA.
	April	Margaret Thatcher, former UK Prime Minister, dies.
	Sept	UK growth returns to historic trend after three years in the doldrums, and a *Financial Times* leader on the 10th declares 'Osborne wins the battle on austerity'.
	Dec	Widespread flooding in the UK.
2014	Sept	Scottish independence referendum: Yes 45% No 55%.
2015	Jan	Syriza win Greek elections and forms government.
	May	Conservatives win UK general election.
	July	Referendum in Greece rejects further austerity measures. Greek government forced to accept Troika conditions for rollover loans.
	Sept	Jeremy Corbyn wins Labour party leadership. John McDonnell announces formation of Economic Advisory Council.
2016	March	Labour announces their fiscal credibility rule.
	May	Sadiq Khan beats Zac Goldsmith to become mayor of London.
	June	EU referendum result: Leave 52% Remain 48%. Cameron resigns. Corbyn loses no confidence vote among MPs by 172 to 40.
	July	Theresa May elected Conservative leader and therefore becomes Prime Minister. Donald Trump confirmed as Republican candidate for President.
	Sept	Jeremy Corbyn beats Owen Smith to retain Labour leadership.

Nov   US general election: Donald Trump beats Hillary
        Clinton.
2017   June   UK general election: In a surprise result Theresa May
        fails to win an overall majority.

INTRODUCTION

At the end of 2011 I started writing my *mainly macro* blog. A key motivation was the poor standard of the public debate about austerity, and as a result most of my blog posts were designed to be read by non-economists. My own academic area includes the study of how changes in government spending and taxes influence the economy, and I knew that the models used by people in my field did not support the policies of the day. Yet this knowledge was rarely given a voice.

There are plenty of economists appearing in the media, but they tend to be City economists because they are much better at making up plausible stories about daily market movements. The financial crisis does not seem to have led the media to question how many of these stories are actually true. However, when it comes to policy issues like austerity City economists are generally more biased and less knowledgeable than academics. In addition, the excellent economists in the Institute of Fiscal Studies (IFS) are experts on the impact of specific taxes and benefits on individual behaviour (part of microeconomics), but not on how austerity might influence total output, employment and inflation (part of macroeconomics). It was this macroeconomic analysis that seemed absent from the public debate, and I hoped in 2011 that by taking the then unusual step of being a UK academic economist who blogs I could make a small difference.

My blog posts tried to explain, in non-technical terms, why the markets did not force the UK to undertake austerity, and why austerity would do serious damage to the economy. As the UK government would all too often point to the Eurozone as the reason why austerity was necessary, I started exploring the real reasons why the Eurozone crisis happened, which were rather different from those given in the media. Although at first I expected my blog posts to be mainly read by my students, I soon found myself interacting with blogging economists in the United States, and discovering that my posts were being read by those advising policymakers in the UK and international institutions such as the International Monetary Fund (IMF). But I also found that many non-economists were reading my blog because they had a desire for real expertise on macroeconomic issues explained in a non-technical way.

At first there was some disagreement between academic economists over austerity, although those that opposed austerity were always a majority. However, once it became clear by 2011/12 that the Eurozone crisis had no implications for other countries like the UK, and as output began to suffer as a result of austerity, the number of economists defending austerity dwindled. Despite this, the policy in the UK continued regardless and the Troika (European Commission, IMF and European Central Bank) in the Eurozone continued to impose ruinous austerity in Greece. As a result I found myself writing about the political economy of austerity: what were the real motives behind the policy, and why was it politically successful.

Part of the answer to the second question was how the media presented macroeconomic arguments. I created the term 'mediamacro' to describe how the media, encouraged by politicians, typically used household analogies when discussing austerity, like 'maxed out credit card'. The media ignored the fact that any first-year economics textbook will tell you that such analogies are completely inappropriate, and that in a recession the government should increase spending or cut taxes and not worry about the deficit. I asked why the media either ignored basic economics, or when occasionally it was acknowledged, treated knowledge as just an opinion, to be always balanced by an opinion that made little economic sense. It seemed as if broadcast media impartiality was becoming a bias against knowledge.

That politicians would try and pull the wool over people's eyes was not surprising. The idea that austerity was necessary because Labour had been profligate in government was powerful politically, which is why Conservative and Liberal Democrat politicians and the right-wing press pushed the idea for all it was worth. The only problem was that it was not true: Labour had not been profligate and the deficit was a result of the biggest recession since World War II. This fact was obvious from looking at the numbers, but it appeared as if no one in the media had ever looked at them. Because neither Labour nor the media challenged these politicians when they constantly repeated the 'clearing up the mess' line, it became something that many assumed to be true when it was in fact false, simply because the media allowed the claims of politicians to go unchallenged.

The failure of the broadcast media to stand up for truth and knowledge gives politicians little incentive to tell the truth. During the Scottish referendum campaign of 2014, nationalists dismissed gloomy estimates produced by widely respected bodies of what an independent Scotland's finances would look like as 'Project Fear', and that tactic came close to winning them independence. That tactic would be used again two years later by the campaign to leave the EU.

In between came the 2015 UK general election. Following the government's rhetoric, the media presented a picture of a strong economy. In reality the opposite was the case. The UK experienced the weakest recovery from a recession for over a century because of austerity, and flat productivity contributed to an unprecedented decline in real wages. Yet the economy appeared to be the government's strong card with the electorate, in part because the media went along with the government line that reducing the deficit rather than increasing living standards was the most important problem for policy. I argued at the time that the false picture of the economy created by mediamacro won the election for the Conservatives, and I still think that is correct.

The term mediamacro implies that there is a problem confined to how the media presents macroeconomics, and I could see that the broadcast media's reliance on City economists could create various biases. The EU referendum was more about the economics of international trade than macroeconomics. Among UK academics, for every economist who thought Brexit would be beneficial there were 22 who thought it would be costly in economic terms.[1] That is as close to unanimous as you will ever get in economics. Yet that unanimous opinion, echoed by the IMF and the Organisation for Economic Co-operation and Development (OECD), was always balanced in the broadcast media by an opposing opinion during the referendum. Voters would have had to work hard to know that what the broadcast media presented as balance was in fact anything but, and as a result I suspect many dismissed the warnings of economists, believing erroneously that the profession was divided.

This dismissal of expertise, by presenting it as just one more opinion by the broadcast media, was not confined to economics. Scare stories like Turkey joining the EU within 10 years were allowed to gain traction rather than being knocked down as ridiculous. The expertise of lawyers about what was possible was balanced against the fantasies of those on the Leave side. The outright lie of £350 million a week extra for the NHS was described by many in the media as 'contested'. The EU referendum became a paradise for politicians peddling lies and fantasies.

When the Leave side narrowly won the referendum, I described it as the triumph of the tabloids. The right-wing tabloid press had filled their pages for years with negative stories about immigrants, and in the months before the referendum these became stories about EU immigrants and the EU more generally. Their reporting about the EU would be better described as propaganda than news. Combined with a broadcast media that put balance above expertise or even truth, and you had a lethal combination that could persuade people to vote for something that would do them harm.

The conventional wisdom is that the partisan press in the UK, and the partisan media like Fox News in the US, has little influence on voters. I thought that unlikely in theory, but empirical proof was more difficult. Partisan media often claimed that they were only reflecting the views of their readers, rather than influencing those views. Yet recent studies by political scientists and economists have told a different story: this partisan media can have a powerful influence on voters and can easily swing elections and referendums.

The right-wing press in the UK and perhaps Fox News in the US would not be so effective in influencing voters if the non-partisan media provided a strong countervailing influence, constantly calling out falsehoods and giving time to facts and expertise. However, I have suggested that in practice, whenever an issue becomes political, the non-partisan media's ability or duty to inform and explain is replaced by an obsession with balance. This obsession can have the effect of devaluing expertise, because in short debates it is very hard for viewers to tell the difference between, say, a climate change scientist representing 97% of his colleagues and a smooth-talking and confident climate change denier.

After the Brexit vote, I wrote how I could see a similar thing happening in the US elections. Fox News pushed Trump of course, and as significantly pushed the image of 'crooked Hilary' which continues to this day. Yet the non-partisan media also talked incessantly about Clinton's emails, and devoted less time to policy questions and the many lies and failings of Donald Trump. In my view the combination of propaganda from sections of the media, and indifference to truth from the rest, played a key role in giving us both, Brexit and Donald Trump.

While the media is important in explaining how Brexit and Trump happened, they cannot explain why we are seeing both emerge now rather than 10 or 20 years ago. To do this requires a discussion of the political economy of neoliberalism and how it has evolved. This was not an area I had expected to write about when I started my blog and called it *mainly macro*, but when you see your own expertise and the expertise of others so completely dismissed by policymakers it becomes imperative to ask why this is happening.

In the last chapter of this book (Chapter 9) I discuss what neoliberalism is about, and how economics is essential to any critique of this ideology. Although neoliberalism may have started by promoting the market, it has increasingly been used to promote policies that reduce the size of the state and facilitate tax cuts for the wealthy. In too many countries the political right saw austerity as a way of reducing the state to an extent that went way beyond what was popular, but which could be achieved through the back door via manufactured concern about the deficit. The right also promoted an anti-immigration policy in part as a scapegoat for the impact of austerity.

To justify austerity and promote anti-immigration views among voters, the partisan media was essential. (In the US there is of course also the race card.) It is hard to get voters to support measures that benefit the wealthy elite over everyone else, so increasingly Conservatives and Republicans promoted socially conservative views to attract socially conservative left-leaning voters, and in the UK to prevent social conservatives more generally voting UKIP (UK Independence Party). As both policies involve deceit (over the true goals of austerity or over the true impact of immigration), expertise about what was really happening was not welcome. Michael Gove told us during the referendum campaign that people had become tired of experts, but it was really ideologues trying to pull the wool over people's eyes that found experts a nuisance.

The partisan media were essential to selling austerity and anti-immigration attitudes, but that also gave this media considerable power. We saw this media use its power to get a President elected whom the Republican hierarchy initially despised, and to bring down a Conservative government to achieve the Brexit that the media barons craved. In the final two posts in this book I argue that neoliberalism has overreached itself, and created with Brexit and Trump a form of authoritarian plutocracy that is a threat to pluralist democracy.

This book contains a selection of my blog posts from 2011 to 2017. As well as the issues discussed above, I have also included posts on the impact of austerity, the rise of Jeremy Corbyn and my brief time in John McDonnell's Economic Advisory Council, and how economists should influence economic policy more generally. The posts are organised into chapters, and each chapter has an introduction. In addition, some posts have preambles or postscripts to fill in any gaps in the narrative or to add information of interest. The posts have been selected so that each chapter tells a complete story. (Partly for that reason, I have included nothing about the post-referendum Brexit negotiations.)

When the idea for this book was first suggested to me I was sceptical. I could see how collecting a small percentage of my posts to tell a coherent story on different issues would save people time in going through everything I had written online. But I wondered whether a book written from scratch with the benefit of hindsight would be better. However, one of the features of all of the topics discussed in this book is that very little hindsight is required. For example, the majority of economists were against austerity from the start. Indeed, part of the message of this book is that the events of the last half-a-dozen years were entirely predictable consequences of poor policy and inadequate media coverage. To emphasise this, I have in each chapter ordered the posts by the date they were written. In addition, I believe there is a virtue in presenting an argument in a set of self-contained short posts, each of which does not require a memory of what had been written before.

I have slightly edited many of the posts for two main reasons. The first is where some text could easily be changed to improve comprehension. I have removed technical discussion that adds nothing to the argument unless you are an economist. The second is to remove many of the links to other blogs when they are not important for the text. One of the things I try to do in blog posts is link to posts by others who are also discussing an issue, because that kind of online conversation is how my own blog became known. However, links of this kind do not translate well to the printed page, so where they are not essential I have removed them from the text.

1

THE
MACROECONOMICS
OF UK AUSTERITY

Introduction

Most of these posts come from 2012. Austerity was in its third year, and the green shoots of economic recovery that had appeared in 2010 had died as a result. However, the policy continued.
My research was all about the impact of changes in government spending and taxes (fiscal policy) on the economy. I knew that cutting government spending just at the point at which the recovery should have started, when interest rates were still stuck at their lower bound, was the opposite of the policy recommended in textbooks and state-of-the-art macroeconomics. Post 1.1, and one of the first I wrote, removed the only sensible argument I could see for austerity. Any irrational behaviour by the financial market over buying government debt would be neutralised by the Bank of England's monetary policy.

Alas, the media preferred the vision of a powerful, dangerous and fickle financial market that I satirise in Post 1.3. There are of course other justifications put forward for austerity, and I try and deal with them all in Post 1.7. In hindsight the one with most durability is the 'burden on future generations' idea, which is discussed in Post 1.6. Post 1.9 is a takedown of part of a Cameron speech trying to justify austerity.

In 2013 Paul Krugman wrote of austerity: 'Its predictions have proved utterly wrong; its founding academic documents haven't just lost their canonized status, they've become the objects of much ridicule.'[1]

I shared that sentiment. But the cost of this policy mistake had been massive (see postscript to Post 1.9 for the overall cost), and despite the views of most economists the politics of austerity remained strong. When the UK economy started growing at last in 2013, even the Financial Times declared that 'Osborne had won the battle on austerity', much to my annoyance (Post 1.11). In the absence of any sensible economic arguments for the policy, my focus turned to why such a damaging policy had been enacted.

Some simple explanations could be easily disposed of. It was not just a forecast error (Post 1.2), or the fault of Gordon Brown (Post 1.4). Although many of austerity's supporters saw it as a means of getting a smaller state (Post 1.10) this was not the wish of a large majority of voters. Unfortunately, as Post 1.12 shows, austerity was not the first major macroeconomic policy error made by the Conservatives. Post 1.13, written in 2017, attempts to provide a comprehensive answer in hindsight for why austerity happened.

Austerity illustrates the gulf that can arise between what the majority of academic economists (correctly) advise and what is politically successful in the short term. Post 1.8 seems particularly prophetic in that regard.

Posts in Chapter 1

1.1
AUSTERITY IS NOT EVEN A SENSIBLE PRECAUTIONARY POLICY WHEN WE HAVE QUANTITATIVE EASING

Thursday, 22 December 2011

There is one very bad, possibly dishonest, argument for austerity today, and that is the idea that cutting government spending will have no impact on the economy, even though we are in a liquidity trap. A liquidity trap in this context is where the central bank thinks it cannot cut interest rates any further, so monetary policy cannot offset the effects of lower government spending. I normally attempt to debunk this argument by going through basic macroeconomic theory to show how, in a recession with unchanged interest rates, cutting government spending is bound to reduce aggregate demand and output.[2] The data backs up the theory when the empirics are properly done.

However, I have in the past had more respect for the following argument, which we might call the case for 'precautionary austerity'. Although there are good reasons why a rapid reduction in government debt is unnecessary, financial markets do not always behave rationally. There is a chance that markets might suddenly panic, and stop buying government debt, forcing up interest rates. As the cost of such an outcome would be very high, macroeconomic policy should do everything it can to avoid it – including reducing debt rapidly – even if that meant deepening the recession.

That is the argument. I was never convinced by it, partly because I think this risk is pretty small. It is certainly wrong to use the Eurozone crisis as evidence otherwise, for reasons explained below. I also agree with Jonathan Portes[3] that the musings of the credit rating agencies tell us nothing about market sentiment. However, Jonathan's post also made me wonder whether the precautionary austerity argument was simply wrong.

Jonathan and others make the argument that there is no way the UK (or US) government will ever default, because they will always prefer to make their central bank buy debt through printing money. While this seemed logical, I had worried about what would happen before this point. It is unlikely that the markets would stop buying debt at any price overnight. Instead, demand for UK government debt would be positive but less than supply, and so interest rates would begin to rise. If interest rates got quite high before the central bank was forced to print money, damage could still be done.

Quantitative Easing (QE) is the process by which, in the UK, the Bank of England buys government debt in an effort to reduce longer-term interest rates. At the moment, every month the Monetary Policy Committee reviews not just the level of short-term interest rates, but also the scale of QE. Suppose, therefore, that interest rates on government debt did start rising because the market started to panic, and yet the economy remained depressed and the outlook for inflation was benign. In these circumstances the Bank would buy government debt as part of its inflation targeting strategy. There would be no need for the government to instruct it to do so. In principle the same logic would apply to the US. If the central bank acted quickly in this way, any significant increase in interest rates would be counteracted by aggressive action by the central bank. Of course this action would involve printing money on a massive scale, but it would be temporary, and so it would not be inflationary.

We do not need to worry about a market panic because of Quantitative Easing. In a sense it is the counterpart to the argument that we have a Eurozone crisis because the ECB (European Central Bank) is so reluctant to act as a lender of last resort to governments. We can go further. Even when markets are behaving rationally, they don't just worry about the fundamentals (in this case the chances of default), but also what other market participants think. If you think there are enough people in the market who might panic, it is rational for you not to buy. But if you also know that there is a residual buyer who will never panic (the central bank), you can just focus on the fundamentals, which in this case includes how long QE will exist as an option. That in turn depends on the outlook for the economy. So QE is not only the fire engine that will put out the fire, it also reduces the chances of a fire occurring in the first place.

The fire engine analogy is often extended to include what economists call moral hazard: the idea that the existence of the fire engine makes house owners less cautious, so fires are more likely. But Quantitative Easing will disappear once the recovery is secure. The central bank will sell back all the debt it now owns, as Japan did in 2006. For this reason it does not remove the need for governments to control debt in the longer term. Instead it just allows them to be more flexible in the short term, while we are at the bottom of a severe recession.

There have been a number of studies trying to assess how effective QE has been in keeping long-term interest rates low. However, perhaps it has a more important precautionary role, which is to eliminate the possibility of a self-fulfilling panic in the government debt market. But if QE does this, why do we need deep austerity now to placate the markets?

POSTSCRIPT

This was the first post I wrote (the blog was just a week old) that got noticed by people I recognised: David Miliband in this case. This remains for me the most vivid personal example of the power of the internet. All I had done to publicise my blog was to include it in my email signoff and on my home page, and I didn't join Twitter for some years.

In terms of the post itself, in my view it put to rest the last justification for austerity left standing. Of course no one in the media ever made this connection between worries that the market might fail to buy government debt and Quantitative Easing, which I guess was why the post was of interest to others. In terms of evidence, no one has presented any that suggests the market was about to stop buying UK debt, and what actually happened is that interest rates on debt fell, suggesting plenty of demand. If you think that falling rates might be a result of austerity, you would then expect the 2010 election result to lead to lower rates, but it had no noticeable impact. All proponents of an imminent crisis have as evidence

*is the opinions of some City economists, and as I argue in Post
1.11, that is not a reliable source of evidence.*

1.2
POLICY ERRORS LIKE 2010 AUSTERITY –
WHAT CAN ACADEMICS DO?
Saturday, 18 February 2012

In an earlier post I claimed that 2010 should be counted as one of
the major errors of UK macroeconomic policy. In fact the claim is
much more general, because 2010 was the year that the consensus
among policymakers in the OECD area shifted from enacting
stimulus to pursuing austerity, with damaging consequences in many
countries. A number of comments and a couple of blogs added to
my speculation on why this error might have occurred. Here I want
to consider more generally what role academics and economists can
play in preventing policy errors, and why this may depend on the
reasons for those errors.

Before coming to that, let me address one common objection to my
view that 2010 was a major policy error at the time, and not just in
hindsight. The objection is that the slowdown in 2011 was due to
factors other than austerity that could not have been foreseen. There
are two problems with this argument. First, the projected speed of
recovery even before these adverse shocks occurred was pitifully slow.
What the IMF described in its 2010 Article IV Consultation[4] as 'solid
UK growth' was actually 2.5% per annum into the medium term,
which on its own admission only gradually closed the output gap.
The OBR's (Office for Budget Responsibility) June 2010 post-budget
forecast also had GDP growth of 1.2% in 2010, 2.3% in 2011, and
never above 3% thereafter. Considering GDP was estimated to have
fallen by 5% in 2009, this was a tepid recovery.

The second, and more important, flaw in this argument is that it
ignores the fact that good policy should allow for risks. Because of

the liquidity trap, or what economists call the zero lower bound for interest rates, there was no insurance policy if bad shocks did occur (as they did). In contrast, if positive shocks had led to a recovery that was too rapid, monetary policy could have been used to cool it down. To put it more simply, austerity was a huge and unnecessary gamble, and the gamble did not pay off. Much the same could be said for many other countries.

One class of explanation for this kind of policy error focuses on hidden agendas. The most obvious in the case of austerity is a desire to reduce the size of the state. As Mark Thoma has said: 'The notion of "expansionary austerity" was the cover, but so long as government shrinks as a result of the policy, the expansionary part is secondary.'[5] I put forward another, more mundane, explanation that is specific to the UK: get the cuts out of the way well before an election, and hope the electorate have short memories. Perhaps an explanation specific to the US might be that it suited those opposed to the President that the economy failed.

If this type of explanation is correct, is there anything that can be done to prevent or expose this kind of subterfuge? In an earlier post I was rather pessimistic. I suggested that it required near unanimity among academics before the media would begin to question the cover stories. Without unanimity, the cover story would just be described as controversial.

Brad DeLong has persistently railed against 'opinions on shape of the Earth differ' type reporting. All too often journalists appear to have only two categories: either something is objectively true or it is controversial. Anything controversial requires evenly balanced reporting. A tragic example from the UK would be the debate over the MMR vaccine. A single paper in *The Lancet* suggesting a link with autism was hyped by the media, despite widespread scepticism among health experts and overwhelming scientific evidence that the vaccine was safe. As a consequence, take-up of the vaccine declined and outbreaks of measles increased.

Even with academic unanimity, there is the possibility that moneyed interests could manufacture controversy through think tanks, as has happened with aspects of climate change debate. Of course, the debate is still worth having, but it is unlikely to change things very much or very quickly.

This pessimism may be a little overdone, however, in the case of austerity. Politicians, above all, want to be re-elected. For that reason the cover story view does require a belief that the harmful impact of (early) austerity will not last long enough for it to matter at the next election. If that is not the case, academics might be able to convince politicians that it may not be in their own interests to undertake the policy.

Which brings me to another class of explanation, which is policymakers fooling themselves. The hidden agenda may still be there, but the difference is that politicians convince themselves that the cover story is also true. In the case of austerity, there are a number of stories politicians can tell themselves. They can believe in expansionary austerity, of course. They could believe that Quantitative Easing will be enough, although I would hope any central banker would tell them that they had no idea what impact QE might have. They might have believed that the recovery was well underway, so any damage done by austerity would not be noticeable.

Does this case also require near unanimity among academics to convince the policymaker they are fooling themselves? There are at least two reasons to suggest it might. First, (macro)economics is not held in the same regard as other sciences, for good reason. I would not go quite as far as one comment which said scientists proclaim facts while economists give out opinions: I think we are somewhere in between these two, but still. Second, the two-way link between ideologies and economics makes it too easy for the politician to dismiss views they do not like by believing they are politically motivated, and it also makes it too easy for the politician to find academics who will tell them the stories they would like to hear.

A third class of explanation for policy mistakes is that they are genuine mistakes. Events may arise which come as a surprise to most academics as well as policymakers, so there is genuine uncertainty. In terms of 2010, I think the probability of Greek default with possible Eurozone contagion was important at changing attitudes among those who might otherwise have been sympathetic to more fiscal stimulus/less austerity. In the case of the UK, it may have been crucial in persuading Nick Clegg and the LibDems to support greater austerity as part of the coalition. What finance minister can sleep easy when there is a chance that they too might be forced down the road being travelled by Greece, Ireland, Spain, Portugal and Italy?

I would argue, following Paul De Grauwe,[6] that this crisis was a crisis of the Eurozone, and not the precursor to a generalised government debt panic. Although that view is gaining increasing acceptance as interest rates on government debt elsewhere continue to fall, at the time this proposition was neither obvious (governments with their own currencies default through inflation and depreciation, and lenders will fear that) nor widely argued.

In situations of this type, academics can in principle have much more influence. Furthermore, the blogosphere allows for an immediacy that might just be able to influence opinions before mistakes are made, and positions become entrenched. In the case of 2010 and austerity, I do not think it would have been enough. The political forces pushing for austerity, the hidden agendas, were too strong, and the panic induced by events in the Eurozone too great. But academics should never become so pessimistic about their potential influence that they give up trying.

POSTSCRIPT

I included this post because the argument that the failure of the UK to recover was down to unforeseen events and not austerity is frequently made. I also included it because it contains a degree of naivety about the influence of economists over political decisions when politicians do not want to listen. At the time I imagined that if almost all economists had been against austerity, rather than just a majority of economists, things might have been different. As Chapter 6 on Brexit relates, almost all economists were united on Brexit, but it made no difference.

1.3
THE FINANCIAL MARKET AS A VENGEFUL GOD
Friday, 6 April 2012

Reading a Jonathan Portes post,[7] I recalled a point in my undergraduate lectures where I have a little fun at the expense of economic pundits from the City. After explaining Uncovered Interest Parity (if you do not know what that is, it does not matter), I tell them that they can now immediately comment on how the foreign exchange market reacts to an increase in interest rates, whatever happens to the exchange rate. If the exchange rate appreciates, that is because domestic assets are more attractive. If the exchange rate does not change, that is because the interest rate increase was already discounted. If the exchange rate depreciates, well the markets were expecting a larger increase.

This is meant to make a serious point about the difficulties in testing this particular theory, but if I'm feeling mischievous I then point out that city pundits always seem to know with certainty why the markets have moved this way or that. Now in goods markets, firms pay market researchers serious money to find out why consumers are or are not buying their products, but in the financial markets this appears unnecessary. Despite market moves being made by thousands of trades and by thousands of people, the motivation for these trades appears clear. It is as if each trade is accompanied by the trader completing the following sentence: 'I bought/sold this currency today because …'. The truth, I reveal to my stunned audience, is that these pundits are just guessing based on no evidence whatsoever.

Of course city pundits have no reason to be honest. When asked 'why has the dollar appreciated?', I would like them to reply 'well no one really knows, but one possible factor might be...'. They never do. If I wanted to be unkind, I might suggest that these pundits want to appear like high priests, with a unique ability to understand the mysterious mind of the market. As high priests have discovered over and over again, if you can convince people that you have a direct line to an otherwise mysterious but powerful deity, you can do rather well for yourself. And sometimes financial markets can appear a bit like vengeful gods, capable of sudden acts of destructive anger that appear to come from nowhere.

If I wanted to ratchet up the unkindness I could go on as follows. It is in the priest's interest to tell the faithful that the god is indeed quite fickle in its mood, and while placid at the moment, it could turn nasty at the slightest provocation. Keep those offerings coming, to make sure that the god stays happy (and don't think about where those offerings go). If you are particularly generous, the priest will promise to give you the heads up if any changes in mood are imminent. If you cannot be a priest yourself, you can always set up as a financial advisor, who will tell people which priests have a better line to the financial market god.

OK, this is a bit silly, but sometimes when listening to policymakers you wonder whether they think this way. Having just gone through a recession largely caused by excessive overconfidence in the financial markets about the ability to manage risks, it is natural to think everything is down to confidence. However, in most situations I think markets and economies react in straightforward and understandable ways. The importance of confidence can be overdone, as it is often a symptom rather than a prime cause. To treat financial markets or the economy as a whole as always behaving like a vengeful god whose mood and confidence can ebb and flow at the slightest provocation is not the way to make good policy.

Jonathan's post also quotes Shakespeare, so how about this from *Julius Caesar*:

> Men at some time are masters of their fates;
> The fault, dear Brutus, is not in our stars,
> But in ourselves, that we are underlings.

1.4
FACTS AND SPIN ABOUT FISCAL POLICY UNDER GORDON BROWN
Monday, 20 August 2012

Figure 1.1 shows UK net debt to GDP from the mid-1970s until the onset of the global financial crisis (GFC). This post is about the right-hand third of this chart, from 1998 to 2007, which was the period during which Gordon Brown was Chancellor.

Figure 1.1: UK net debt as a percentage of GDP (financial years)

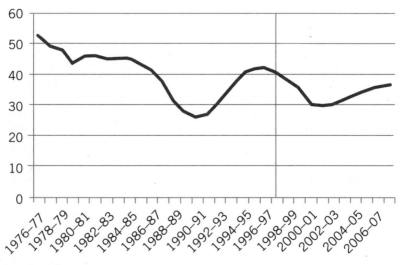

Source: OBR.

In general, looking at figures for debt can give you a rather misleading impression of what fiscal policy is doing, particularly over short intervals. However, having finished trawling through budget reports and other data for a paper I am writing, I can safely say that this chart tells a pretty accurate story. In the first two years of his Chancellorship, Brown continued his predecessor's policy of tightening fiscal policy. The budget moved into small surplus, so that the debt-to-GDP ratio fell to near 30% of GDP. Policy then shifted in the opposite direction, with a peak deficit of over 3% of GDP, a period which included substantial additional funding to the NHS. The remaining five budgets were either broadly neutral or mildly contractionary in the way they moved policy, but as this was starting from a significant deficit, the net result was a continuing (if moderating) rise in debt.

Why was fiscal policy insufficiently tight over most of this period? Despite what Gordon Brown said at the end of his term, I do not think this had anything to do with the business cycle. In one sense there is nothing unusual to explain: we are used to politicians being reluctant to raise taxes by enough to cover their spending, which leads to what economists call deficit bias. However this should not have happened this time because policy was being constrained by two fiscal rules designed to prevent this. So what went wrong with the rules?

The first answer is in one sense rather mundane. The rules, as all sensible fiscal rules should, tried to correct for the economic cycle. However, rather than use cyclically adjusted deficit figures, Gordon Brown's rules looked at average deficits over the course of an economic cycle. That allowed Brown to trade off excessively tight policy in the early years against too loose policy towards the end, and still (just) meet his rule. As we can see from the chart, debt ends up about where it started under his stewardship, which also roughly coincided with a full cycle.

Was this intended? The answer is to some extent not. This brings us to the second reason policy was too loose, and that is forecast error. One of the striking things about reading through the budget reports is how persistent these errors were. Outturns seemed always more favourable than expected over the first part of this period, until they became persistently unfavourable in the second. The former encouraged forecasters to believe that higher than expected tax receipts represented a structural shift, and they were reluctant to give up that view in the second period. Unlucky or an aspect of wishful thinking that is often part of deficit bias?

To their credit, the current Conservative-led government learnt from both these mistakes. Most notably, they set up the independent Office for Budget Responsibility with the task of producing forecasts without any wishful thinking. In addition, their fiscal mandate is also defined in terms of a cyclically adjusted deficit figure, which does not have the backwards-looking bias inherent in averaging over the past cycle. Their mistake is in trying to meet that mandate when the recovery had only just begun.

What this chart does not show are the actions of a spendthrift Chancellor who left the economy in a dire state just before the global financial crisis. He stopped being Chancellor with debt roughly where it was when he started, and a deficit only moderately above the level required to keep it there. The spin that our current woes are the result of the awful mess Gordon Brown left the UK economy in is a distortion based on a half-truth. The half-truth is that it would have been better if fiscal policy had been tighter, leaving debt at 30% rather than 37% when the recession hit. The distortion is that the high deficit and debt when Labour left office in 2010 were a consequence of the recession, and commendable attempts to limit its impact on output and employment.

POSTSCRIPT

I think it is worth amplifying the final paragraph, based on subsequent comments to this post. Many people think as follows. Even if most of the 2010 deficit was due to the recession and only a small part was the result of earlier deficits, if that small part had not been there it would have made austerity that much less painful. The mistake here is to think that reducing the deficit in a liquidity trap was inevitable. It is not, because the deficit reduction can be postponed until the recovery is well under way and the liquidity trap has gone. If you are not in a liquidity trap, reducing government spending need not lead to lower output because monetary policy can offset the negative demand impact of lower government spending.

As a result, the social welfare cost of the failure to reduce the deficit by around 1% of GDP in 2007 is a bit too much spending in 2007, and a bit too little whenever the liquidity trap is over. There are no aggregate effects on inflation or unemployment. This is why Labour's failure to reduce the deficit before the global financial crisis is a distinctly minor mistake.

This post was picked up by Jeremy Warner of the Daily Telegraph, in a piece with the headline 'Oh boy! There was nothing wrong with fiscal policy under Labour, says top economics prof'.[8] It was a typical hatchet job. I responded with a post on 20 June, where I think I gave as good as I got. I ended with these words:

> Yet some journalists really do believe the myth [of Labour profligacy]. How can they do so, when it is a myth that is easy to unravel? Well maybe the same way they can take a piece of text, and so obviously misrepresent what it says. The same way they can have a headline which is not just untrue, but which the headline writer knows is untrue.

It was enough to earn a more polite and courteous reply from Warner. Predator became prey a few months later in Post 1.10.

1.5
WHEN POLICY IGNORES EVIDENCE: BADGERS AND AUSTERITY
Monday, 15 October 2012

In the wood next to our house live at least one fox and maybe some badgers. We have seen badgers around, but it was only this summer that we first saw a badger walking (or more accurately sniffing) its way through our garden. It caused great excitement. On a walk from our house is someone who keeps on their smallholding a small number of alpacas. Except the last time we passed two were missing. They had been put down, because they had tested positive for TB. The risk that the others, and nearby cattle, might get the disease was too great. Tragically, autopsies found no trace of TB: the initial tests are not 100% accurate.

Badgers get, and spread, TB. As a result, the UK government is about to begin a large-scale cull of badgers in Gloucestershire and Somerset. No one likes the idea of killing badgers. But cattle (or occasionally alpacas) dying from TB is no fun either. So the badger cull is just one of those necessary bad things that have to be done to prevent something even worse happening. Environmentalists are up in arms, but that is just because badgers look cute and cattle do not.

Except that is not what the evidence suggests. Following various small-scale randomised badger-culling trials, the UK government set up an independent group of scientists (the ISG) to evaluate the evidence. In 2007 the government published the report. It concluded as follows:

> The ISG's work – most of which has already been published in peer-reviewed scientific journals – has reached two key conclusions. First, while badgers are clearly a source of cattle TB, careful evaluation of our own and others' data indicates that badger culling can make no meaningful contribution to cattle TB control in Britain. Indeed, some policies under consideration are likely to make matters worse rather than

better. Second, weaknesses in cattle testing regimes mean that cattle themselves contribute significantly to the persistence and spread of disease in all areas where TB occurs, and in some parts of Britain are likely to be the main source of infection. Scientific findings indicate that the rising incidence of disease can be reversed, and geographical spread contained, by the rigid application of cattle-based control measures alone.[9]

On 14 October 2012, 30 eminent UK and US scientists published a letter in the *Observer*. They write: 'As scientists with expertise in managing wildlife and wildlife diseases, we believe the complexities of TB transmission mean that licensed culling risks increasing cattle TB rather than reducing it.'[10] One of the signatories described the government's policy as crazy, and suggested vaccination and biosecurity was a better solution. The *Guardian* reports the chair of the ISG as saying: 'I just don't know anyone who is really informed who thinks this is a good idea.'[11] The current government chief scientist said: 'I continue to engage with Defra [the relevant government ministry] on the evidence base concerning the development of bovine TB policy. I am content that the evidence base, including uncertainties and evidence gaps, has been communicated effectively to ministers.' In other words, ministers know what scientists are saying and have decided to ignore them.

So what is going on? One of the strongest pressure groups in the UK is the National Farmers' Union (NFU), and many of their members naturally care a great deal about the health of cattle. To say that the NFU has a strong influence on policy at Defra is a bit like saying that the position of the sun has a strong influence on whether it is night or day. The NFU are convinced that culling badgers will reduce the incidence of TB in cattle, and government policy is following that belief, rather than the scientific advice it commissioned. The BBC reports Defra Minister David Heath as saying: 'No-one wants to kill badgers but the science is clear that we will not get on top of this disease without tackling it in both wildlife and cattle.'[12] Dare I say weasel words.

I would not be the first to draw a link between research and evidence in epidemiology and macroeconomics. Neither is a science where experiments can be easily devised to definitively prove ideas right or wrong. In both fields evidence can be messy. With austerity we did not have randomised trials: we had one almost globalised trial, starting in 2010, and one 80 years earlier during the Great Depression. The evidence this time round is becoming clear: the harmful effects are much greater than many had assumed.

As I know about macroeconomics rather than epidemiology, I'm tempted to think the policy on badgers is the greater political sin. I'm all too aware of the conflicting messages the academic community have been giving policymakers. Although TB in cattle is an emotionally charged issue, I doubt that it attracts the ideological baggage that seems to infect macro. However, perhaps the two cases are not so different. The problem with austerity is that too many people of influence just know that high government debt is always and everywhere a bad thing. Too many think it is just obvious that when a Eurozone country has difficulties in selling debt that must imply cutting it back as quickly as possible, in the same way that it is obvious that killing badgers must reduce the spread of TB. And perhaps too many people see badger culls as part of a battle between farmers and environmentalists, just as austerity is a weapon in a battle over the size of the state.

Maybe we are just naive in thinking that as the evidence against austerity accumulates the policy will change. Unfortunately the influence of academics on policy is much weaker than many imagine. While I would never advocate a totally uncritical acceptance of the views of scientists, we are an awfully long way from that position, as unfortunately many badgers are about to find out.

1.6
AUSTERITY, DEBT BURDENS AND HYPOCRISY
Sunday, 21 October 2012

After the weekend march against UK austerity, I saw a government minister on TV justifying their fiscal plans. One of the arguments he used was that it was necessary for the sake of our children. In these circumstances I can quite understand the urge to dismiss such arguments as invalid. Part of this urge comes from knowing that, in many cases, the argument about debt being a burden on future generations represents simple hypocrisy.

How do I know this? Because often exactly the same people championing austerity also argue that we cannot take action to reduce future climate change because the current costs will be too great. The UK government's spin was that it would be the greenest government ever, but its policy is quite the opposite. The Republican Party in the US also resists any action to reduce climate change because of the current costs of doing so (at least when they are not denying climate change exists). The connection? Both issues involve trading off costs to the current generation (austerity, measures to reduce climate change) with costs to future generations (higher taxes, climate change itself). If you really believe that we must reduce debt right now (rather than after the economy has recovered) because of the impact debt will have on future generations, then you should also be doing everything you can right now to reduce carbon emissions.

But just because some of those who use the 'we are doing it for our children' argument to justify today's austerity are doing so hypocritically does not mean the argument is wrong. However, although concerns about intergenerational equity are valid, they are unlikely to be critical to the austerity debate. Probably most major economic issues involve some element of redistribution, and in practice the device of compensating the losers is not an option. Take monetary policy, for example. We currently have low real interest rates, which benefits some but harms others. Do we let the fact that savers are worse off as a result of this policy hinder the central bank from keeping interest rates low? Of course not.

In the case of reducing debt today through austerity, there are other factors which have distributional consequences going in the other direction. To the extent that we have austerity through lower investment in infrastructure or education, it is the young more than the old who will be hurt by this policy. As important, high unemployment among the young today can have lasting effects on their welfare, and their children's welfare. More generally, persistent effects of this kind can mean that an entire future generation may be worse off as a result of austerity.

So it is not that 'burden of debt' arguments are always wrong, but that they are just not that important in the context of the current austerity debate. The welfare loss to future generations of delaying debt reduction by 10 years is small relative to the massive loss of resources and welfare caused by austerity today. If we are worried about future generations, a far cheaper way of helping them is to take action to mitigate the impact of climate change.

1.7
BEING RUDE ABOUT AUSTERITY
Sunday, 4 November 2012

PREAMBLE

Just when you think you have refuted one justification for austerity, another pops up. Sometimes the one that pops up is the same as one you refuted some time ago. One of those justifications was that austerity would increase confidence, and greater confidence would increase output. It was a completely circular argument, because confidence would only increase if austerity was good for the economy, which of course it is not. So

I wrote an all-purpose list of possible justifications for austerity and (very briefly) why they are wrong. It is designed to apply to all countries, not just the UK. Inevitably the brevity has costs: for periphery Eurozone countries, for example, I should have noted that the ECB through its inactivity put them in this position, as Chapter 2 explains.

How rude should I be about policymakers? Some may think this a strange question, but I personally have quite a high regard for them. Having spent some of my formative years working in government, I can certainly appreciate the difficulties they face. Sure, there are unspoken (in public) political imperatives that drive a lot of policy, but I don't think politicians' public concern with social welfare is entirely a façade, and it is certainly not among most of those who work for them: quite the opposite, in fact. So when I wrote the following about belief in the confidence fairy, I did worry I was allowing rhetoric to get the better of me.

Now to believe in fairies you need pretty good evidence, and that is just what we do not have. A few economists think they saw some in the data, but that is not enough – nothing like enough – to justify inflicting this scale of pain on so many. Most other economists saw nothing. Unfortunately too many people just wanted to believe in the confidence fairy. Normally we find those who really do believe in 'real' fairies either rather amusing or rather strange. Unfortunately some of those who believed in the confidence fairy were put in charge of running our economies.

Now, in mitigation, I have to say that the 2010 switch from fiscal expansion to austerity does make me very angry. I'd like to think that this is just because of the immense harm it is doing, but there is something else as well. It represents the abrogation of knowledge: knowledge which, largely through accident, I was particularly aware of. I think this is something that even economists who are not macroeconomists, and not just non-economists, do not fully appreciate. In the mid-2000s my main research was on monetary and fiscal policy interactions, and this was a field that appeared to be characterised by considerable common ground, and certainly not by alternative 'schools of thought'. Some of this knowledge began to be applied in 2008/9, and even an institution like the IMF, which was famed for its fiscal conservatism, was quite happy applying that knowledge.

It is as if you are a doctor, treating a patient with proven but also state-of-the-art medication. The patient is not well but the treatment you are applying is working. Then suddenly the hospital administrator tells you to stop, because the drugs are expensive and they would like to try some spiritual healing instead. And, in case you ask, the financial crisis did not suddenly render the sum of macroeconomic knowledge accumulated over the previous decades obsolete (whether embodied in textbooks or state-of-the-art models).

But in a sense all this makes trying to be dispassionate about the reasons for the switch to austerity all the more important. So here is a list. I give them marks out of 10, where the lower the mark the more rudeness is justified.

'Our government cannot sell any debt.' Here I draw a sharp distinction between those in the Eurozone periphery, and those outside. For those inside, I think the choice between austerity and default (there was no other option) was very difficult, and I would only have minor criticisms: sometimes a failure to adopt the right fiscal mix, sometimes going further than was necessary, and sometimes being naive about the position and motivation of their creditors (perhaps through collective guilt). So 8/10: rudeness not appropriate. For those outside these countries (UK, US, many in the ECB, Commission and Germany), a very different assessment – see below.

'After Greece, it could be anyone next' or more simply **'Panic!'** Many policymakers convinced themselves that markets, in refusing to buy certain countries' debt, were behaving irrationally – after all, we had just had a financial crisis where they also seemed to behave in this way (either before, or during, or both). In these circumstances, 'confidence' becomes the word of the moment, and appeasement to a particular reading of market sentiment understandable (although still wrong). Here I give (6−2x)/10, where x is the number of years after 2010. I can forgive policymakers being confused in the panic of 2010, but by 2011 we understood much better what was going on, and the evidence by 2012 that this was a particular Eurozone problem generated by ECB behaviour became so clear that even the ECB understood. (As you can see, 2/10 means I can be rude!)

'We want our money back.' A reason that is only relevant to those who lent to certain Eurozone economies. A common enough human motive, generally coupled with a belief that creditors bear no responsibility for properly assessing risk. Not a good way to lend money (see 2007/8 and earlier), and certainly not a good basis for macroeconomic policy. Also largely self-defeating, as Chapter 2, Post 2.4 suggests. Does not deserve a mark.

'The recovery is well under way, so now is the time to deal with debt.' What this argument has going for it is that at some point it becomes correct. In addition there are policy lags, and forecasting is difficult. But it is also true in macro that timing is everything. The argument was wrong in 2010, because it failed to take seriously the asymmetric nature of the consequences of forecast errors (see Post 1.2). So (6−3x)/10. By now those who advocated austerity on this basis should have changed their minds, which some have done, to their credit (and I mean that − it is difficult to admit mistakes).

'Monetary policy can take care of demand.' What I have called zero lower bound denial. There is perhaps some evidence that this belief was part of the UK Conservative Party mindset, but I think it is more prevalent among some bloggers, or economists who are not macroeconomists or who 'missed' the lost decade in Japan and who thought the Great Depression was just history. There, I've revealed my mark by my language again: 2/10. A slight variant in the UK is 'without austerity, interest rates would have been higher because inflation would have been higher', which owes a great deal to hindsight (and higher VAT).

'We need to reduce the size of the state' (apart, perhaps, from the bit that buys military hardware). 0/10, not for the belief itself (that is mostly politics, with very little macro), but for duplicity. Less than 0/10 for the variant that says what the state does in another country is a waste of money, because even if it happens to be true it combines duplicity with imperialism.

'What aggregate demand problem?' or more succinctly demand denial. A strange belief that supply creates its own demand, which is obviously incorrect in a monetary economy but which resurfaces from time to time. 0/10.

'Reducing debt is virtuous.' I hesitate to include this, because I do not seriously think any policymakers actually believe it (they are often the same people who happily spend or cut taxes in a boom). The macroeconomics is obviously silly. Not everyone can run a budget surplus (so 0/10). Unfortunately this kind of economics as morality does seem to influence some people. The argument that 'we cannot waste any time tackling the problem of debt' faces similar problems.

So there you have it, and yes, I do feel much better having written this all down. But will it stop me being rude in the future?

1.8
THE FINAL VERDICT ON GEORGE OSBORNE AS CHANCELLOR
Saturday, 23 February 2013

This may well turn out to be the low point in the political fortunes of George Osborne. Of course the loss of Moody's AAA means nothing whatsoever. His opposite number Ed Balls gets it right:

> It would be a big mistake to get carried away with what Moody's or any other credit rating agency says. Tonight's verdict does not change the fact that the credit rating agencies have made major misjudgements over recent years, not least in giving top ratings to US sub-prime mortgages before the global financial crash. But what matters is the economic reality that the credit rating agencies are responding to. Moody's themselves say the main driver of their decision is the weak growth in Britain's economy.[13]

For the Chancellor, from now on things may start to get better, if only because they have become so bad. The UK may just avoid a triple dip recession, and may even grow at more than the snail's pace predicted by forecasters. Any growth will be talked up as if it is a new dawn, and people will want to forget the last few years as quickly as they can. This may even be enough to see a Conservative government elected in 2015. In that case, George Osborne as politician will be vindicated. But this blog is about economics (mainly). As far as macroeconomics is concerned, nothing that will come can repair the damage that has been done over the last two-and-a-half years. Hence the finality of my title.

It would be foolish to argue that all of the UK's economic woes are down to its Chancellor. The financial crisis has generated some particular problems for the UK, which most Chancellors of the Exchequer would have struggled with. What George Osborne did with his austerity programme was the equivalent of putting a sick patient on a starvation diet accompanied by cold showers. The UK economy without accelerated austerity would still have been in poor shape, but under George Osborne it has been a disaster.

It is perhaps telling that the best we can say for the record of the last two-and-a-half years is that maybe the statisticians have got the numbers wrong. Maybe more of nominal GDP growth is real and less is inflation. Without such a major rewrite of the data, the record is dismal. Effectively no growth, during a period in which we would normally expect a significant recovery, a recovery that had already begun before he took over. Those who say that the employment numbers are not so bad completely miss the point (journalists please note): if the numbers are right it seems that productivity and the supply side of the UK economy have also stalled in the last few years, implying that the loss of output could even be permanent. A temporary loss of output (and the increase in unemployment or lower real wages that goes with it) is bad enough, but to permanently reduce output forever is some achievement. For once, the word disaster is not an exaggeration.

What about that terrible legacy the previous government had given him, which he never fails to mention? Absolute nonsense. The record of the previous government was far from perfect, but they did not create a horrible mess that he had to put right. What about the debt crisis? The panic of 2010 might have justified promises of future austerity, perhaps with immediate action which demonstrated intent in ways that did least harm to aggregate demand. When I was asked by one of his advisors what this might involve, I suggested temporarily raising estate taxes (death duties) – what better way to show you are deadly serious about reducing the deficit than doing something that had big political costs for you, but with a relatively small impact on demand? Yet for a Chancellor where politics is key, what we got instead was front-loaded austerity, which even Nick Clegg has recently acknowledged[14] was in areas that did maximum damage to the economy.

After the panic of 2010 was over, when it became clear that the debt crisis was really a Eurozone crisis and UK long-term interest rates declined with the fortunes of the economy, we should have had a major change of policy. There were many possibilities besides conventional stimulus, such as balanced budget fiscal expansion (higher government spending and tax increases, which if both are temporary increases output), or changes to the monetary policy regime. But these would all have involved political costs, so instead we had short-term tinkering coupled with the prospect of more austerity beyond the next election.

Can he blame the advice of others? Sure there was bad advice from some influential quarters, but there were also plenty (a majority, indeed) of reputable economists who correctly warned of the dangers the policy involved. So austerity was always a gamble: a gamble that the UK economy was strong enough to be able to offset the undoubted negative impact of accelerated austerity. It was not.

So what was the prize that led to this gamble? Again it had little to do with macroeconomic policy. As Paul Krugman has pointed out many times, the 'debt problem' is seen by many on the right as a useful cover to reduce the size of the state. Seen through this lens, the details of the austerity programme make much more sense. A focus on demand 'rich' items like investment, local authority spending and welfare, and avoiding temporary increases in taxes that have a much lighter demand impact? This makes sense because the aim is to permanently reduce the size of the state. George Osborne was prepared to take a gamble with the economy for political ends.

Of course all Chancellors are politicians. Most would take small liberties with the macroeconomics to gain political advantage: for example before 1997 by delaying raising interest rates until after the party conference, or after 1997 by being a little too optimistic about tax receipts to minimise unpopular tax increases. However, in most cases these are the equivalent of minor indiscretions, which do not fundamentally alter the fortunes of the economy. The centrepiece of Osborne's strategy was accelerated austerity for political ends, and it stopped the recovery dead.

So my final verdict on George Osborne? He is a political tactician who time and again has put party political gain ahead of the economic interests of the economy. We see this in many 'small' things, like the details of his budgets, to more important things, like his support for government policy on immigration or Europe. It is defined by both what he has not done (total inaction on monetary policy, where unlike others he has considerable power), as well as what he has done (accelerated austerity). The politics may still come good for him, but the damage to the UK economy his action and inaction has caused is final.

POSTSCRIPT

When I wrote the second paragraph of this post I was probably hoping it would not be true, but unfortunately I was being unusually prescient. With the benefit of the hindsight of half-a-dozen years, I do not think I would change one word of this post. That someone who caused so much harm (see Post 1.9) should end up editing London's major newspaper tells you much about the UK at the moment.

1.9
LOOKING FOR A ROBUST DEFENCE OF AUSTERITY
Thursday, 7 March 2013

So, driving home today, I was told by the BBC that the Prime Minister had just made a 'robust' defence of his government's economic policies. One definition of robust (for an object) is 'sturdy in construction'. Well, let us see, by looking at some of the sections discussing the fiscal strategy.[15]

(1) 'First, the deficit. This deficit didn't suddenly appear purely as a result of the global financial crisis. It was driven by persistent, reckless and completely unaffordable government spending and

borrowing over many years. By 2008, we already had a structural deficit of more than 7 per cent – the biggest in the G7.'

UK GDP fell by 1% in 2008. In the financial year 2007/8, the cyclically adjusted budget deficit according to the OBR was 1.6% of GDP. As I explained in Post 1.4, probably a little too high, but hardly 'reckless and completely unaffordable'.

(2) 'There are some people who think we don't have to take all these tough decisions to deal with our debts. They say that our focus on deficit reduction is damaging growth. And what we need to do is to spend more and borrow more. It's as if they think there's some magic money tree. Well let me tell you a plain truth: there isn't.'

People and companies borrow all the time. I do not think they believe in a 'magic money tree'. People and firms borrow more when the cost of borrowing is very cheap – that is common sense. The government is trying to encourage individuals and firms to borrow more. So why is it good for the private sector to borrow more to invest in good projects when the cost of borrowing is cheap, but when the government does the same thing it involves believing in magic?

(3) 'As the independent Office for Budget Responsibility has made clear ... growth has been depressed by the financial crisis ... the problems in the Eurozone ... and a 60 per cent rise in oil prices between August 2010 and April 2011. They are absolutely clear that the deficit reduction plan is not responsible. In fact, quite the opposite.'

If this were true, then one would seriously wonder about the competence of the OBR. There has been much recent debate about the size of multipliers, but not the sign: greater austerity almost certainly reduces growth. The theoretical plausibility and empirical evidence for expansionary austerity is practically zero. However, as far as I am aware, the OBR has never said that austerity has had no impact on growth. What they have talked about is why growth has been lower *than they expected* back in 2010. As they had austerity built into their forecasts of 2010, then they have naturally looked elsewhere for events they were not expecting. So this statement deliberately misrepresents what the OBR has been saying, to imply that the OBR believes in expansionary austerity. But the Prime Minister knows that the OBR will let this misrepresentation of its views pass – which is a shame.

(4) 'Last month's downgrade was the starkest possible reminder of the debt problem we face. If we don't deal with it … interest rates will rise, homes will be repossessed and businesses will go bust…'

Interest rates might rise if the markets thought that the UK government might default on its debt or if the UK was about to enter an inflationary spiral, but there is no sign of that (in fact, quite the opposite), for very good reasons.

(5) 'So those who think we can afford to slow down the rate of fiscal consolidation by borrowing and spending more are jeopardising the nation's finances … and they are putting at risk the livelihoods of families up and down the country. Labour's central argument is exactly that. They say that by borrowing more they would miraculously end up borrowing less. Let me just say that again: they think borrowing more money would mean borrowing less. Yes, it really is as incredible as that. The Institute of Fiscal Studies has completely demolished this argument.'

The argument that by borrowing more you may end up borrowing less has been set out in DeLong and Summers (2012).[16] If you search for references to these authors on the IFS website, or for both on Google, nothing comes up, so I do not know what demolition is being referred to here.

(6) 'But we are making the right choices. If there was another way I would take it. But there is no alternative.'

The resort to TINA is the ultimate 'reveal': if the arguments for the policy being pursued have been lost, the evidence is stacking up against you, and there are plenty of perfectly feasible alternatives, then assert as dogmatically ('robustly') as possible that you are pursuing the only possible path.

POSTSCRIPT

Occasionally I have used my blog to 'take apart' political speeches, so I thought I should include one in this volume. But there is also an interesting coda to my point (3) above. Shortly after I published this post, the OBR's Director Robert Chote wrote a letter to the Prime Minister in which he said: 'For the avoidance of doubt, I think it is important to point out that every forecast published by the OBR since the June 2010 Budget has incorporated the widely held assumption that tax increases and spending cuts reduce economic growth in the short term.'

It was intended to be a rebuke, and was seen that way in the press. Whether the letter had anything to do with my blog post I have no idea. However, by then I knew many people within the UK's economic institutions read my blog, so it is not entirely impossible that there was some connection, and to some extent what I wrote in (3) was a deliberate provocation.

In posts not included here I used the OBR's assessment of the impact of austerity to calculate a lower bound for the total amount of resources lost because of austerity: £4,000 per household. This is a lower bound in part because the OBR assumes rather low multipliers (the direct and indirect impact of particular cuts), but also because I assume that by 2013 UK GDP had regained all the ground lost by austerity, which seems very unlikely. The true cost of UK austerity could easily be two or three times this figure. If you asked me what my best guess was, I would say £10,000 per household by 2015.

1.10
THE SCANDAL OF THE AUSTERITY DECEPTION
Monday, 23 September 2013

The assistant editor of the *Daily Telegraph*, Jeremy Warner, after some comments on some recent posts by Paul Krugman and myself, writes:[17] 'In the end, you are either a big-state person, or a small-state person, and what big-state people hate about austerity is that its primary purpose is to shrink the size of government spending.' And the final paragraph starts: 'The bottom line is that you can only really make serious inroads into the size of the state during an economic crisis. This may be pro-cyclical, but there is never any appetite for it in the good times; it can only be done in the bad.'

There is the old joke that there are just two kinds of people in the world, those who think there are two kinds of people and those who don't. The trouble with following an ideology is that you tend to make this 'with us or against us' division on what is seen as fundamental. In these terms I am a non-person, because I have no idea what the ideal size of the state should be (although I suspect within an ideology that defines itself by the virtues of a small state that makes me 'one of them'). For me, the intellectual case against austerity has nothing to do with the size of the state. The key argument I and others are making for those who want a smaller state is that it is folly to try to achieve it in a recession when interest rates are at the zero lower bound.

The problem for 'small state people' like Warner is that 'there is never any appetite for it in the good times'. I can only interpret this as meaning that in good times people appear to be quite content with the size of the state they have (see the postscript), and will not elect a government which aims to reduce the size of the state. So why are things different in a crisis? Do people's preferences over the size of the state relative to GDP really change when we are in recession? Or could it be that in the current crisis people are told that government debt is 'out of control', and that a reduction in government spending is necessary to bring the nation's finances to order. Cuts in government spending are being justified by the need to reduce debt and not because of the virtues of a small state.

Reducing the size of the state temporarily to reduce debt and reducing it permanently are rather different things. There is apparently no appetite for the latter, so why not push for the former as a way of achieving the latter? As a political ruse it sounds very clever, and it is currently working in the Eurozone, US and UK. But it remains a ruse: a giant deception played on electorates across the globe.

So no wonder Jeremy Warner is tired of the austerity debate. As he says, 'if you attempt to rip big chunks of government demand out of the economy, it is bound to have negative short term consequences'. Seeing the government you support trying to avoid making this admission must be painful. It would have been much more honest to say that the loss of output was worth it for the long-term benefits that a small state would (allegedly) bring, but that is not the argument that governments are making: instead it was all about a 'debt crisis'. This becomes even more painful when the intellectual basis for the debt crisis argument falls away.

Surely this deception is scandalous. The *Telegraph* played a major role in the MPs' expenses affair. Many UK MPs had been overinflating their expenses because they believed their salaries were unjustifiably low as the public never had the appetite to increase them. So the end justified the means. The *Telegraph* quite rightly exposed this practice, and those MPs were held to account. Yet in financial terms the cost of the austerity deception is infinitely greater. To some, the end (a smaller state) justifies both the cost (percentages of output lost) and the means (telling people it is all about a debt crisis). Yet it involves deceiving electorates around the world, which is why no government politician is ever going to be as honest as Jeremy Warner has been.

POSTSCRIPT

About a year later I wrote a post about the data on preferences for a smaller and larger state, from the British Social Attitudes survey. When this is reported in the press, we are often only shown the 'higher' and 'same' lines, which tend to react with a lag to the actual share of government spending in output. What is left out of such a comparison is the line for those wanting a smaller state, which never rises above 10% of the population (Figure 1.2).

Figure 1.2: British Social Attitudes Survey, National Centre for Social Research

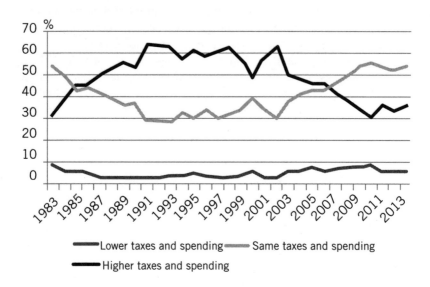

━━ Lower taxes and spending ━━ Same taxes and spending
━━ Higher taxes and spending

There is, and never has been, any public mandate for any renewed shrinking of the state. As I wrote:

> *The big change over time has not involved public attitudes, but the political position on economic issues of the Conservative Party. Just like the Republicans in the US, it has moved substantially to the right, beginning with*

Thatcher, and continuing under Cameron. Just as with the Tea Party in the US, there is a sizeable minority that wants to go further. However this rightward shift does not reflect majority opinion, and so when enough alternatives exist, as in Scotland, votes have drifted away from the Conservatives to more moderate centre-right parties. In a two-party system like the US, or with a voting system that favours the two main incumbent parties like the UK, that cannot happen.

No wonder small-state politicians leapt at the chance to use deficit deceit to achieve their goals.

1.11
ECONOMIC STANDARDS
Saturday, 4 January 2014

PREAMBLE

The following post reflects the specific circumstances of 2013. The UK economy finally started growing. It did not grow by more than pre-crisis trends, but after years of almost no growth it felt like a relief. The government used that mood to proclaim that austerity had been a success. This was just silly, but predictable. In one of my first posts in February 2012 I had written this:

What I am prepared to predict is the reaction of some when growth does return (as it may be in the US, and as it might one day in the UK and the Eurozone). My prediction is that some people will say that growth shows those Keynesian prophets of doom were all wrong. Look, the patient has recovered just fine without the need for any fiscal stimulus medicine.

It is silly because economic theory predicts that austerity will reduce growth for a few years, not permanently. Any economist knows this. As a result, average growth after years of stagnation is an indictment of austerity, and not proof it was the right policy. In one post I imagined a politician somehow temporarily closing 5% of the economy down for a few years. It would be ludicrous to celebrate the growth rate when this 5% starting up again, rather than question why they had wasted 5% of economic resources for the preceding few years.

I was particular incensed at a Financial Times *leader with the headline 'Osborne Wins the Battle on Austerity' (10 September 2013). In a separate post I compared it to a leader in the* New Scientist *saying that politicians have won the climate change argument because of recent heavy snow. In this post I use this event to make an important distinction between most academics and many City economists.*

I have used the following analogy before, but it remains pertinent. Imagine you are an academic scientist who is genuinely sceptical about climate change. I have met them so I know they exist. You are asked by a journalist whether the current spell of cold weather disproves manmade global warming. Perhaps you are tempted to say yes, or 'yes, although', because it would encourage scepticism. But I'm almost certain you would instead say 'of course not'. You would then give the journalist a little lecture about probabilities, averages, trends and so forth. It is exactly the same answer that a scientist who believes in climate change would give. You do not give the wrong answer just because it is convenient to your overall argument, because you are an academic and a scientist. You have standards.

Now imagine (maybe you do not need to) that you are an economist and you are asked by a journalist 'Has George Osborne's "plan A" [fiscal austerity] been vindicated by the recovery in 2013?' There is only one correct answer to this question – no. It is the correct answer, *even if you believe plan A is the right policy.* But when the *Financial Times* asked this question in its end of 2013 survey, about half of the 80-odd economists answered yes. However, many of the economists asked were City economists, and only a dozen of those surveyed were academic economists. Among the academic economists, only two said yes.

I rather like an analogy from Chris Dillow:[18] 'To give Osborne credit for the recovery is like praising a taxi-driver for getting us home when he has taken us on a two-hour detour.' Chris says that the mistake of saying yes is an example of outcome bias. For some maybe, but for a trained economist it is no excuse. I think, like Paul Krugman, that it is just political opportunism.

It is important to understand that this has nothing to do with whether austerity was a good or bad policy. What a supporter of austerity should reply is 'No, but I still believe austerity is the right policy for the following reasons'. If they are being generous they might even say 'the fact that the recovery has been so delayed could be evidence against austerity'. But for an economist, a recovery four years after the recession is never going to be evidence that *supports austerity*.

Unfortunately when some economists enter a political arena (using political in its widest sense), there is a danger that they leave their scientific standards behind. Thankfully only two academics answered yes on this occasion, but many more City economists did so. Perhaps this is because some City economists are hired to say things that clients like hearing, or perhaps they have lower scientific standards. Whatever the explanation, this suggests a clear difference between the two groups if you want good objective advice on broad policy issues.

You could say I am naive to expect anything else. As a great deal of politics is about economics, then economics is also bound to be political, and cannot hope to have the same integrity as a science. There is a weak form of this proposition with which I agree: economic ideas are influenced by ideology, and it is foolish to pretend otherwise. But our reaction should be to expose these influences and try and reduce them, rather than shrugging our shoulders. What I refuse to accept is that economics cannot be an evidence-based discipline.

So, if the hypothesis is 'austerity is the appropriate policy' and the evidence is 'the economy recovered in 2013', any economist can only give one response: the evidence does not support the hypothesis. Just because the question is political does not justify saying otherwise. In fact, being in a political arena means it is all the more important to maintain scientific standards. That is why we call economics a discipline.

1.12
LEFT, RIGHT AND MACROECONOMIC COMPETENCE
Sunday, 23 November 2014

Does a political party's place on the left–right spectrum influence its macroeconomic competence? It should be obvious that, for any individual country, looking at some macro outcome (like growth) and drawing some conclusion can be meaningless. For example, growth under Republican presidents has been far worse than under Democratic presidents, but that could so easily be down to luck rather than judgement. To make headway we need to think of mechanisms and particular instances when they applied.

In the US, for example, there is a belief on the right that cutting taxes will increase tax revenue, a belief that is also clearly wrong. So you would expect Republican administrations that acted on that belief to run up bigger budget deficits than their Democratic counterparts, and that seems to be what they do. That may not be the whole story, but at least it is a mechanism that seems to fit. However, it seems like a story that is rather specific to the US, at least for the moment.

Just now you could argue that parties of the right are more prone to austerity, because they want a smaller state than those of the left, and austerity can be used as a cover to undertake policies that reduce the size of the state. In a situation where interest rates are stuck at zero that has the damaging macroeconomic consequences that we are seeing today. However, this is a story that is specific to liquidity traps.

An alternative source could be different views about the relative costs of inflation and unemployment. You might expect governments of the left to have higher inflation and those of the right to have higher unemployment. While that mechanism loses much of its force when you have independent central banks, it can resurface in a liquidity trap.

A final left/right difference that might impact on macroeconomic outcomes is different views on the need for state intervention. Those on the right might favour less intervention, leading them to favour simple rules, and to argue against the use of fiscal policy for macroeconomic stabilisation.

Is any of the above helpful in looking at UK policy since 1979? I use this place and period as a case study because I am most familiar with it. In the past I have talked about three major macroeconomic policy errors over this period, all of which occurred when the Conservatives were in power. However that alone proves nothing: Labour was in power for fewer years and might have been lucky. (If you want to call the gradual liberalisation of financial controls that facilitated the financial crisis a macroeconomic policy error that would make four, but I do not think anyone would seriously argue that this occurred under Labour because they were more predisposed to market liberalisation than the Conservatives.)

The period starts with Margaret Thatcher and the brief experiment with monetarism. Here you could use the inflation/unemployment contrast: the policy succeeded in getting inflation down very rapidly, but at high costs in terms of unemployment, which persisted because of hysteresis effects (an economic term for mechanisms that make high unemployment persistent). A secondary question is whether, given any particular preferences between inflation and unemployment, the policy was inefficient because it attempted to run monetary policy according to a simple rule which failed. Many at the time argued it was, because it put far too much of the burden of lost output on the traded sector, which in turn was because the policy inevitably generated a large appreciation in the exchange rate.

The 1990 recession can also be linked to left/right influences. The rise in inflation that preceded the recession (and to some extent made it necessary) was partly down to Nigel Lawson's tax cuts. I have been told by one insider that the key wish at the time was to cut the top rate of tax, but it was felt that to do this alone would be politically damaging, so tax cuts were made across the board. That was not the only reason for the late-1980s boom as there was also the decline in the aggregate savings ratio that in my view had a great deal to do with financial deregulation, but it was a factor.

The macroeconomic failure that everyone knows about from that period was the forced exit from the ERM (exchange rate mechanism) in 1992, and that was costly because it made monetary policy too tight beforehand. Although you could say that fixing the exchange rate is a simple rule that the right might prefer, that would be stretching things: ERM entry was favoured by Labour as well (although with the notable exception of Bryan Gould). According to my own and colleagues' analysis at the National Institute,[19] the entry rate was too high, which might follow from a preference for low inflation, although it could just have been a choice based on poor macroeconomic analysis.

Inflation targeting followed the ERM debacle, and it was augmented by central bank independence at the start of the Labour government of 1997. One major decision that, if it had gone the other way, we might be scoring as a major error would have been if the UK had joined the euro in 2003. Post 8.3 in Chapter 8 argues that the decision not to was based on an intelligent and well-researched application of current academic knowledge (subsequently vindicated by additional but related problems that academics did not anticipate), rather than any left/right policy preference.

Which brings us to George Osborne. I have just finished the first draft of a paper that appraises the coalition's macroeconomic policy, and an interesting question that arises from that is why the coalition went for austerity despite the liquidity trap. While the 2010 Eurozone crisis might explain the change of mind of the minority partners in the coalition, it does not explain Conservative policy, which was against fiscal stimulus in 2009. If you look at some of Osborne's speeches (and I'm not sure there is much else to go on), the rationale for austerity was a belief that monetary policy was sufficient to stabilise the economy, even in a liquidity trap. At the time that represented a minority view among macroeconomists. It could be explained in left/right terms in various ways: a dislike of additional state intervention, taking a risk that would lead to higher unemployment rather than higher inflation, or a devious way of reducing the size of the state.

So we have three major UK macroeconomic policy errors: the monetarist experiment of Thatcher; ERM entry and exit (and the boom that preceded it); and current austerity. In all three cases it is possible to link these *to some extent* to right-wing political preferences. It may be equally possible to go back further and link the increased inflation of the 1970s to a left-wing dislike of unemployment, but I cannot do that from memory alone so it would require some additional work going over the detailed history of that period.

However, one additional point strikes me. Two of these three errors can be attributed to following a minority academic view. That monetarism was a minority academic view in the UK in the early 1980s became clear with the famous letter from 364 economists in 1981. In UK right-wing mythology that episode represents the triumph of Thatcher over the academics. The Labour/Brown period perhaps represented a high point in the influence of academic economists within government, and the analysis behind the 2003 entry decision was an example of that. A belief that fiscal policy is not required in a liquidity trap is a minority academic view.

It may seem odd to some that those on the right might be more disposed to ignore mainstream academic opinion within economics, but of course academic economics can be described as the analysis of market failure. No one looking at debate in the US would dispute that minority academic views, or a more general anti-intellectualism, finds an easier home on the right than the left at the moment. Of course you can also find anti-intellectualism on the left, and my distant memories of the UK in the mid-1970s suggest that during this period they might have been at least as prevalent as those on the right. What may have happened over the last few decades is that what is currently called the left has become ideology-light, and therefore more receptive to academic expertise and evidence-based policy.

1.13
HOW DID THE UK AUSTERITY MISTAKE HAPPEN?
Monday, 14 August 2017

As the global financial crisis and consequent recession were in progress, the Labour government looked at how fiscal stimulus could be used to moderate its impact. This would increase the budget deficit that was already rising as a result of the recession, but they knew that cutting interest rates alone would be insufficient to deal with this crisis, and that you do not worry about the deficit in a recession. That is Econ 101 – basic macroeconomics – and it is 100% correct.

Here Osborne and his advisors saw a political opportunity. Before the recession, fiscal policy had been all about meeting the government's fiscal rules about debt and deficits, because monetary policy looked after smoothing the business cycle. There had been much discussion about the extent to which Gordon Brown had been fiddling these rules. Osborne could therefore make political capital over the rising deficit, particularly if he could suggest the deficit represented fiscal profligacy rather than the result of the recession.

But what about Econ 101? The advice he was given (I suspect) was reflected in a speech he gave in 2009.[20] This gave a short account of the history of macroeconomic thought, and described how the New

Keynesian model underpinned his macroeconomic policy. It said that in today's world the consensus is that monetary policy not fiscal policy dealt with moderating booms and recessions. Yet it failed to mention that this idea no longer worked when nominal interest rates hit their lower bound. And that unconventional monetary policy was powerless in the New Keynesian model. The speech was given a month after interest rates hit their lower bound.

The speech also said nothing about expansionary austerity, or the need to appease the markets. That would all come later. This also suggests that Osborne's focus on the deficit was a simple but devastating macroeconomic error, a result of just not doing your homework. It was an incredible error to make, as the fact that interest rates had hit their lower bound was all over the financial press. If the media had been in touch with academic economics they would have pounced on this black hole in the speech. (Maybe this is complete coincidence, but his main economic advisor, Rupert Harrison, had previously worked at the IFS, where they do not really do macro. This advice served him well in other respects, such as establishing the form of his fiscal rule – which would help limit the impact of austerity after 2011 – and creating the OBR.)

As an economic choice his policy was crucially out of date, but as a political choice it was almost brilliant. The line he pushed on the deficit came to dominate the media narrative, which I was later to describe as mediamacro. It did not win the 2010 election outright, but it went on to win the 2015 election. I say almost brilliant, because it is proving the undoing of his successor. The economic damage done by cutting government spending at the one and only time monetary policy could not offset its impact was immense. I think it is no exaggeration to call it the most damaging UK macroeconomic policy mistake in my lifetime as an economist.

It was damaging in part because politics drove two additional features of his policy after he became Chancellor in 2010. First, the austerity policy would have had less economic impact if most measures had been delayed until later into the five-year term of the coalition government. But that would have meant deep cuts before the next election, and Osborne could see that would do political damage. Second, although the fiscal rule did not require it, public investment was cut back sharply in the first few years, because investment is often easiest to cut. Those cuts in public investment alone could have reduced GDP by 3%.

By 2010 you need to introduce other actors who played a part in these mistakes. The Treasury did what the Treasury unfortunately often does, and put public spending control above the macroeconomic health of the country. The Governor of the Bank of England pretended that losing his main instrument didn't matter, even though I'm told the MPC had almost no idea what impact unconventional monetary policy would have. If either institution had acted better perhaps the damage done by the austerity policy could have been moderated, but we will never know.

However, the main damage was done when the Conservatives were still in opposition. Did the policy of opposing fiscal stimulus start off as a policy to reduce the size of the state under cover of deficit reduction: what I call deficit deceit? Or was it just something to beat Labour with: the first in what proved to be a long line of bad economic judgements simply designed to wrong-foot his opponents. Without the actors involved telling us, I think it is impossible for us to tell. However there are two things I think we can clearly say.

First, if it started as ignorance rather than deceit, it turned into the latter as Osborne prepared to repeat the policy all over again before the 2015 election, while at the same time cutting taxes. Second, if it started as ignorance it is far too kind to call it a mistake. It is similar to someone who has never learnt to drive taking a car onto the highway and causing mayhem. It reflects a cavalier attitude to economic expertise that has its roots back in the early days of Thatcherism.

POSTSCRIPT

The discussion above focuses on the UK. When you look at the US and the Eurozone, which also undertook austerity in 2010, the role of ideology is a common factor, as I argue in a paper I gave as a keynote speech to a conference organised by the Royal Irish Academy.[21] In that paper I suggest that in the UK, US and Eurozone as a whole austerity was completely unnecessary and avoidable, and I explore the political economy factors that allowed this damaging policy to happen (see also Post 8.9).

I mentioned in the post that Osborne's speech in 2009 setting out his macroeconomic strategy was at least 10 years out of date, because it ignored the re-emerging problem of a liquidity trap that had hit Japan in the 1990s. Perhaps this is an example of the 'practical men' that Keynes described as absorbing some of the wisdom of 'academic scribblers' of 'a few years back'. Another piece of received wisdom was deficit bias, which described the tendency that many economists discussed before the financial crisis for deficits and debt to tend to rise over time in many countries (not the UK). This might help explain why some viewed deficit reduction as a virtue, although in a liquidity trap it is anything but.

As they say, a little knowledge can be a dangerous thing. Those of us working on the frontline of monetary and fiscal interaction, or who had studied economic history or looked at the lost decade in Japan, knew that this 'received wisdom' broke down when interest rates hit their lower bound. We knew that this liquidity trap was absolutely not the time to worry about deficits, and if you did so you would cause tremendous damage. And we were right.

2

EUROZONE

Introduction

The popular understanding of the Eurozone crisis is that various periphery Eurozone governments overspent and as a result found it difficult to sell their debt on the markets. During the crisis the media would ask whether measures being taken to reduce budget deficits were enough to convince the markets. This completely failed to see why the crisis happened in the Eurozone and not elsewhere.

To understand the Eurozone crisis you need to know how it ended. In September 2012 the European Central Bank (ECB) introduced OMT (outright monetary transactions). OMT was in essence an unlimited commitment to buy the debt of particular countries: to be what economists call a lender of last resort. What created the Eurozone crisis between 2010 and 2012 was the ECB's refusal to act as a lender of last resort to individual Eurozone governments.

Governments with their own central bank cannot be forced to default by the markets, because the central bank will step in and buy any unsold debt. As I described in the first post of Chapter 1, in the UK the Bank of England did this as part of its unconventional monetary policy. For institutions and individuals lending to these governments, having the central bank as the lender of last resort removes the risk of a forced default. Even if the rest of the market fails to buy the debt, the government will not be pushed into default.

In contrast, as long as the ECB refused to act as a lender of last resort to Eurozone governments, Eurozone government debt was much riskier and much more susceptible to market panic. So the crisis started by Greece (which really did borrow too much) was allowed to spread to other countries where public finances were sound. Once OMT was put in place the crisis quickly subsided, and did not start up even when Greek default again became possible in 2015. As Post 2.1 shows, these points were understood well before OMT was introduced.

The consequences of the delay in introducing OMT were immense. Austerity occurred in all Eurozone countries, not just the periphery, with large costs in terms of a second recession and lost resources, as outlined in Post 2.6. The immediate culprit for this austerity-led recession was a more stringent set of fiscal rules, but in Post 2.2 I argue that the crisis actually means that centrally imposed rules are unnecessary, and in Post 2.3 I suggest that decentralisation of fiscal control is a better way forward than further union.

Austerity was partly, as elsewhere, ideological deceit. As I recount in Post 2.5, when France tried to reduce its deficit by raising taxes rather than cutting spending it was told that this was not what austerity was about. Another important factor was the relative position of Germany within the Eurozone. Before the financial crisis Germany had in effect undercut its neighbours, and Post 2.12 asks whether this was deliberate or unintentional. Whichever it was, Post 2.1 shows that this meant it was in Germany's narrow interests to allow deflation in the Eurozone as a whole.

THE LIES WE WERE TOLD

Post *2.7* asks whether it was self-interest or ideology that influenced German policy. The strength of anti-Keynesian views in Germany is a continuing puzzle (Post *2.11*). What is even more of a puzzle for me is why other countries allowed either German self-interest or ideology to plunge the Eurozone into a second recession, and the fantasy in Post *2.9* tries to illustrate this by imagining if it had been France rather than Germany that had tried to dictate events.

The Eurozone country hit hardest by austerity is of course Greece. While some austerity in Greece was inevitable, what actually happened was far worse than it need have been, as I outline in Post *2.4*. In Post *2.8* I make a comparison that some may find over the top, but which I hope conveys the role of ideological conviction in the continuing Greek tragedy. Post *2.10* discusses events in 2015.

Posts in Chapter 2

2.1
THE EUROZONE AS ONE COUNTRY
Thursday, 19 April 2012

The Eurozone is undertaking more austerity than either the US or the UK, yet its overall budgetary position is much more favourable than either of these two countries. Can this be right, at a time when the Eurozone is in recession? If we thought about the Eurozone as a single country, then clearly it is not. Everything that is wrong with current UK policy would be even more wrong in the Eurozone. The question I ask here is whether the fact that it is not one country changes this assessment.

The Eurozone is like one country in having a single central bank. The ECB's nominal interest rate is stuck at its equivalent of the zero lower bound (ZLB). This makes the Eurozone's situation no different from the US or the UK. A recession in which interest rates are at the zero lower bound is not the time to undertake austerity. The Euro area as a whole should be reducing its underlying budget deficit much more slowly. It needs a large fiscal stimulus relative to current plans. But can we translate this aggregate conclusion into action to be undertaken at the individual country level?

I do not think a social planner in charge of the Eurozone that treated all its citizens equally would have a problem. They would reason as follows. In aggregate we need a large stimulus relative to existing plans. In addition, because in Germany inflation before the crisis was lower than in other member countries, we need a significant inflation differential between Germany and non-Germany to open up. Suppose 2% is the optimal inflation rate, and we need a 2% gap between Germany and non-Germany (which is probably a lower bound on the inflation gap required). We could have 2% (Germany) and 0% (non-Germany), or 3% and 1%. The latter will be preferred because it is better to spread the pain of being away from 2% equally. In addition, the difficulty of reducing inflation when it is already near zero is well known, so it would be less costly to raise inflation in Germany. A large part of the stimulus would therefore go to Germany, raising inflation above the optimal level from the German national point of view.

But this is academic, as we do not have a Eurozone central planner. In principle non-Germany could compensate Germany to achieve the optimal aggregate outcome, but it is unclear what non-Germany has to offer. So let us take it as a constraint that Germany will not adopt a large stimulus. (It may also do its best to counteract the impact of any expansionary ECB policy on its own economy.) This means that we cannot have as large a stimulus for the Eurozone as a whole as we could if it was one country. We have to go for 2% and 0% rather than 3% and 1%, which means lower Eurozone output. But does it mean the current level of austerity is correct?

At present austerity in non-Germany is being driven by each country's bond market. If the Eurozone really was one country, which issued Eurozone debt, this would not be happening. Just as savers are happy to buy UK or US debt, they would happily buy Eurozone debt. (No one buying UK debt is too worried about the widening North–South divide in the UK!) The Eurozone is highly unlikely to default.

Germany has ruled out Eurobonds, so are we back to our previous problem? No, because the ECB can act as if they existed, by (indirectly) buying national governments debt when the market will not, and therefore acting as a sovereign lender of last resort. Buyers of non-German debt are worried about default, and the ECB can rule out default by being the buyer of last resort. Although the ECB is buying some debt, it is not making the kind of unconditional promises that are required for a sovereign lender of last resort. My own view (and more importantly others) is that the ECB is too concerned about moral hazard, and not concerned enough about the impact of austerity on non-German output, with the result that we are seeing much more austerity than is necessary. The ECB could still exercise fiscal discipline by varying the rate at which it capped the interest rate on non-German debt.

Instead the ECB appears to be using market sentiment as an index of national fiscal discipline. This puts national governments in an impossible position. These governments can try and demonstrate that they will not default by piling on the austerity, but in the process they may actually be making their longer-term fiscal positions worse, as well as unnecessarily increasing unemployment.

Using market sentiment as an indicator of fiscal sobriety is particularly inappropriate at the moment, as market concerns may be much more focused on the health of national banking systems and the knock-on effects if governments are required to rescue national banks. To the extent that this is true, austerity will make things worse. As the economy contracts, more loans go bad, and banks' balance sheets worsen. Without clear signals and statements from the ECB that no further fiscal tightening is required, there is a real danger that national governments may continue to tighten too quickly.

Viewing the Eurozone as a single country clearly indicates a substantial easing of both fiscal and monetary policy. German national self-interest, combined with the need for non-German competitiveness to improve, does moderate the amount of fiscal easing that can occur, but there is no reason why the ECB should reduce aggregate inflation on this account. However, the amount of aggregate fiscal austerity that this implies is still considerably less than is currently being enacted. Here the ECB has the ability to remove the constraint imposed by national government bond markets, and it should do so before the degree of austerity currently being enacted does lasting damage to the sustainability of the Eurozone.

2.2
SHOULD THE EUROZONE'S FISCAL RULES BE ABOLISHED?
Sunday, 18 November 2012

Yes, I know it sounds an outlandish question, but it is unclear to me what the rationale is for fiscal controls imposed at the Eurozone level. A simplistic answer is that they are designed to stop future debt crises. However, if you ask any Eurozone government whether it wants to avoid another debt crisis, they would say emphatically yes. And this is not just words – they are taking highly unpopular measures to reduce their current deficits. So why do these efforts need to be augmented and directed from the European/Eurozone level?

Let's go right back to the formation of the euro. A standard rationalisation for the Stability and Growth Pact (SGP) was the following. With its own currency, there is market discipline on a government spending too much or taxing too little. As government deficits rise, so do interest rates. This may be because deficits lead to excess demand and inflation, and the central bank raises interest rates to counteract this, or it may be because inflation or default risk increases. Put that same economy into a monetary union, and that discipline is diluted. In particular, there is only a union-wide interest rate, and the impact on inflation in the monetary union as a whole may be small. Individual union members may therefore not internalise the impact that their deficits have on the union.

So it was thought that a monetary union reduces fiscal discipline, and therefore it needs to do something to reverse that. Hence the SGP. Events seemed to confirm this model in the years after the formation of the euro. Interest rates on government debt for all member countries tended to converge, and fiscal discipline was very hard to maintain. But the former now looks like an aberration, caused perhaps by a combination of a belief that no Eurozone economy would ever default, and a general pre-crisis downgrading of risk.

What we now have appears to be precisely the reverse of the argument behind the SGP. Market discipline is too great: interest rates on government debt for certain Eurozone members are 'too high', leading to a danger of self-fulfilling default. Markets react much more to increases in individual Eurozone members' government debt than similar increases in other countries, mainly because the former do not have a 'lender of last resort' – their own central bank. The ECB's OMT is designed to counteract that tendency, but because OMT is discretionary, no country can presume it will operate, particularly if they are profligate.

So do markets reduce fiscal discipline within the Eurozone, or intensify it? It seems very difficult to believe that we will go back to the pre-2007 situation any time soon, given the extent of the current crisis. If this is true, where is the rationalisation for generalised fiscal controls at the European level? If there is more market discipline within the Eurozone than outside it, there is no need for Eurozone-imposed fiscal controls to supplement that market discipline.

An important distinction here is between conditionality ex ante and ex post a debt crisis. Conditionality ex post, when institutions or other countries provide loans the market will not provide, is inevitable. However the myriad fiscal rules that replace the SGP are ex ante, and apply to countries with no incipient debt crisis (like the Netherlands, for example). In the rest of the world, we have the IMF, and the only ex ante conditionality it imposes is the need to cooperate in Article IV consultations. Why is the Eurozone so different?

One argument is that recent events show clear contagion within the Eurozone. Greek problems raised interest rates for other Eurozone members, in a way that might not happen to, say, South Korea if Japan defaulted. However, I would suggest that this was largely due to uncertainty about what the ECB would do. To say we need the Eurozone's fiscal rules because the way the Eurozone handles a debt crisis is unclear sounds lame indeed.

Another argument is that if emergency loans are required, other Eurozone countries will suffer potential losses on those loans, so they have an interest in preventing crises ex ante. However, exactly the same is true for the IMF and the rest of the world. Indeed, my own view is that it would be far better, post-OMT, if any emergency loans for a future Greece were provided by the IMF alone, because that reduces potential conflicts of interest.

So why is the Eurozone obsessed with its fiscal rules? I can think of one clearly bad reason. (Actually I can think of many bad reasons, but this post is already long.) Eurozone governments still do not know what to do if a future Greece emerges. How does it differentiate between a future Greece (where default is required) and a future Ireland (where it is not)? The answer at the moment seems to be that the fiscal rules will ensure that there will never be another Greece. That sounds like wishful thinking, particularly if other countries join. Unfortunately here the Eurozone has form. A common response before 2000 to those who argued that the Eurozone needed a strategy for dealing with asymmetric shocks was that this was not a problem because the formation of the Eurozone will itself eliminate asymmetric shocks. We all know what happened next.

2.3
IS A MONETARY UNION WITHOUT FISCAL/ POLITICAL UNION DOOMED?
Sunday, 24 February 2013

This seems to be a very common view at the moment. The view that the Eurozone will have to move to fiscal union, which implies some form of political union, comes from two directions:

- Those working in the political unions that are the United States or the United Kingdom know that combined monetary and fiscal unions can work. From this perspective, the monetary-only union of the Eurozone was a largely untried experiment, and it is failing. The perpetual crisis of the markets may be over as a result of OMT (the ECB's programme to become a conditional lender of last resort) but the crisis that is unemployment in the periphery just gets worse.

- Within the Eurozone itself, there has always been a powerful lobby for further integration. It is therefore not surprising that actors like the Commission see further integration as the longer-term solution to the Eurozone's problems.

Yet we should be very cautious about making generalisations from a single observation. It may be worth reminding ourselves about why the Eurozone has not been a fair test of monetary union without fiscal union:

- The crisis of competitiveness was partly a result of a mistaken belief in the market that default risk on everyone's debt was similar to German debt, a mistake that is unlikely to occur again in decades. In the years before the recession, no attempt was made to use fiscal policy to offset overheating in periphery countries.

- In probably only one case, Greece, was there a clear problem of underlying fiscal excess. Yet instead of recognising the need for default early on, the union made a futile attempt to avoid it by replacing private debt with intergovernmental lending, which had disastrous consequences. This major and avoidable error produced the worst moment of the crisis, when Greece was threatened with exit. It continues to impose a disastrous degree of austerity on Greece.

- The fiscal position of other Eurozone economies became critical because the ECB refused to act as a lender of last resort. If the ECB had introduced its OMT programme two years earlier than it did, the crisis might well have dissipated very quickly. This is hardly wisdom from hindsight. Market reaction always had much more to do with the ECB than the fiscal position of the countries involved, an observation that research confirms.

- The current double-dip recession in the Eurozone is largely about a collective failure of fiscal and monetary policy. The position of the Eurozone would look significantly better if the ECB acted more like the US Fed, and if Germany and other fiscally untroubled economies were less obsessed with austerity. Neither has much to do with the absence of fiscal union.

To use evidence from one very badly designed test case to condemn the whole concept of monetary union without political union is far too hasty. It is also potentially very dangerous. We should not forget that monetary union itself was encouraged by a belief that the fixed exchange rate regime that preceded EMU was untenable because of market pressure. The lesson of Eurozone failure so far is mainly about bad design, rather than disproof of concept. If this failure leads to a fiscal and monetary union imposed from above on an unwilling electorate, by an elite that played such a big part in creating the current failure, we may go on to find out that a badly conceived political union could be even more disastrous than a badly designed monetary union.

POSTSCRIPT

The view expressed in this and the previous post remains very much a minority opinion both within and outside the Eurozone, for the reasons given in this post. In particular, one of the fundamental lessons from the Eurozone crisis and the continuing control over Greece has not been learnt, as some proposals for a European replacement for the IMF unfortunately show. That lesson is that Eurozone countries should never be involved in deciding whether problem countries default or not, and should never bail them out. The tragedy of Greece, discussed in some of the following posts, shows that this puts far too much power into the hands of creditors.

There has, however, been one development in the direction I advocate. All Eurozone countries are now required to have independent fiscal councils (like the Office for Budget Responsibility in the UK). There is also now a formal apparatus that allows these councils to coordinate and express views to the Commission. On 25 October 2017 I wrote about how this apparatus could form the basis for preserving subsidiarity in fiscal policy making, but also help deal with problems when national control failed.

2.4
THE STUPID CRUELTY OF THE CREDITOR
Friday, 19 April 2013

In the Middle Ages those who could not afford to pay their debts were sent to prison by their creditors. An efficient solution to the moral hazard problem? Hardly, because the chances that the debtor could earn some money to repay something to the creditor from a prison cell were not high. So countries gradually developed rather more civilised bankruptcy laws, like Chapter 11 in the US.

Yet we are seeing the equivalent of these medieval practices in Europe at the moment. Arguably the harm being inflicted on the people of Greece by its creditors is even more cruel, and more stupid. More cruel, because the harm is being done to those totally innocent of the original contract. More stupid, because those doing the damage cannot see what they are doing, either by refusing to open an economics textbook, or believing that they somehow know better.

Just look at the numbers in Table 2.1, from the latest OECD economic outlook.

Table 2.1: The Greek macroeconomic disaster

	2010	2011	2012	2013	2014
Government consumption growth (%)	−8.7	−5.2	−5.9	−7.1	−4.0
Underlying primary surplus (% GDP)	−3.6	1.3	4.2	6.5	7.6
Output growth (%)	−4.9	−7.1	−6.3	−4.5	−1.3
Unemployment (%)	12.5	17.7	23.6	26.7	27.2

Why is this happening? Because the Eurozone governments that foolishly bailed out Greece after the crisis first developed in 2010/11 want all their money back.

But surely, you may say, those who lent money to the Greek government are entitled to have their money back (with interest). No one was forcing the Greek government to accept these loans, and the conditions that go with them. The creditors are justified in doing everything they can to pressure the Greeks to repay their debts, including threatening Greece with expulsion from the Eurozone. The fact that this is causing great human suffering and misery is just one of those unfortunate things, and perhaps a necessary lesson to make others think more carefully before electing governments that secretly run up unsustainable debts.

If that is what you think, then I would suggest this view is the moral equivalent of locking debtors up in prison. It is also as stupid, because the damage being done to the Greek economy and its politics is making the scale of the eventual default greater than if some debt relief was allowed now. A fiscal contraction of this scale, in a country with no independent monetary policy, was bound to do this much damage. Any macro textbook tells you that. Those who believe that reducing one component of demand just changes its mix rather than its overall level display an ignorance which in this case is close to criminal.

But, you may say, the Greek economy has become uncompetitive, and wages need to fall if the economy wants to stay part of the Eurozone. There is no escaping macroeconomic pain. True some deflation was necessary, but deflation on this scale is totally wasteful, and the immense harm it is doing is therefore avoidable. Once again, very simple macroeconomics tells you this. And the core of the Eurozone is making this competitiveness correction as difficult to achieve as possible by keeping overall inflation low. You might say that this chaos is required to achieve necessary structural reform. I seem to remember someone else once had a similar idea: Mao called it perpetual revolution.

Unfortunately this would not be the first time creditors have laid waste to cities in an effort to recover debts. In contrast, after World War II the Allies wrote off 93% of the Nazi-era debt and postponed collection of other debts for nearly half a century. So Germany, whose debt-to-GDP ratio in 1939 was 675%, had a debt load of about 12% in the early 1950s – far less than that of the victorious Allies – helping to produce post-war Germany's economic miracle.

The lesson from the 1920s had been learnt. Whether this was done out of self-interest, because a vibrant post-war Germany benefited everyone, or compassion, I do not know. But whichever it was, the creditors of the Eurozone could use some of that wisdom right now.

2.5
FRANCE AND THE COMMISSION
Tuesday, 3 September 2013

France is subject to the Fiscal Compact's 3% budget deficit target like everyone else in the Eurozone. European Commissioner Olli Rehn is the chief enforcer of these rules. In May the Commission granted France, along with a few other countries, two years' grace before they needed to achieve that target.

Figure 2.1 shows OECD numbers and forecasts for various fiscal measures in France. The financial balance relates to the 3% target. The underlying balance essentially cyclically adjusts this. As you can see, the key reason that France is not meeting the 3% target is depressed output. The OECD estimates the output gap in 2013 will be nearly –4%, rising in magnitude to –4.5% in 2014. The underlying primary balance is the best indicator of what government policy is doing: fiscal policy has been tightening ever since a sharp expansion following the 2008/9 recession.

Figure 2.1: OECD fiscal measures in France

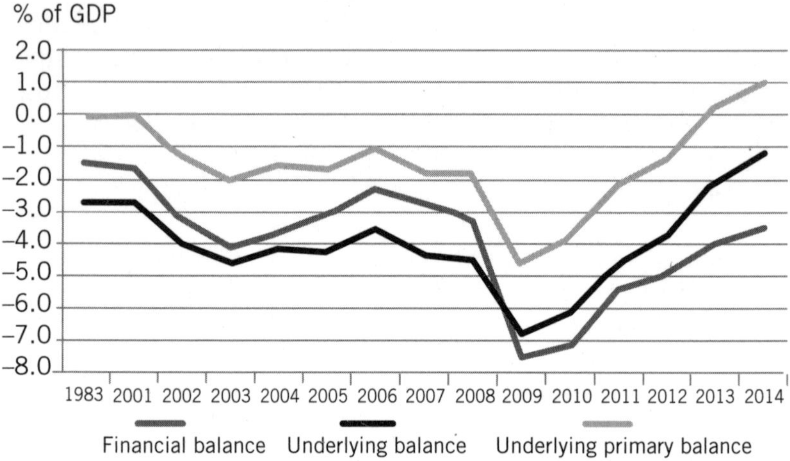
% of GDP
2.0
1.0
0.0
–1.0
–2.0
–3.0
–4.0
–5.0
–6.0
–7.0
–8.0
1983 2001 2002 2003 2004 2005 2006 2007 2008 2009 2010 2011 2012 2013 2014
Financial balance
Underlying balance
Underlying primary balance

Source: OECD Economic Outlook Statistical Appendix.

So far, so typical of the Eurozone and elsewhere. However, what makes France relatively unusual is the pattern of this tightening. It has achieved this fiscal contraction entirely through tax increases rather than spending cuts. The first best thing to do, of course, is to delay fiscal tightening until the output gap has closed. The Eurozone's fiscal rules will not allow that, and instead in the current context encourage pro-cyclical fiscal policy. I have never met a macroeconomist who advocated pro-cyclical fiscal policy, but of course those behind the Fiscal Compact know best.

If you have to follow the Fiscal Compact, then from the point of view of doing least damage to the economy in a recession any temporary fiscal tightening should focus more on tax increases than spending cuts. You might, for example, try to meet the Fiscal Compact rules in the short term through temporary tax hikes, and follow with more permanent spending cuts and/or tax increases once the economy recovers. To a first approximation that appears to be what the left-wing government in France is trying to do, most notoriously by temporary increases in the top tax rate.

My argument has always been based on straightforward macroeconomic theory, but this is fully supported by empirical work. It is therefore entirely predictable that European Commissioner Olli Rehn should take completely the opposite point of view. He is quoted as saying that new taxes would 'destroy growth and handicap the creation of jobs'. 'Budgetary discipline must come from a reduction in public spending and not from new taxes', he added.[1]

Now I'm not sure whether that counts as advice or instruction: within the Eurozone it is increasingly difficult to tell. I suppose you could argue that Rehn's concern is more about the longer-term size of the French state, and that his obvious belief that the French state is too big comes purely from worries about the implications for macroeconomic performance. But what struck me was simply this: in the election of April 2012 the French people elected a left-wing government that had a clear platform of achieving fiscal consolidation partly through tax increases. Even if the Commissioner thinks that is a foolish thing to do, that is their choice.

It is one thing to have a set of fiscal rules that focus on overall budget deficits: however misguided those rules may be, the French government did agree to them. What I do not think any Eurozone government signed up to was having the Commission tell them what the size of their own state should be. With these remarks, together with its insistence that various Eurozone countries undertake certain 'reforms', the Commission appears to be doing its best to create a de facto fiscal union. The only problem, of course, is that the French did not elect Olli Rehn.

2.6
THE 'OFFICIAL' COST OF AUSTERITY
Monday, 28 October 2013

Well, not quite, but probably as close as we will ever get. In a new paper,[2] Jan in't Veld uses the European Commission's QUEST model to estimate the impact of fiscal consolidation in the Eurozone (EZ) from 2011 to 2013. The numbers in Table 2.2 include spillover effects from other EZ country fiscal consolidations, so they are best interpreted as the impact of overall EZ fiscal consolidation over this period. There are at least two important things to note about the exercise. First, they do not attempt to analyse the impact of the particular mix between cuts in spending and increases in taxes applied in each country. Instead the 'input' is simply the change in the general government primary structural balance each year, which is assumed to be equally balanced between expenditure and revenue measures. Second, to a first approximation this fiscal consolidation is assumed to lead to no change in short- or long-term real interest rates during the 2011–13 period.

Table 2.2: GDP losses due to Eurozone fiscal consolidation (including spillovers) 2011–13

	Impact on GDP (2013)	Cumulative Impact (2011–13)
Germany	3.9%	8.1%
France	4.8%	9.1%
Spain	5.4%	9.7%
Ireland	4.5%	8.4%
Greece	8.1%	18.0%

Source: From Jan in't Veld (2013) 'Fiscal consolidations and spillovers in the Euro area periphery and core,' *European Economy Economic Papers* 506, Table 5.

Of course many would argue that had countries like Spain or Greece not undertaken this degree of austerity, long-term interest rates might have been even higher than they actually were. However a significant amount of fiscal consolidation took place in Germany, and this had significant spillover effects on other EZ countries. It is difficult to see why that consolidation was required to ease funding pressures.

The assumption that consolidation is evenly divided between spending cuts and tax increases is important. As the paper shows, the Quest model indicates that consolidation implemented through spending cuts has about twice the short-run multiplier as consolidation through higher taxes, but of course this is exactly what theory would suggest. In a forward-looking model like this it also matters a great deal how agents perceive the permanence of these policy changes.

Of course Quest is just one DSGE (Dynamic Stochastic General Equilibrium) model, which just happens to be maintained by the Commission. An earlier study by Holland and Portes had important differences in detail, but the bottom line was similar: EZ GDP was 4% lower in 2013, and the cumulated GDP loss was 8.6%.[3] These numbers are of course large, and so it is quite reasonable to say that the proximate cause of the second EZ recession is simply austerity.

Now many would argue that much of this was forced by the 2010 crisis. There seems to be a mood of fatalism among many in Europe that this was all largely unavoidable. I think that is quite wrong. Some fiscal tightening in Greece was inevitable, but if EZ policymakers had taken a much more realistic view about how much debt had to be written off, we could have avoided the current disaster. What ended the EZ crisis was not austerity but OMT: if that had been rolled out in 2010 rather than 2012, other periphery countries could also have adjusted more gradually. And of course fiscal consolidation in Germany and some other core countries was not required at all. If instead we had seen fiscal expansion there, to counter the problem of hitting the ZLB, then the overall impact of fiscal policy on EZ GDP need not have been negative. (Section 5 of Jan in't Veld's paper looks at the impact of such a stimulus.) That means that over three years nearly 10% of Eurozone GDP has been needlessly lost through mistakes in policy. This is not the wild claim of a mad macroeconomist, but what simple analysis backed up by mainstream models tell us.

One final point. The UK equivalent to these 'official' numbers are the OBR's estimates of the impact of fiscal consolidation on the UK. While they are significant in size, they are smaller than these EZ numbers. The OBR estimates that UK GDP in 2013 is about 1.5% lower as a result of fiscal consolidation, and the cumulated GDP loss due to fiscal tightening from 2010 to 2013 is a bit above 5%. There is a good reason and a bad reason for this difference. First, the UK is a more open economy than the EZ as a whole, and we would expect openness to cushion the impact of fiscal consolidation. Second, the OBR's numbers are more crudely derived, based on multipliers that take no account of the zero lower bound or deep recession. The numbers from the Quest model allow for both, which of course raises the size of the fiscal impact.

POSTSCRIPT

The paper I discuss here included the normal disclaimer: 'The views expressed are the author's alone and do not necessarily correspond to those of the European Commission.' It is certainly true that the Commission typically takes a more rosy view.

The paper's author, Jan in't Veld, wrote a couple of comments on this post, which you can read below the original. I do not think they warrant changing the main text, but you can judge for yourself. (If I get comments on any post where I think some change is warranted, I do change the text.)

I returned to this theme in subsequent posts, as other studies of the impact of fiscal policy on the Eurozone economy were published. These tended either to be of the same order of magnitude as the numbers above, or greater. One particular study also confirmed that the Eurozone crisis would have been greatly reduced if more countercyclical policy had been conducted in periphery countries before the financial crisis, and if OMT had been implemented earlier.[4]

2.7
THE REAL PROBLEM WITH GERMAN MACROECONOMIC POLICY
Sunday, 3 November 2013

Paul Krugman has been laying into Germany in the past few days. I think it might be interesting to look at two possible defences for the German position. The first is that they are doing what any government would do, which is act in their national interest. The second is that, for from being at the centre of the Eurozone's problems, they have been holding it together.

Take the national interest argument first. If the EZ really had an EZ government that took decisions in the overall EZ interest (see Post 2.1), then given the problems with ECB monetary policy (whether self-inflicted or otherwise), EZ fiscal policy should be expansionary rather than contractionary. Given the needs of periphery countries, this implies fiscal expansion in Germany. The problem is that this appears not to be in the German national interest, because growth has been relatively healthy in Germany, unemployment is low and inflation not that low (Table 2.3).

While this performance is nothing to write home about, it is also not enough to overcome the longstanding distrust in Germany of countercyclical fiscal policy. Why risk inflation going above 2% when unemployment is less than half the EZ average?

Table 2.3: The latest OECD forecasts (and outturns) from the September OECD Economic Outlook

	2012	2013	2014
Consumer prices	2.1	1.6	2.0
Unemployment	5.1	5.0	4.7
GDP growth	0.4	1.3	2.1
Output gap	0.1	−0.8	−0.2

Pointing out that the macroeconomic interests of Germany and the EZ as a whole conflict is important, because (for some at least) it strengthens the arguments for fiscal union. It is almost the fiscal equivalent to the arguments for monetary union in the 1990s. Pre-euro we had a quasi-fixed exchange rate system where French and Italian monetary policy was effectively tied to what the Bundesbank wanted, and the Bundesbank's job was to focus on Germany. This all came to a head after German unification, when German monetary policy was tightened as the rest of Europe was suffering a period of low growth. The parallel is not exact because today Germany does not dictate fiscal policy outside Germany: well, at least not in theory.

From this perspective, arguments about the German current account surplus are beside the point. Macroeconomic policy should not be geared to current account surpluses or deficits, but to economic fundamentals like unemployment and inflation. In the absence of fiscal union, German macroeconomic policy looks OK from a German point of view.

The second defence of the German position is that, far from acting selfishly, it is providing the financial glue which is holding the EZ together, through EU bailouts of the periphery. As it becomes increasingly clear that some part of the funds provided by the Troika to Greece will have to be written off, this point of view can only strengthen in Germany.

I think both lines of defence are quite powerful, yet I think they are in danger of missing the point. The problem with German macroeconomic policy is not that it is acting in the national interest, or otherwise, but that it is based on a discredited and harmful set of ideas. In particular there are three key myths that are leading German policy making astray.

Myth 1: The EZ crisis stemmed from fiscal irresponsibility in the periphery EZ countries, and the crisis can only be solved by reversing this through harsh austerity.

Reality: The crisis was at least as much to do with private as public sector excess.

Myth 2: An anti-Keynesian view that fiscal policy has no place in managing aggregate demand, which can be safely left in the hands of the ECB as long as the ECB sticks to its job of keeping inflation below 2%.

Reality: The Keynesian argument against austerity at the zero lower bound is correct. Keynesians also argue, correctly, that restoring competitiveness in a monetary union is much more difficult when inflation in your key competitor country is low.

Myth 3: To be independent, central banks must never buy government debt, as this indicates fiscal dominance.

Reality: EZ governments need the ECB to (potentially) act as a sovereign lender of last resort, to prevent self-fulfilling market panics. The introduction of OMT demonstrated this.

To see how these myths have distorted German policy, let's start with the assistance Germany has provided to the periphery. Myth 1 has led to a focus on austerity, and a reluctance to see the pressure for austerity eased. Myth 2 means that the damage caused by this austerity is discounted, and Myth 3 leads to reluctance to let the ECB help reduce market pressure. In short, the money that Germany has or will provide could have been much better spent. Ironically it could have been better spent in Germany, boosting domestic demand, which would have helped raise demand and inflation in Germany (the latter being the sacrifice Germany would make to help keep the EZ together), which would have done much more to help the periphery adjust their competitiveness at lower cost. Myth 2 prevents Germany from seeing this, although it is quite clear from macroeconomic models (see Post 2.6). The financing needs of the periphery would have been much reduced if more Greek debt had been written off, and had German resistance (Myth 3) not delayed OMT until September 2012.

These myths have also damaged Germany's own narrow domestic interests. Myths 1 and 2, besides leading to harsh austerity in the EZ periphery, has also led to fiscal contraction in the core, which has reduced German GDP and led to inflation below 2% this year. The Fiscal Compact, despite slight softening around the edges, is a deeply flawed and damaging policy which comes directly from Myths 1 and 2.

So the problem is not with Germany, but with the macroeconomic myths that seem to be so deeply embedded in current policy. I do not think Germany has been simply acting in its own national interest, but the myths prevent it seeing that its current account surpluses are a key part of the problem and why some overheating in Germany is the best solution for the EZ as a whole. Although these three myths have a particular ordoliberal flavour, they are not so very different from similar myths expounded by politicians and the occasional economist in the US, the UK and elsewhere in Europe. The myths are the problem.

POSTSCRIPT

This theme is one I would return to often, in part because of articles by German economist Michael Burda that pushed the self-interest viewpoint, and also because it is difficult to establish a clear reason for anti-Keynesian views in Germany (see Post 2.11). However, I do not think my views have changed fundamentally. In essence while German domestic policy has followed self-interest, its influence on other Eurozone countries has done much harm. This influence was less obviously in Germany's national interest, and instead reflected the interest of particular politicians (Greece) or reflected outdated macroeconomic ideas.

2.8
THE SHARP BUT EFFECTUAL REMEDY
Friday, 7 March 2014

Mario Draghi, head of the ECB, declared the Eurozone as an 'island of stability' yesterday as he announced no change in policy. He was referring to the impact of the Ukrainian crisis, but I think it serves for macroeconomic policy as a whole. Inflation is well below target, and there is a negative output gap of nearly 4% according to the OECD. Unemployment remains at 12%. There is a recovery from recession, but it is weak and fragile.

So the Eurozone is stable, stuck in a bad place, a place that looks a lot like Japan in the 1990s. The central bank's inflation target is either unclear or one-sided, and the ECB should not wait until there is deflation (below-zero inflation) before doing more than sitting on its hands.

Yet complacency is not confined to the ECB. We had a second Eurozone recession because fiscal austerity has been acute in some member countries, and it has not been offset elsewhere. If you think that is because the Eurozone is a monetary union and not a fiscal union, ask yourself this: if overall fiscal policy was being determined in Brussels rather than by individual national governments, would it be so very different today? I suspect we would be seeing similar overall austerity as the 'Eurozone government' obsessed with reducing debt. Given their relative competitive positions, that would mean 'stability' in parts of the Eurozone and severe recessions elsewhere, much as we have now.

...

[D]rastic reductions to municipality budgets have led to a scaling back of several activities (eg, mosquito spraying programmes), which, in combination with other factors, has allowed the re-emergence of locally transmitted malaria for the first time in 40 years ...

a 21% rise in stillbirths between 2008 and 2011 ... attributed to reduced access to prenatal health services for pregnant women.

These are statements not about some poor African nation, but about Greece, from a recent paper in *The Lancet*.[5] The title of the paper is 'Greece's health crisis: from austerity to denialism'. By denialism the authors mean the following:

Greek citizens ... are subject to one of the most radical programmes of welfare-state retrenchment in recent times, which in turn affects population health. Yet despite this clear evidence, there has been little agreement about the causal role of austerity. There is a broad consensus that the social sector in Greece was in grave need of reform, with widespread corruption, misuse of patronage, and inefficiencies, and many commentators have noted that the crisis presented an opportunity to introduce long-overdue changes. Greek Government officials, and several sympathetic commentators, have argued that the introduction of the wide ranging changes and deep public-spending cuts have not damaged health and, indeed, might lead to long-term improvements. However, the scientific literature presents a different picture. In view of this detailed body of evidence for the harmful effects of austerity on health, the failure of public recognition of the issue by successive Greek Governments and international agencies is remarkable.

...

Between 1846 and 1851 about a million died of starvation and epidemic disease in the Irish potato famine. The general consensus today is that although this famine began as an extraordinary natural catastrophe, its impact was made much worse by the actions (or lack of action) of the British government, headed by the Whig Lord John Russell. As Jim Donnelly describes, there seem to be three ideologies that held the 'British political élite and the middle classes in their grip, and largely determined the decisions not to adopt the possible relief measures'. These were 'the economic doctrines of laissez-faire, the Protestant evangelical belief in divine Providence, and the deep-dyed ethnic prejudice against the Catholic Irish'. The system of agriculture in Ireland was perceived in Britain to be riddled with inefficiency and abuse. The British civil servant Charles Trevelyan, chiefly responsible for administering Irish relief policy, wrote that the famine was 'the sharp but effectual remedy by which the cure is likely to be effected'.[6]

There is a debate about the humanity and personal responsibility of Charles Trevelyan. Yet his actions were hardly idiosyncratic. The Lord Lieutenant of Ireland, the Earl of Clarendon, wrote a letter to Prime Minister Russell on 26 April 1849 expressing his feelings about lack of aid from the British House of Commons:[7] 'I do not think there is another legislature in Europe that would disregard such suffering as now exists in the west of Ireland, or coldly persist in a policy of extermination.' The *Economist* magazine strongly supported the laissez-faire line pursued by Trevelyan and Russell. Were the governing elite collectively evil, as they provided armed guards for the shipping of huge quantities of grain away from the same areas affected by the blight? We could just say people act in their own interests, but this underestimates the power of ideas and ideologies.

...

Of course the Irish famine is different in degree and form to the difficulties being faced by many in some Eurozone economies. But the similarities should worry us. There is the widespread view that the inefficiencies and corruption that exist in these economies are a key factor in explaining the difficulties these countries are in. Worse still is the idea that severe austerity is necessary to ensure 'structural reform' takes place to reduce these inefficiencies. There is also a common belief today that various economic processes cannot be interfered with and contracts have to be upheld, which are not very different from beliefs held by the British government in the 1840s. When the 'effectual remedy' leads directly to suffering, the evidence that it does so is ignored, as the *Lancet* paper argues is happening in Greece today.

If you think that the problems in Greece and elsewhere are clearly self-inflicted, rather than the result of an act of God, like potato blight, consider this: the Greek government borrowed way too much and concealed that fact, but this was hidden from the Greek people as much as anyone else. Just because politicians are elected, does that make the people as a whole responsible for everything they do? Are they more responsible than those who lent the government this money, or in the case of other Eurozone countries lent money to banks that were subsequently bailed out with no public discussion?

In Victorian times there was a belief that the debtor must be made to repay their debts whatever hardship that entails, and with minimal cost to the creditor. We think we live in more enlightened times today, but at least the individuals in debtor prisons normally signed the contracts they were being held to. In the case of Greece and elsewhere their leaders signed on their population's behalf.

If you say that the law must be followed, well the British government was also protecting the rule of law when it ensured that those shipments of grain left famine-stricken Ireland. Are those shipments of grain so very different from the flows of money now leaving Greece and elsewhere to pay the interest on government debt? Our attitude to famines is a little more enlightened than it was in the 1840s, but perhaps some of that enlightenment is needed elsewhere.

2.9
EUROZONE ASYMMETRIES
Sunday, 5 October 2014

Suppose a large Eurozone country, let's call it France, decided that it needs to substantially increase its minimum wage in order to reduce poverty. The increase is sufficiently large that it leads to a sustained increase in average French wage inflation, which in turn decreases the competitiveness of France relative to the rest of the Eurozone. France cannot be permanently uncompetitive, so the obvious consequence would be that France has to endure a subsequent period in which its relative inflation was below the Eurozone average.

However, this would require a period where French unemployment was above its natural rate. French politicians declare that this would be politically unacceptable to French voters; instead they suggest that French inflation should remain at 2%, and the remainder of the Eurozone should increase their inflation rate to 4% for a time (giving an average Eurozone inflation rate of over 3%) to ensure France regains competitiveness. Now this would not normally be possible, because the ECB's inflation target is 2%. However, the influence of France on the ECB is such that the ECB fails to raise interest rates in time to prevent 3% average inflation, and subsequently keeps interest rates low because they repeatedly forecast inflation falling back down to 2% in due course.

The rest of the Eurozone would understandably be upset at having to endure 4% inflation. Some countries might suggest that perhaps, in the absence of ECB action, they could tighten fiscal policy to get their inflation below 4%. However France refuses to countenance changes to agreed fiscal targets, and instead suggests that what is really required is for other countries to adopt a similar increase in the minimum wage to the one originally undertaken in France. The French head of the ECB gives a speech which intimates that the ECB might be prepared to raise interest rates a little bit in exchange for other countries introducing this 'structural reform' to their minimum wage levels. The French government also hints that it might be prepared to allow very limited fiscal contraction outside of France, but only if this took the form of tax increases rather than public expenditure cuts.

Your reaction to this little imaginary story is that it couldn't possibly happen because other Eurozone countries would not permit it to happen. My suggestion is that Germany rather than France is doing exactly this at the moment, except that in their case it started with a period where German wage inflation was below the Eurozone average. In fact what Germany is doing is worse, because inflation asymmetries and debt deflation mean that the output costs of achieving zero inflation outside Germany to regain non-German competitiveness are far greater than the costs associated with 4% inflation in my story. German control of the ECB might not be as complete and simple as I imagined French influence in the story above, but it has the advantage that interest rates have hit the zero lower bound, and the threat that anything unconventional could be declared illegal. And in this real-world story I too wonder why other Eurozone countries allow Germany to get away with it.

2.10
GREECE: OF PARENTS AND CHILDREN, ECONOMISTS AND POLITICIANS
Tuesday, 21 April 2015

Chris Giles in the *Financial Times* describes how non-Greek policymakers (let's still call them the Troika) see themselves like parents trying to deal with the 'antics' of the problem child: Syriza in Greece. These parents may sometimes want to act as if the child is grown up (though they believe it is not), sometimes they want to be disciplinarians. As a description of how the Troika view themselves, and present themselves to the public, the analogy rings true. It certainly accords with the constant stream of articles in the press predicting an impending crisis because the Greeks 'refuse to be reasonable'.

In *FT Alphaville* Peter Doyle writes about a recent meeting at the Brookings Institution in Washington, the highly respected US social science research/policy think tank. In that meeting Wolfgang Schäuble and Yanis Varoufakis, finance ministers of Germany and Greece, gave back-to-back presentations. He describes how 'Schäuble was avuncular, self-effacing, and Germanic, and was tolerated rather than warmly embraced by his hosts'. In contrast 'when Varoufakis spoke, eyes burning with anger, his hosts were animatedly engaged'. The audience actively sympathised with the position of Greece, and asked 'how it felt to be right but penniless'. He writes 'There was no doubt where the hosts' sympathies lay between their two guests.'[8]

I am not surprised at all by this account. The arguments that many of us have made about how far Greece has moved and what agonies it has endured in order to satisfy the unrealistic wishes of its creditors are I think widely shared among our colleagues. We know that if Greece was not part of the Eurozone, but just another of a long line of countries that have borrowed too much and had to partially default, its remaining creditors would be in a weak position now that Greece has achieved primary surpluses (taxes>government spending). The reason why the Troika is not so weak is that they have additional threats that come from being the issuer of the Greek currency.

It is important to understand what the current negotiations are about. Running a primary surplus means that Greece no longer needs additional borrowing. It just needs to be able to roll over its existing debts. Part of the argument is about how large a primary surplus Greece should run. Common sense would say that further austerity should be avoided so that the economy can fully recover, when it will have much greater resources to be able to pay back loans. Instead the creditors want more austerity to achieve large primary surpluses. Of course the former course of action is better for Greece: which would be better for the creditors is unclear! The negotiations are also about imposing additional structural reforms. Greece has already undertaken many, and is prepared to go further, but the Troika wants yet more.

From the perspective of the Eurozone and IMF, this is all extremely small beer. You would think the key players on that side had more important things to do with their time. The material advantages to be gained by the Troika playing tough are minimal from their perspective, but the threats hanging over the Greek economy are damaging: not just to investment, but also to the very primary surpluses that the Troika needs. So why do the Troika insist on continuing with brinkmanship? Can it be that this is really about ensuring that an elected government that challenges the dominant Eurozone political and economic ideology must be forced to fail?

In a recent post (8.8) that I (jokingly) entitled 'Should economists rule?' I suggested that much of the debate about the delegation of economic policy to economic experts was really an issue about political transparency rather than diminished democracy. Elected politicians normally always have ultimate control. Sometimes 'delegation' amounts to little more than making the advice they receive transparent: contracting out the fiscal forecast to the OBR would be an example. All that democracy loses in this case is the ability of politicians to conceal or manipulate the advice they receive, and to fool the public as a result. Greece may be (unfortunately) a good example of how far politicians are prepared to go in misleading their own electorates to cover up their mistakes and achieve their own political ends.

POSTSCRIPT

It is fashionable today to blame Syriza, and particularly its then finance minister Yanis Varoufakis, for being hopelessly naive in trying to get a better and more reasonable deal. For the record, I was also naive in posts written before this one, because I had believed both that Germany would not want to throw Greece out of the Eurozone and that the so-called independent ECB would not cut off the supply of euros to Greece. As I say in this post, it is Greece wanting to stay in the Eurozone that gave the Troika its power.

Having power does not of course mean that you should use it. There is no excuse for deliberately keeping a country in poverty simply to avoid the embarrassment of admitting you used Greece to bail out your own banks and that you will not get the money back. In July 2015 Dani Rodrik, Thomas Piketty, Heiner Flassbeck, Jeffrey Sachs and I wrote an open letter to Angela Merkel (published in the Guardian, Le Monde, The Nation *and* Der Tagesspiegel*)[9] asking for some of Greece's debt to be forgiven, much as Europe's debt was forgiven in the 1950s. Instead Germany and much of the rest of the EU preferred to pretend that they were the adults in the room and exercise their power over Greece, and most of the media went along with the pretence.*

2.11
WHAT IS IT ABOUT GERMAN ECONOMICS?
Tuesday, 9 June 2015

I recently had the privilege to speak in Berlin at the 10th anniversary celebration of the Macroeconomic Policy Institute (IMK). You could describe the IMK group within Germany in various ways (see below), but one would be an island of Keynesian thinking in a sea that was rather hostile to Keynesian ideas.

As my talk focused on how Keynesian ideas are pretty mainstream elsewhere, this raises an obvious puzzle: why does macroeconomics in Germany seem to be an outlier? Given the damage done by austerity in the Eurozone, and the central role that the views of German policymakers have played in that, this is a question I have asked for many years. The textbooks used to teach macroeconomics in Germany seem to be as Keynesian as elsewhere, yet Peter Bofinger is the only Keynesian on their Council of Economic Experts, and he confirmed to me how typical this minority status is.

There are two explanations that are popular outside Germany that I now think on their own are inadequate. The first is that Germans are preoccupied by inflation as a result of the hyperinflation of the Weimar Republic, and that this spills over into their attitude to government debt. A second idea is that Germans are culturally debt averse, and people normally note that the German for debt is also their word for guilt. The trouble with both stories is that they imply that German government debt should be much lower than in other countries, but it is not. (In 2000, the German government's net financial liabilities as a percentage of GDP were at the same level as France, and slightly above the UK and US.)

A mistake here may be to focus too much on macroeconomics. Germany has recently introduced a minimum wage: much later than in the UK or US. I think it would be fair to say that German economists generally advised against this. In the UK and US the opinion of economists on the minimum wage issue is much more balanced, largely because there is a great deal of academic evidence that at a moderate level the minimum wage does not reduce employment significantly. So here German economics also appears to be an outlier.

Many people have heard of ordoliberalism (Post 9.3). It would be easy to equate ordoliberalism with neoliberalism, and argue that German attitudes simply reflect the ideological dominance of neo/ordoliberal ideas. However, because ordoliberalism recognises actual departures from an ideal of perfect markets and the need for state action in dealing with those departures (for example, monopoly), it is potentially much more amenable to New Keynesian ideas than neoliberalism. Yet in practice ordoliberalism does not appear to allow such flexibility. It is as if in some respects economic thinking in Germany has not moved on since the 1970s: Keynesian ideas are still viewed as anti-market rather than correcting market failure, and views on the minimum wage have not taken on board market distortions like monopsony. But that observation simply prompts the question of why in these respects German economics has remained isolated from mainstream academic ideas.

One of the distinctive characteristics of the German economy appears to be very far from neoliberalism, and that is co-determination: the importance of workers' organisations in management, and more generally the recognition that unions play an important role in the economy. Yet I wonder whether this may have had an unintended consequence: the polarisation and politicisation of economic policy advice. The IMK is part of the Hans Böckler Foundation, which is linked to the German Confederation of Trade Unions. The IMK was set up in part to provide a counterweight to existing think tanks with strong links to companies and employers. If conflict over wages is institutionalised at the national level, perhaps the influence of ideology on economic policy, in so far as it influences that conflict, is bound to be greater.

The 'Hamburger Appell' of 2005, signed by more than 250 German economists, is clearly anti-Keynesian. The intellectual rationale given there is unclear, but one theme is that a more effective way of increasing employment is to increase international competitiveness by holding down domestic costs. Now if you are part of a fixed exchange rate regime or a monetary union, and you have, for institutional reasons, an ability to influence domestic wage costs which other countries that belong to the regime do not have, then it may make perfect Keynesian sense to use that instrument. This is exactly what happened (deliberately or not) from 2000 to 2007, which is a major reason why Germany is currently not suffering the recession being experienced by the Eurozone as a whole. Of course, unlike a fiscal stimulus, it is a beggar-my-neighbour policy, because demand increases at the expense of other countries in the regime: for the regime as a whole a flexible exchange rate will offset the impact of lower costs on competitiveness.

As you can see, I remain some way from answering the question posed in the title of this post, but I think I'm a bit further forward than I was.

2.12
WAS GERMAN UNDERCUTTING DELIBERATE?
Wednesday, 2 December 2015

In what I described elsewhere as the untold story of the Eurozone crisis, Germany held nominal wage increases below the level of other core Eurozone countries, gradually gaining a large competitive advantage over them. This had a number of consequences, but perhaps the most important is that when the Great Recession hit, Germany was much better placed than all the other Eurozone countries. (It is essentially a zero-sum game, because the euro exchange rate moves to influence overall Eurozone competitiveness, which is why I describe it as Germany undercutting its Eurozone neighbours.)

Up until now I have always been careful to avoid describing this as a deliberate beggar-my-neighbour policy. But one of the five members of Germany's Council of Economic Experts, Peter Bofinger, writes:

In 1999, when the Eurozone started, Germany was confronted with an unemployment rate that was too high by German standards, although it was still below the EZ average. The solution to the unemployment problem was typical of Germany's corporatist system. Already in 1995 Klaus Zwickel, boss of the powerful labour union IG Metall, made the proposal of a Bündnis für Arbeit (pact for work). He explicitly declared his willingness to accept a stagnation of real wages, i.e. nominal wage increases that compensate for inflation only, if the employers were willing to create new jobs (Wolf 2000). This led to the Bündnis für Arbeit, Ausbildung und Wettbewerbsfähigkeit (pact for work, education and competitiveness), which was established by Gerhard Schröder in 1998. On 20 January 2000, trade unions and employers associations explicitly declared that productivity increases should not be used for increases in real wages but for agreements that increase employment. In essence, 'wage moderation' is an explicit attempt to devalue the real exchange rate internally.[10]

You still hear people say that the DM was overvalued when it converted to the euro, but my research at the time suggested otherwise, and it is difficult to argue against the view that with today's current balance surplus of over 7% of GDP the real exchange rate in Germany is grossly undervalued (that is, it is too competitive relative to other Eurozone countries).

It is hard to overstate the importance of all this. German employers and employees connived in a policy that would take jobs away from their Eurozone partners. Whether this was done knowingly, or because of a belief is some kind of wage-fund doctrine, or something else, I do not know. But it makes Germany, a country with perhaps a unique ability to cooperate on an internal devaluation of this kind, a dangerous country to form a currency union with. The thing I find extraordinary about all this is that Germany's neighbours seemed to have let it happen without a whisper of recognition or complaint (see Post 2.9).

3

THE
CONSEQUENCES
OF AUSTERITY

Introduction

While Chapter 1 very much concentrates on the macroeconomics of austerity, and the politics of why it happened, this chapter looks at some of the consequences. Post 3.1 relates a particularly egregious example of stigmatising those receiving benefits to justify welfare cuts. Post 3.5 talks about how austerity, along with other measures, were skewed to hit the poor. Post 3.4 looks at flooding, which was also partly a consequence of austerity, although few in the media made the link. Post 3.7 looks at the NHS, and how the word 'protected' was abused to disguise the impact of austerity.

The remaining posts focus on political implications. In Post 3.2 I link declines in real wages in the UK and the Netherlands to the rise of the far right in each country. Post 3.3 looks at how Cameron's attempt to change the image of the Conservatives away from the 'nasty party', as it was described by Theresa May, was being derailed by austerity. It is a bit of a stretch, but I do think the closeness of the Scottish independence vote owed a lot to austerity. Post 3.6, written just before the vote, lambastes the Scottish National Party (SNP) over its denial of the short-term fiscal costs of independence.

Posts in Chapter 3

3.1
NASTY POLITICS IN HARD TIMES
Monday, 8 April 2013

This is a post about morality rather than economics, and as a result I am rather unsure about whether I should be writing it at all. Yet it is something that I have kept thinking about over the last few days, even though I would rather put it out of my mind. So perhaps this is blogging as therapy.

When jobs are scarce, people become understandably more exercised about the idea that some people are getting an income from the state without trying to find a job, just as they imagine that immigrants are 'stealing' what jobs there are. Such views are encouraged by the tabloid press. The tabloids are our equivalent of Fox News.

There has recently been a particularly egregious example of this in the UK. For those UK readers I just have to say the Philpott case and the *Daily Mail*, and they can skip the rest of the paragraph. For those outside of the UK, a criminal case recently came to an end where someone called Mick Philpott and two others were jailed for killing their six children by burning down their house. It was not murder: the individuals intended to rescue their children and frame someone else as part of a custody battle, but the 'plan' did not work out. A tragic case, and as the architect of the plan, Philpott received a very heavy sentence for manslaughter. Philpott had 17 children by five different women, and received large amounts of money in benefit payments. Which allowed the *Daily Mail* newspaper to print the headline 'Vile Product of Welfare UK'. Not to be outdone, the *Sun* said 'Let's hope this is the last time the state unwittingly subsidises the manslaughter of children'.

This all takes place at the same time as the government's welfare reforms are starting to be implemented. I am far from an expert in this area, so I have not talked about these reforms in this blog, although I did recently note how they are expected to reverse recent declines in child poverty. That aside, whether these reforms make sense or not is beside the point here. What is important is that one of the government's stated aims is to make the system more efficient, because in times of austerity money needs to be saved.

It is clear that the problem of the welfare state allowing, let alone encouraging, certain people to remain unemployed and have large families is not the main issue in trying to make the welfare system more efficient. To quote the *Economist*:

> Though most of them seem to end up in newspapers, in 2011 there were just 130 families in the country with ten children claiming at least one out-of-work benefit. Only 8% of benefit claimants have three or more children. What evidence there is suggests that on average, unemployed people have similar numbers of children to employed people.[1]

What we do know is that the vast majority of welfare payments go to people who are trying to find a job but cannot because jobs are scarce, or who are disabled, or who do have a job which is very poorly paid. These are people that most citizens in the UK would never want to exchange places with, and they deserve our sympathy and support. So what do you do if you are a public figure who knows these facts, and a national newspaper like the *Daily Mail* not only distorts the truth with its headlines, but by implication paints all those receiving welfare in such horrible colours?

I would suggest any decent person would try to bring the debate back to reality. At the very least you might say the following: 'The Philpott case is an individual tragedy. Children have died in that case. I think that is where we should let that case lie. I would not want to connect that to the much wider need to reform our welfare system.' That is what Danny Alexander, the (LibDem) Chief Secretary to the Treasury said. But this is what his boss, the Chancellor George Osborne, said:

> Philpott is responsible for these absolutely horrendous crimes and these are crimes that have shocked the nation. The courts are responsible for sentencing him, but I think there is a question for government and for society about the welfare state

– and the taxpayers who pay for the welfare state – subsidising lifestyles like that, and I think that debate needs to be had.[2]

So he sees no problem with the *Daily Mail*'s headline. Regular readers will know that I think George Osborne has been a hopeless Chancellor, and in addition that he has subordinated his economic task to the urge to make political capital. Yet even I was surprised by this attempt to use the tragic deaths of six children in a bizarre and unique case to try and score political points.

People can make up their own minds about the morality of this. Or you might take a cynical view: that all politicians will take any opportunity they can to make populist points, and that there is no morality left in politics. In which case the last thing Ed Miliband should have said is:

> do you exploit tragedy, like the Philpott tragedy? The right place for Mr Philpott is behind bars, but do you exploit the deaths of six children to try and make a political point about the welfare system, and at the same time say to people that this is somehow a common truth about people on benefits?

Perhaps there is just a little morality left in politics, whichever side you are on.

3.2
THE CENTRE CANNOT HOLD?
Monday, 12 August 2013

Everyone knows about the return of extremist politics as a result of austerity in Greece. The link between economic depression and far right extremism in the 1930s is also well documented. Yet I suspect there is a tendency to assume that this kind of thing only happens in 'immature' democracies. This assumption is wrong, as both the Netherlands and the UK currently show.

The Netherlands has been run by a parliament since at least 1848. Coalitions are the norm rather than the exception, and there is a general desire to achieve consensus on important political issues. Before the formation of the Eurozone, the extreme right in the Netherlands could be described as marginal, which was not the case in France, for example. Yet recent opinion polls suggest that if elections were held now, the far-right Freedom Party would become the largest party in parliament. The left-wing Socialists have also been taking support away from the centre-left Labour Party. What the two extreme parties have in common compared to the mainstream is opposition to further fiscal austerity.

So far, there has been a depressing consensus among the more centrist political parties in the Netherlands that they need to follow the Eurozone's fiscal rules. The economy is in recession: GDP fell by 1% in 2012, and will probably fall by a similar amount this year. Unemployment is rising: Figure 3.1 shows OECD forecasts and also OECD estimates of the output gap. Of course this has increased the budget deficit, and so we have had a series of austerity measures in an attempt to keep the deficit at 3% of GDP to stay within the Eurozone's fiscal rules. When the Freedom Party, which was part of a right-wing coalition, refused to support these cuts in 2012, they were passed by a coalition of the centre, egged on by the European Commission.

Of course the Netherlands, unlike Greece or Ireland or Portugal, has no problem funding its budget deficits, so here austerity is very much a political choice. Recent polls suggest the public has had enough, and that as a result support for the euro itself is suffering. The union movement has been active in its opposition, but more recently prominent business organisations have also begun to question austerity, although predictably their opposition has focused on tax increases rather than cuts to welfare. Coen Teulings, who departed as head of the highly respected CPB Netherlands Bureau for Economic Policy Analysis in April (the Dutch fiscal council), was vocal in his opposition to recent cuts, but the central bank has been much more supportive of austerity (as Post 8.9 suggests, this is not unusual central bank behaviour).

Figure 3.1: OECD economic outlook estimates for the Netherlands

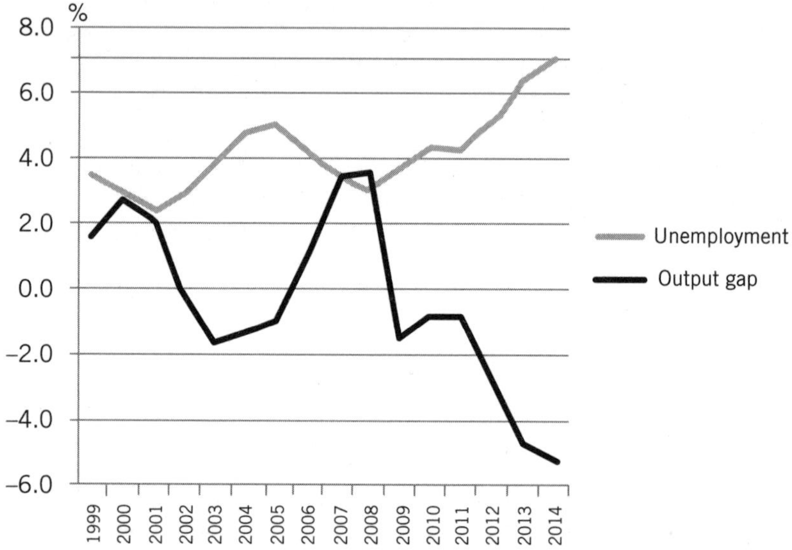

Source: OECD Economic Outlook Statistical Appendix.

The UK has also seen the emergence of a politically successful far right party, UKIP. This is also unusual from a historical perspective: since Oswald Mosley the UK has had a proud tradition of resisting parties of the far right. UKIP's popularity is not normally linked directly to austerity, but instead to widespread hostility to both immigration and the European Union. As a result, the Conservative Party has taken economically damaging positions on both issues in an attempt to reduce UKIP's appeal. Yet the link between concerns about immigration on the one hand and unemployment and low wages on the other is fairly obvious. Despite all the valiant attempts by Jonathan Portes and others to focus on the evidence, this is one of those cases where the combination of tabloid media hype, partisan political advantage and 'common sense' normally wins, and as a result the UK Labour Party seems to spend much of its time trying to ape the Conservatives.

Why has support for the far right grown in the UK and the Netherlands, while in France, for example, the far right did not make a breakthrough in 2012? No doubt a complete answer would be quite complex. However it is worth noting that the UK and the Netherlands have both experienced sharp falls in real wages in the recent past. The OECD expects real compensation per employee to have declined by a total of about 4.5% in the three years 2011–13 in the Netherlands, and by about 5% in the UK. The decline in the euro area as a whole has been much smaller, at less than 2%. In France real wages have increased a little in all three years. Figures recently calculated by the House of Commons library show a similar picture, with only Greece and Portugal doing as badly as the UK and Netherlands since mid-2010.[3]

In both the UK and the Netherlands we have recession and fiscal austerity, where the recession has been associated with marked falls in real wages as well as increases in unemployment. In both cases I would argue that there has been no effective opposition to fiscal austerity from the political centre, which helps encourage support for the political extremes. But that is probably as far as the similarity goes, because the position of the centre-left Labour Party in the two countries is very different.

In the UK the Labour Party is in opposition. It seems their general tactic on issues like austerity or immigration is not to question the underlying assumptions on which government policy is based. Perhaps the idea is to avoid being branded as irresponsible (austerity) or out of touch (immigration), while hoping to retain the support of those who do strongly oppose government policy. This position has so far been tenable partly because there is no strong party to the left of Labour. We may have to wait until 2015 to see if this strategy is successful.

The position of the Labour Party in the Netherlands is more immediately problematic. It is now part of the coalition enacting cuts. The Socialist Party, which is to the left of Labour and which does not support austerity, has moved ahead of Labour in the polls. In April there was a 'social accord', where the unions and business groups signed up to the budget deal proposed by the government. Further cuts are now required beyond those agreed in April to meet the fiscal rules, and the unions (and perhaps business leaders) are now actively campaigning against austerity. Yet it will be hard for the centre-right to ask Brussels for a reprieve, as their leader and Prime Minister, Mark Rutte, has followed Germany in taking a hard line on the 3% deficit limit and the Commission's enforcement of it. The reasons for Labour to back additional austerity are much less clear.

So in the Netherlands and elsewhere in Europe, on the issue of the stupidity of pro-cyclical fiscal policy, it is only the views of politicians on the far left or far right that match those of the majority of macroeconomists. Given the social, economic and political consequences of declining real wages and rising unemployment, which fiscal austerity only makes worse, this is both a very sad and rather dangerous state of affairs.

POSTSCRIPT

This was written when terms like populism were not commonly used, and when I was not knowledgeable enough to use them. I would now focus on the irony that in the Netherlands only the populist parties were supporting views about austerity that most academic economists agreed with.

I got a lot of comments on this post complaining about my use of far right to describe UKIP. The more cogent criticisms said that UKIP was a party focused on the EU, as its name suggests, and as such was to an extent outside the normal left–right spectrum. The mistake here is to think that an obsession with the EU is independent of that spectrum, when you generally find those who are so obsessed on the extremes of UK politics. And for good reason, because only at those extremes is the EU seen as a serious constraint on what can be done. One of the great achievements of the far right was how they turned an issue which few voters cared about before the referendum campaigning started into a (slim) majority to leave.

3.3
THE CONSERVATIVES AND THE GHOST OF CHRISTMAS PAST
Saturday, 21 December 2013

In October 2002 Theresa May, the then Chairman of the Conservative Party, said to her party's conference: 'There's a lot we need to do in this party of ours. Our base is too narrow and so, occasionally, are our sympathies. You know what some people call us – the Nasty Party.' That tag owes something to the contrast between the public images of Margaret Thatcher and Tony Blair: the Iron Lady compared to Blair's easy informality. In terms of policies it is not totally clear that the label was deserved. Poverty increased, but the poor were not denigrated. Unions were broken, but many felt the unions had become too powerful and selfish in their use of power. The state was reduced by privatising utilities, but the welfare state was not seriously diminished. Unemployment rose substantially, but inflation had to be brought under control. But whether deserved or not, I think May was right in her observation.

David Cameron also appears to have believed that the Conservatives had this image problem, and in opposition he aimed to create the idea of a modern, compassionate Conservative Party. Hoodies were to be hugged, environmental goals embraced and, most tellingly of all, rather than deny the relevance of 'society', he wanted to create a 'Big Society'. I am not concerned here about how real or radical these changes were, but instead just note that he felt a change of image was necessary to end the Conservative's run of election defeats. The fact that they did not win the 2010 election outright perhaps suggests the strength and toxicity of the nasty brand.

What a difference a few years make. As the government finds it more and more difficult to cut government spending on goods and services, it aims austerity at welfare spending. There is plenty that has already happened. As to the future, Paul Johnson of the IFS[4] estimates that huge cuts in welfare spending are required to meet the goals of the latest Autumn Statement, particularly if state pensions are ring-fenced, yet this appears to be Osborne's preferred option. The Conservative's current Party Chairman and an influential MP have recently suggested restricting benefits for those with more than two children, to encourage 'more responsible' decisions about procreation. Never mind the impact this would have on those children.

Changes to welfare already introduced, together with falling real wages, have led to a huge rise in the use of food banks in the UK. According to the Trussell Trust, one of the main operators of voluntary food banks, 346,992 people received a minimum of three days' emergency food from their food banks in 2012–13, compared to 26,000 in 2008–9. Of those helped in 2012–13, 126,889 (36.6%) were children.[5] The Red Cross is to start distributing food aid in the UK, for the first time since World War II. A letter from doctors to the *British Medical Journal* talks about a potential public health emergency involving malnutrition. It is undeniable that benefit changes are a big factor behind these developments, yet the government seems intent on hiding this fact.

Actions are of course more important than rhetoric, but rhetoric can help define image. It is undeniable that ministers, including the Prime Minister and Chancellor, have attempted to portray the poor and unemployed as personally responsible for their position due to some character failure. Even a proud institution like HM Treasury cannot resist talking about 'hard-working families'. This phrase looks like going the same way as 'taxpayers' money', becoming a routine slight against either the unemployed or the poor. Both Cameron and Osborne will be too careful to emulate Romney's 47% moment, but too many Conservative MPs appear to share the attitudes of some of those on the US right.

So what accounts for this U-turn from compassion to disparagement? The recession is one answer, which has hardened social attitudes. The success of UKIP, whose policies show a striking similarity to the preoccupations of certain right-wing newspapers, is another. Yet it seems incredible that a political calculation that appeared valid before 2010 can have been so completely reversed in just a few years. Even Theresa May, whose speech started this blog, has joined in on the act. There are those vans of course, but asking landlords to check the immigration status of tenants is an incredibly stupid and harmful policy. We will see in 2015 whether it pays to be nasty.

Yet even if the strategy works in the short term, and even recognising that politicians often do questionable things to gain votes, this just seems a step too far. It is one thing to create hardship because you believe this is a necessary price to improve the system or reduce its cost. Perhaps you really believe that cutting the top rate of tax at the same time as cutting welfare will benefit everyone eventually. But it is quite another thing to try and deflect any criticism by unjustly blaming those who earn too little, or who are trying to find work. That just seems immoral.

I suspect Cameron as the Compassionate Conservative would have agreed. He would have also noted that, although nastiness might accord with voter sentiments today, at some point in the future voters in more generous times will have no problem forgetting this, and will just remember the Conservatives as the nasty party. As Christmas approaches, Charles Dickens' *A Christmas Carol* seems apt.

3.4
UK FLOODING: ANOTHER AUSTERITY CHRISTMAS PRESENT
Saturday, 28 December 2013

The big UK news at the end of 2013 has been flooding caused by heavy rain. The Prime Minister naturally toured some of the worst-affected areas, but the reaction he got was not what he might have hoped in terms of media coverage. Was this hostility fair? Figure 3.2 is taken from 'Flood defences in England', House of Commons Library.

Figure 3.2: Flood defences in England

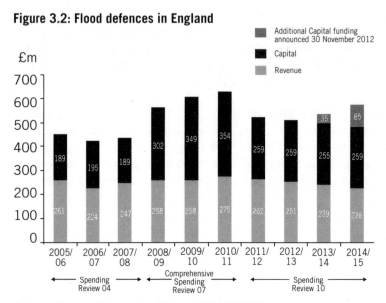

Source: House of Commons Library, SN/SC/5755.

Until 2010, flood defence spending by the government had been steadily increasing: between 1997 and 2010 spending increased by 75% in real terms. There are good reasons why spending should be increasing. One is that climate change is likely to substantially increase the chances of periods of severe rainfall. Flood damage currently costs over £1 billion a year, but the Environment Agency has estimated this figure could rise to £27 billion by 2080.

When the current government came to power, its 2010 comprehensive spending review reduced spending by 20% in real terms, according to the Committee on Climate Change. Following floods in 2012 the government provided a small amount of additional money: shown in the top sections of the last two bars in Figure 3.2. So instead of continuing to raise spending to deal with a growing threat, the government cut back spending as part of its austerity programme.

It is a distraction to try and link specific episodes of flooding to spending cutbacks. These things work on probabilities. It is also a distraction to obsess about whether spending has gone up or down in real terms. The government will claim that spending on 'frontline' defences has not fallen because of 'efficiency savings' elsewhere and partnerships with local authorities, but the real point is this: the recession presented the government with a huge opportunity to bring forward the many existing plans to enhance the UK's flood defences at a time when labour was cheap and borrowing costs very low. It chose not to take advantage of that opportunity, ostensibly because of a potential debt crisis but in reality because of an ideological distaste for public spending. Over the next decade or two, many people will pay the price for that decision, either directly as their homes and businesses are flooded, or indirectly through higher insurance premiums.

POSTSCRIPT

The hostility I reference at the start of the post was against the Environment Agency, while the reason I wrote the post was because I saw flooding as a particularly obvious cost of austerity. Yet after I wrote this post I became surprised by two aspects of nearly all the media coverage: that hardly anyone in the media referenced the data shown above (allowing the Prime Minister to get away with claims that the government had not cut spending), and that the connection between the flooding and austerity was not made.

Subsequent posts noted that in 2007 the Labour government established the Pitt review, which recommended increased spending on flood defences[6] to counteract the expected exceptional rainfall due to climate change. This was the reason for the increases in spending from 2008 to 2010. Labour introduced regulations on land use with the specific aim of reducing flood damage. The coalition government scrapped these regulations, and made the cuts shown in Figure 3.2. After this post, in November 2014, as part of Osborne's spending review, local authority spending on flood defences was cut by a third.

In short, UK flooding should have been a scandal for the government. But with the honourable exception of David Carrington in the Guardian, *the media treated flooding events as natural disasters and conspicuously failed to make the link to austerity. Cameron calculated that an appearance in wellies at each flood site would be enough to assuage public concern, and the media allowed him to get away with that.*

3.5
HITTING THE POOR AND THE DISABLED
Saturday, 12 July 2014

In the UK, Wales has a degree of regional autonomy. This has helped shed some light on two aspects of UK government policy: taking income from the disabled and the working poor.

The Welsh government asked the highly respected Institute of Fiscal Studies (IFS) to examine the cumulative impact of the coalition government's tax and benefit reforms up until April 2015. Ideally we would like such an assessment for the UK, but the government has said this would be 'difficult' and 'meaningless'. However there is no reason why findings for Wales should be very different to the UK as a whole, and the Welsh government, run by Labour, had no inhibitions about asking the IFS to do this for Wales.

In terms of income distribution, the report's findings are summarised in Figure 3.3.

The chart speaks for itself, except to say that UC and PIP stand for the new Universal Credit and Personal Independence Payments schemes, which will not have their full impact until beyond 2015.

The study also looks at how this breaks down among particular groups. Pensioners fare relatively well, losing only 0.5% of income as a result of all these changes. In contrast, the working age disabled are hit relatively badly, suffering on average a 6.5% loss. Yet this loss may pale into insignificance compared to the fear that has been created by the government's new assessment procedures, contracted out to private firms whose methods are confidential.

Figure 3.3: IFS income distribution assessment for Wales

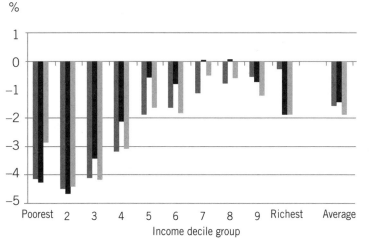

Source: Summary of gains and losses across the income distribution, 2014–15 prices. From 'The distributional effects of the UK government's tax and welfare reforms in Wales: an update' by David Phillips, IFS.

You might cynically think that this kind of thing is an inevitable result of austerity, where help to the poor and disabled is considered a luxury that society can no longer afford. Certainly the UK is not alone here. However the second policy has nothing to do with austerity. As part of its drive to reduce 'red tape', the government abolished the Agricultural Wages Board (AWB), the last surviving wages council which set minimum terms and conditions for agricultural workers. The government's argument was that the Board hindered 'flexibility' in the labour market, and that it duplicated the role of the national minimum wage.

The last argument is simplistic. Although the AWB set a basic hourly rate very similar to the national minimum wage, it also set overtime rates, which as anyone living near a farm will know, are particularly relevant to farm workers. The importance of this can be found from the government's own impact assessment of abolition, which suggests a transfer of as much as £33.4 million from farm workers to farm owners as a result of abolishing the AWB. (Farm workers are poorly paid on average: in 2011 the average wage was £8.17 per hour, compared to a minimum wage of £6.08.)

As to the need to increase market flexibility by reducing external intervention, this is particularly rich given the scale of public subsidies received by this sector. This government has fought hard to maintain the subsidies from Europe that go to large farms, so no free market there. Farm workers themselves are particularly powerless compared to their employers, which is why the AWB was the one wages council that the previous Conservative government did not abolish in 1993.

What has this got to do with Wales? The Welsh government argued that it had the power to keep an AWB for Wales. The UK government disagreed, and took this all the way to the Supreme Court, but last Wednesday it lost. So Welsh farm workers will retain some protection.

I would love to say that these two cases are isolated examples, but they are not. Conservative ministers have recently proposed additional restrictions on the right to strike, requiring over 50% of all eligible members to vote in favour of strike action before a strike can be called. This is a strikingly stupid idea, and is essentially just an attempt to further weaken an already weak trade union movement. In terms of the future of the welfare state, the Chancellor's plans for future austerity require yet further reductions. With pensions protected, this means the disabled will be in the firing line once again.

POSTSCRIPT

I have written a few posts about the impact of austerity on income distribution, so it may seem strange to include one that deals with Wales (although it is very similar to the rest of the UK). The reason relates to the second half of the post, about abolishing the Agricultural Wages Board. From what I can gather this was abolished on the extremely misleading grounds that it was no longer necessary because of the minimum wage. Someone who worked inside government at the time told me that the arguments against abolition I make here were simply not considered.

3.6
SCOTLAND AND THE SNP: FOOLING YOURSELVES AND DECEIVING OTHERS
Thursday, 11 September 2014

PREAMBLE

I wrote a number of posts before the Scottish Independence vote, but the one below became my most widely read post by far. If the SNP had won that vote, the consequences for Scotland would have been even worse than those described here, because the world oil price collapsed shortly afterwards. It would not be the last time I would bemoan politicians dismissing economic costs with the phrase 'Project Fear'.

There are many laudable reasons to campaign for Scottish independence. But how far should those who passionately want independence be prepared to go to achieve that goal? Should they, for example, deceive the Scottish people about the basic economics involved? That seems to be what is happening right now. The more I look at the numbers, the clearer it becomes that over the next

THE LIES WE WERE TOLD

five or ten years there would more, not less, fiscal austerity under independence.

The Institute for Fiscal Studies is widely respected as an independent and impartial source of expertise on everything to do with government spending, borrowing and taxation in the UK. It has produced a detailed analysis of the fiscal (tax and spending) outlook for an independent Scotland, compared to what would happen if Scotland stayed in the UK. It has no axe to grind on this issue, and a considerable reputation to maintain.

The analysis is unequivocal. Scotland's fiscal position would be worse as a result of leaving the UK for two main reasons. First, demographic trends are less favourable. Second, revenues from the North Sea are expected to decline. This tells us that under current policies Scotland would be getting an increasingly good deal out of being part of the UK. To put it another way, the rest of the UK would be transferring resources to Scotland at an increasing rate, giving Scotland time to adjust to these trends and cushioning their impact. Paying back, if you like, for all the earlier years when North Sea oil production was at its peak.

The SNP does not agree with this analysis. The main reason in the near term is that they have more optimistic projections for North Sea Oil. The IFS analysis uses OBR (Office for Budget Responsibility) projections which have in the recent past not been biased in any one direction. So how does the Scottish government get more optimistic numbers? It seems that, whenever there is room for doubt, they assume whatever gives you a higher number. In my youth I did a lot of forecasting, and I learnt how to be very suspicious of a series of individual judgements all of which tended to move something important in same direction. It is basically fiddling the analysis to get the answer you want. Either wishful thinking or deception.

I personally would criticise the IFS analysis in one respect. It assumes that Scotland would have to pay the same rate of interest on its debt as the UK. This has to be wrong. Even under the most favourable assumption of a new Scottish currency, Scotland could easily have to pay around 1% more to borrow than the UK. In its original analysis the IFS looked at the implications of that,[7] and the numbers are large.

So what would this mean? Could Scotland just borrow more? I am all for borrowing to cover temporary reductions in income, due to recessions for example, which is why I have been so critical of current austerity. However, as the IFS shows, North Sea oil income is falling long term, so this is not a temporary problem. Now it could be that the gap will be covered in the longer term by the kind of increases in productivity and labour supply that the Scottish government assumes. Governments that try to borrow today in the hope of a more optimistic future are not behaving very responsibly. However, it seems unlikely that Scotland would be able to behave irresponsibly, whatever the currency regime. It would either be stopped by fiscal rules imposed by the remaining UK, or markets that did not share the SNP's optimism about longer-term growth. So this means, over the next five or ten years, either additional spending cuts (to those already planned by the UK government), or (I hope more realistically) tax increases.

Is this a knockdown argument in favour of voting No? Of course not: there is nothing wrong in making a short-term economic sacrifice for the hope of longer-term benefits or for political goals. But that is not the SNP's case, and it is not what they are telling the Scottish people. Is this deception deliberate? I suspect it is more the delusions of people who want something so much they cast aside all doubts and problems.

This is certainly the impression I get from reading a lot of literature as I researched this post. The arguments in the *Wee Blue Book*[8] are exactly that: no sustained economic argument, but just a collection of random quotes and debating points to make a problem go away. When the future fiscal position is raised, we are so often told about the past. I too think that past North Sea oil was squandered, but grievance does not put money into a future Scottish government's coffers. I read that forecasting the future is too uncertain, from people who I am sure think about their future income when planning their personal spending. I read about how economists are always disagreeing, when in this case they are pretty united. (Of course you can always find a few who think otherwise, just as you can find one or two who think austerity is expansionary.)

When I was reading this literature, I kept thinking I had seen this kind of thing before: being in denial about macroeconomic fundamentals because they interfered with a major institutional change that was driven by politics. Then I realised what it was: the formation of the Eurozone in 2000. Once again economists were clear and pretty united about what the key macroeconomic problem was ('asymmetric shocks'), and just like now this was met with wishful thinking that somehow it just wouldn't happen. It did, and the Eurozone is still living with the consequences.

So maybe that also explains why I feel so strongly this time around. I have no political skin in this game: a certain affection for the concept of the union, but nothing strong enough to make me even tempted to distort my macroeconomics in its favour. If the Scottish people want to make a short-term economic sacrifice in the hope of longer-term gains and political freedom that is their choice. But they should make that choice knowing what it is, and not be deceived into believing that these costs do not exist.

3.7
IS THIS THE RIGHT WAY TO SHRINK THE STATE (NHS EDITION)?
Thursday, 26 November 2015)

In terms of changes since his July budget, the basic story of the Autumn Statement is that George Osborne has used more favourable tax forecasts from the OBR to ease up a little on planned spending cuts. The stress here is on 'a little'. We still have sharp fiscal tightening, with the OBR's estimate of the cyclically adjusted budget deficit showing a turnaround worth 4% of GDP between 2015/16 and 2019/20. (That is nearly as much as the contraction from 2009/10 until 2015/16. The turnaround in the actual deficit is slightly larger.) While the US and euro area ease off on fiscal consolidation, George wants to carry on.

In an article in the *Independent* I make two key points.[9] With all these cuts, we are told about 'protected departments'. This is classic spin: employ words which the media will use endlessly that do not mean what most people think they mean. The second is that if the goal is to reduce the size of the state, this seems a remarkably incompetent way of doing it. Rather than look at what the state does and strategically decide what we could do without, the method seems to be to keep cutting until a crisis becomes visible. I do not think enough is made of this government's incompetence. I want to illustrate both points by looking at health.

Let's start with this nice chart from John Appleby of The King's Fund (Figure 3.4).[10] It should be shown every time anyone claims that NHS spending under this government has been protected.

For reasons that are well known, the share of spending on health pretty well everywhere has been rising steadily since World War II. Try to reverse that and you get a crisis. Try to reverse that when you are also slashing local authority spending for community help, so that elderly patients cannot be discharged into local authority care, and you get a major crisis.

But that is not the only sign of incompetence. Under the coalition Cameron undertook a massive reorganisation of the NHS, which was badly conceived and used up precious resources. (Perhaps the biggest political failure of the Liberal Democrats in coalition was to allow this reorganisation to go through.) Then before the last election the Conservatives thought it would be a clever strategy to establish a 'seven-day a week' health service. To try and justify that policy, Health Minister Jeremy Hunt made dodgy use of data[11] to argue that health outcomes were worse if you were admitted to hospital at the weekend. Did no one tell him that this might lead some to do themselves harm by trying to delay going into hospital?

Figure 3.4: King's Fund data on NHS spending

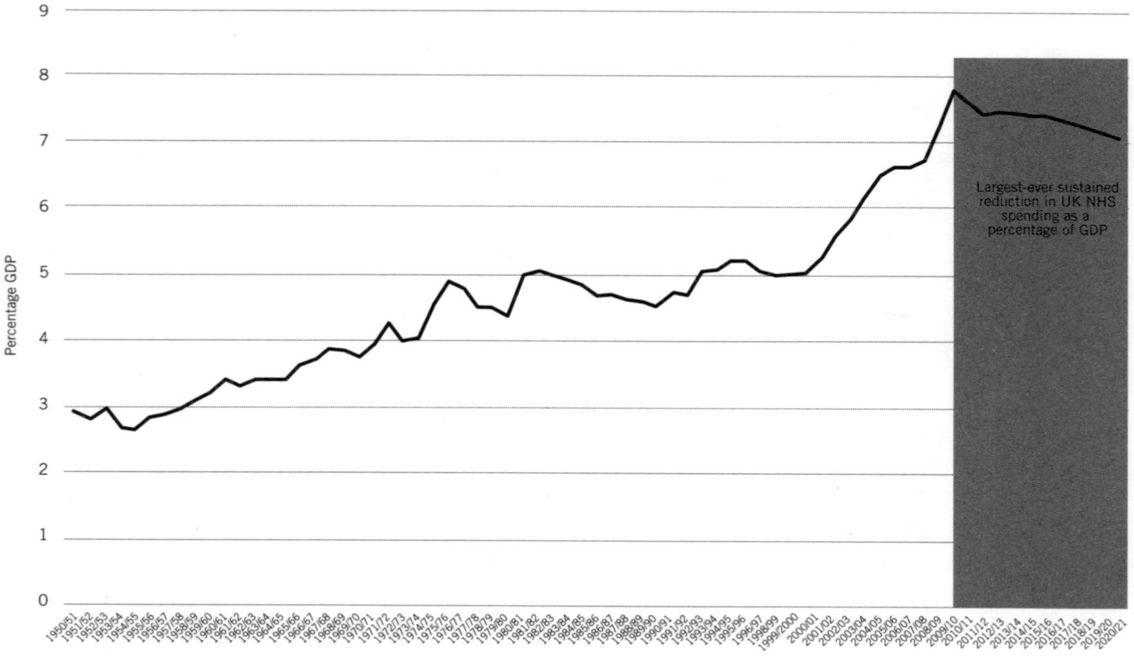

Largest-ever sustained reduction in UK NHS spending as a percentage of GDP

Percentage GDP

Source: John Appleby (2015) 'NHS spending: squeezed as never before', The King's Fund, 20 October.

There is no money to fund this new policy, so Hunt has tried to restructure junior doctors' contracts to pay for it. With many junior doctors already leaving the UK to work overseas, this was the last straw and they have voted overwhelmingly to go on strike. In 2012 training places for nurses were cut, so now hospitals have to use more expensive agency nurses. All this indicates basic incompetence by those who ultimately are responsible for the NHS.

It was this kind of thing that I had in mind when I wrote: 'It is difficult to know which is worse: duplicity to achieve an ideological goal or pursuing that goal incompetently.'[12]

4

THE
2015 UK
GENERAL ELECTION

Introduction

In my view mediamacro (how macroeconomics is presented in the media) was critical to the 2015 election result. Post 4.1 sets the scene, by looking at the apparent contradiction between Conservative claims that the economy was strong and Labour claims about a cost of living crisis. The reality, outlined in Post 4.2, was that the economy was not strong in any meaningful sense, and had performed poorly under the coalition relative to the previous Labour government. Post 4.3 looks at the role of business leaders in elections.

To emphasise the chasm between economic reality and how things were portrayed by the media, I published shortly before the election a series of posts on 'mediamacro myths', of which Post 4.4 is a summary. Needless to say, economic reporting did not improve. In the last few days of the campaign the broadcast media focused on the Conservative line that a Labour–SNP coalition would bring chaos. In Post 4.5 I explain why it was another myth: as I wrote, 'If you want chaos, see what will happen to the Conservative party during the EU referendum'. But it was a powerful myth because it appealed to English nationalism, and also because there was no one arguing against it.

Post 4.6 sets out why mediamacro was a key factor behind the Conservative success. There was also, as I suggest in Post 4.7, a large element of luck. But the luck should not obscure my claim that had the media reported macroeconomic facts rather than mediamacro myths, the Conservatives would not have won, and among other things we would still be in the EU. And of course luck runs out eventually.

Posts in Chapter 4

4.1
THE UK FEEL-GOOD FACTOR
Thursday, 20 November 2014

If UK GDP growth has been so good (OK, I'm exaggerating) over the last two years, and the economy is growing faster than the Eurozone and Japan, why are most people still worse off than before the recession?

The first reason is straightforward. A large amount of the increase in GDP we have seen since 2007 is the result of there being more people in the UK. Figure 4.1 plots real GDP and real GDP per capita, where I've normalised the second series so it starts at the same point in 2007 Q1.

While the level of GDP in the second quarter of 2014 was well past its 2007 peak, the level of GDP per head was below that peak. GDP per head is a much better measure of how prosperous each individual

Figure 4.1: Real GDP and real GDP per capita

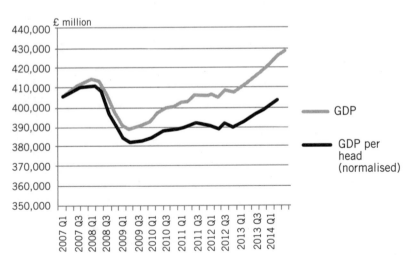

Source: ONS (Office for National Statistics).

person in the UK feels. (Incidentally, GDP per head in the US and Japan in 2013 exceeded 2007 levels. UK levels in 2013 relative to 2007 were similar to the Eurozone, but going up in the UK, down in the EZ.)

There are two other important differences between total GDP and how prosperous consumers feel. The first is how GDP is distributed between wages, profits and taxes. Figure 4.2 shows the shares of these three items (plus an 'other' category that includes self-employment income) over the same period.

Figure 4.2: Breakdown of real GDP by income share

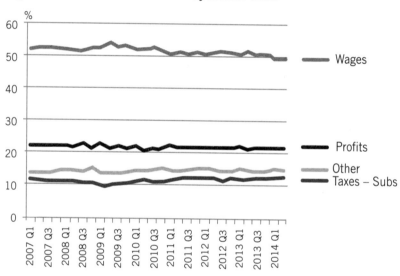

Source: ONS (Office for National Statistics).

The top line is the share of 'wages' (compensation of employees) in GDP. Movements have not been dramatic, but this share is now lower than in 2007. A major reason for this is straightforward: higher indirect taxes. VAT was reduced in 2009, but restored in 2010, and raised again in 2011. Austerity has played a part in reducing real incomes. You might think another factor is changes in direct taxes and benefits, but cuts in taxes have largely offset cuts in benefits on average (but not for those in the lower quarter of the income distribution).

The second important factor is what economists call the terms of trade. We buy many overseas goods, so if their price has been rising relative to the price of goods produced in the UK, we will feel poorer. Here the major change occurred in 2008, with the large depreciation in sterling, although higher commodity prices will also have had an impact.

This leads to some data that is increasingly quoted in the media, which is the average earnings index relative to the consumer price index. People have been getting excited by the fact that the two measures are now growing at roughly the same rate, and when you look at the time series for real earnings from 2007 to today you can see why (Figure 4.3).

Figure 4.3: Real earnings from 2007

Source: ONS (Office for National Statistics).

Real earnings were over 8% lower in 2014Q2 compared to their average in 2007. This overstates how much poorer we are on average for various reasons, but poorer we certainly are. Real disposable income per head was about 2.5% lower in 2013 than 2007. Consumption per head in 2013 was also substantially lower than in 2007, and also lower than it was in 2005 and 2006. And if you think that was because 2007 was a debt-fuelled consumer boom, you are wrong. In fact, according to the latest data from the ONS, the savings ratio in 2013 was a little below its level in 2007.

So although GDP may be higher than before the recession, when we take account of the fact that there are more people in the UK, government takes more in indirect taxes, and import prices have risen much faster than the price of UK output, the data really shows that we are significantly poorer.

4.2
TO ALL UK JOURNALISTS
Thursday, 29 January 2015

To all UK journalists who plan to talk about the economy over the next 100 days. Here is a very simple fact. GDP per head (a much better guide to average prosperity than GDP itself) grew at an average rate of less than 1% in the four years from 2010 to 2014. In the previous 13 years (1997 to 2010), growth averaged over 1.5%. So growth in GDP per head was more than 50% higher under Labour than under the Conservatives, even though the biggest recession since the 1930s is included in the Labour period!

You have all read, and perhaps written, that the Conservatives will focus on the economy, because they think that is their strong point. Compared to their performance on other issues, maybe it is their strong point. But relative to the previous administration, this simple fact suggests otherwise.

George Osborne says: 'Britain has had the fastest growing major economy in the world in 2014.'[1] However, GDP per head in the UK in 2014 remains below 2007 levels, but it had exceeded those levels in the US and Japan by 2013. The UK is not bottom of the league in these terms only because the Eurozone's performance has been so poor. That GDP per head growth under 1.9% in 2014 can be trumpeted as a great success when it is no more than average growth between 1971 and 2010, and when we should be recovering from a huge recession, shows how diminished our expectations have become.

In terms of a historical comparison between the record of this government and the previous administration Labour has no case to answer, because its performance is miles better. I am sure a supporter of the current government would say at this point that they had to clear up the mess that Labour created. But just think what such an excuse implies:

- The Great Recession was in 2009, so it is included in the Labour government's growth average, not that of the current government. You can see the impact of the recession on the average (the red line) in Figure 4.4. Are they really saying that the mess Labour left was worse than the impact of the global financial crisis?

- This excuse implies that bringing the government deficit down rapidly (austerity) meant that GDP growth is bound to be lower. This is something that the government's critics have long argued, and which the OBR agrees with, but the government has always denied. Is the government now admitting that austerity was (really) bad for growth?

- If a government was elected just after a major recession, you would normally expect the exact opposite from these figures to be true. The new government would benefit from the recovery from the recession, while its predecessor's average would be weighed down by the recession itself. So in any normal world, you would expect GDP per head to have grown much more rapidly over the last four years than any long-run average. The fact that it has grown by considerably less means that the government should have a lot of explaining to do.

Growth under Labour, including the Great Recession, was 50% better than under the coalition. So please, if you want to make your reporting on the economy over the next 100 days objective, use this fact. If the Conservatives win this election because enough people believe that they are more competent than the previous government at handling the economy, it will be a devastating verdict – on the UK media and its journalists.

Figure 4.4: Quarter on previous year's quarter growth in UK GDP per head, 1997Q2 to 2014Q3

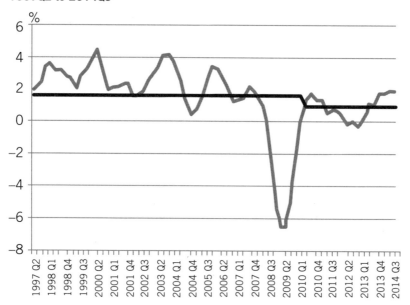

Source: ONS (Office for National Statistics).

4.3
INEQUALITY, BUSINESS LEADERS AND MORE DELUSIONS ON THE LEFT
Saturday, 7 February 2015

The Blair governments did a lot to fight poverty, but were famously relaxed about inequality, or more specifically the earnings of the 1%. For many in those governments this reflected their own views, but it also reflected a political calculation. The calculation went as follows. To win, Labour needed to be seen as competent to run the economy. The media all too often look to business leaders to answer that question. So Labour needed to be business friendly. Now being business friendly should mean creating an environment that business can thrive in. However to get the approval of business leaders you also need to create an environment where business leaders can thrive personally, and they are very much part of the 1%. QED.

Labour today is not following this strategy. First, Miliband has said quite clearly that he sees tackling inequality as a major issue:

> Now I have heard some people say they don't know what we stand for. So let me take the opportunity today to spell it out in the simplest of terms. It is what I stood for when I won the leadership of this party. And it is what I stand for today. This country is too unequal. And we need to change it.

Second, it has two policies that directly impinge on the 1%: the mansion tax and restoring the 50p income tax band.

There are some on the left who dismiss these measures as marginal. One of the comments on an earlier post said that 'When it comes to the broad trend of ever greater inequality there really is no meaningful difference between the main parties'. This seems to me a colossal tactical error. To see why, you only have to note what has happened over the last week in the UK. Various business leaders have proclaimed that a Labour government would be a disaster. Stefano Pessina, who among other things runs the Boots chain, declined to elaborate on why exactly Labour would be a disaster.[2] In contrast, he was quite clear that the UK leaving the EU would be a big mistake, which of course is much more likely to happen under a Conservative government!

There is an obvious inference. Labour would not so much be bad for business, but bad for business leaders personally. Another possibility is that they think Labour would be much tougher on business tax avoidance than the Conservatives, but saying this in public would be embarrassing. They, unlike some on the left, recognise that Miliband is not Blair, and that there has been a key shift in the direction of Labour policy. So they will do what they can to stop Labour winning. Labour in turn has responded by attacking the tax avoidance practised by many of these companies. This is the beginnings of a major battle.

There are at least two important implications. First, the non-partisan media need to understand what is going on. Getting business leaders to comment on the relative merits of the two main parties' programmes is no longer a neutral decision – it is giving additional airtime to one side. Second, everyone who cares about inequality needs to realise the importance of this election. Inequality is a key election issue, and there is a very meaningful difference between the two main sides. Certain business leaders clearly understand that.

POSTSCRIPT

On 1 April 2015, a survey of mainly academic economists[3]
was published in which 66% disagreed with the statement
that 'austerity policies of the coalition government have had
a positive effect on aggregate economic activity'. Some of the
media picked up the story, and I was interviewed on the BBC's
World at One *about it. However on the same day a letter from*
100 'business leaders' was published in the Daily Telegraph
saying that the Conservatives have better policies for business.

Now this letter was not a survey (it is, by definition, a biased sample), and given this post it was hardly news. Despite this, the letter rather than the economists' survey was lead item on the BBC news. In terms of prominence and duration of coverage in the broadcast media, the letter beat the survey hands down. This post explains why that was a choice that did not represent balanced coverage.

4.4
MEDIAMACRO MYTHS: SUMMING UP
Wednesday, 29 April 2015

The story presented in much of the UK media is simple and intuitive. The previous government messed up: it spent too much, and it left the UK economy on the brink of financial meltdown. The coalition came to the rescue: clearing up the mess was tough at first, but now it is all coming good.

In previous posts I have shown that this is almost complete fiction. The increase in the government's budget deficit under Labour was all about the recession, which in turn was created by the global financial crisis. There was no prospect of a UK financial crisis in 2010, which meant that austerity was not something the government was forced to undertake. Reducing the deficit could have been left until the recovery was secure (and, crucially, interest rates had risen above their lower bound), but the coalition chose to do otherwise. As a result they delayed the recovery by three years, at great cost. Even since 2013 we have simply seen a return to normal growth rates: there has been no catching up of lost ground. In that sense, growth under the coalition hardly deserves the term recovery, and we have seen an unprecedented lack of growth in living standards. Productivity growth has been non-existent, yet the government has feted the employment growth that is its counterpart.

The government's claims of macroeconomic success can therefore be dismissed without saying a word about the nature of the GDP growth that has taken place. But what growth there has been is itself worryingly unbalanced. Growth is too dependent on consumption, there is not enough investment, and the current account deficit is very large.

A large part of the media sees their role as supporting the government's line, however far from the truth it may be. For whatever reason, most of the remaining media has bought this line, and failed to expose it as fiction. Even a headline in the *Guardian* yesterday talked about 'rip-roaring growth rates of 2013 and 2014' when growth in GDP per head in those years was at best just average, and growth in income per head non-existent.

It is still commonplace to hear media commentators say that the economy is doing great, and ask why the government is not reaping the benefit in terms of political support. In truth the puzzle is the opposite: given how poor economic performance under the coalition has been, and that this poor performance has hit most people in their pockets, the real puzzle is why so many people think the government is economically competent. And the answer to that puzzle in turn lies in the myths that mediamacro has allowed to go unchallenged. Perhaps the latest figures, showing just 0.3% growth in 2015Q1, might begin to dent them, but a remarkable feature of these myths is that they seem impervious to actual data.

I coined the term mediamacro because I obviously find it strange that public discourse on the macroeconomic fortunes of the UK economy seems so different from what the data and simple economics would suggest. For once I can be the one-handed economist that Truman demanded, because the evidence is so clear and the economics so uncontentious. But mediamacro has implications well beyond macroeconomics. If the media has been capable of distorting reality by so much for so long in this case, are there other areas where it has done the same, and what does that tell us about the health of our democracy?

4.5
CHAOS THEORY
Thursday, 30 April 2015

Some polls suggest that the Conservatives have finally found a scare story that works. We probably will not know how large or long-lasting it will be until after the election. However, as scare stories are generally myths, I thought it would be worth asking why this one has stuck whereas earlier attempts have failed.

Here were some earlier but unsuccessful attempts.

- 'Labour will bankrupt the economy, again.' Given mediamacro, this should have worked. But I suspect this line was ruined when Cameron started to promise to tax less and spend more and reduce the deficit. You cannot base your fiscal policy on home economics and then ignore the household accounts.

- 'Labour will put up your taxes' flopped, perhaps because voters didn't mind too much if this helps save the NHS. A smaller state is just not popular, which is probably one reason why they had to make so much of deficit reduction.

- The 'Miliband looks funny' strategy fell apart when people realised he was rather better than much of the press made out. The problem here was that there was no half-truth to build a myth upon (beside a rather dark one), but the Conservatives believed their own propaganda.

So why has the Lab + SNP = chaos line worked? A myth it certainly is. If you want chaos, see what will happen to the Conservative party during the EU referendum.

With my mediamacro experience, I can think of three reasons why this myth has stuck. First, a successful myth has to be based on a half-truth, and the half-truth is that the SNP would have some influence on any Labour government. Not much, because to vote down a Labour government would be a huge gamble for the SNP. Their support in Scotland could disappear overnight if they could be charged with letting a Conservative government back in without due cause. But clearly there would be some influence, which is only right in a democracy.

Second, the non-partisan media finds it difficult to counter a myth when no major political party is calling it a myth, particularly during an election. The SNP has encouraged the myth: some would unkindly say because they want a Conservative government, but even if that is not true they want to talk up the influence they would have on Labour. Labour itself does not want to promote the idea that they could happily work with the SNP because they in turn want to scare former Labour Scottish voters from voting SNP. With no political party challenging the chaos myth, the broadcast media finds it very difficult to do so off its own bat.

Third, this is new territory, with few reference points, so people cannot use their own experience of similar situations in the past. The parallel with austerity would be the Eurozone crisis.

But before I convince myself, there may be something less myth-like and more basic going on here: pure and simple nationalism. Although many on the left would like to believe that the Scottish independence referendum marked a new engagement with politics away from the Westminster elite, it could also just be an example of the political power of nationalism. And if nationalism can have so much force north of the border, it is not surprising that there should not be at least some echo of this in England. English feelings of resentment and unfairness might be perfectly justified, but their monetary and political importance is tiny compared to the huge differences between the political parties on other issues. But nationalism does not respect that kind of calculus.

So maybe this all has nothing to do with chaos theory, but is simply about a more basic strategy: divide and rule.

4.6
UK ELECTION: IT WAS MEDIAMACRO WOT WON IT

Sunday, 3 May 2015

After the UK general election in 1992, which the Conservatives won to the surprise of many, the Murdoch-owned tabloid newspaper the *Sun* splashed the headline 'It's The Sun Wot Won It'. The headline is infamous enough to have its own Wikipedia entry. I want to argue that what I call mediamacro won the 2015 election for the Conservatives.

Since the 2010 elections, YouGov has asked the following question: 'Here is a list of problems facing the country. Could you say for each of them which political party you think would handle the problem best?' Table 4.1 compares the Labour lead in this poll just after the 2010 elections and today.

Table 4.1: Labour lead after the 2010 elections and today

Issue	Lab lead 6/7 June 2010	26/27 April 2015	Difference
NHS	−1	14	+15
Immigration	−26	−6	+20
Law and Order	−21	−12	+9
Education	−4	6	+10
Taxation	−10	−8	+2
Unemployment	−7	−4	+3
Economy in General	−11	−18	-7

Source: YouGov.

Ignoring the normal academic caveats, the message is clear: the only topic on which the Conservatives are doing better today than shortly after they won the last election is their handling of the economy in general.

Yet when you look at any standard criteria of economic performance, the economy has done terribly during the coalition's term of office. There is no doubt about this: numbers from GDP per head to real wages all tell a similar story. Average living standards have not increased, which means that they have fallen for many, a result which is almost unprecedented over a five-year period. How much of this is the result of government policy is debatable, but that is not a debate that you see in the media. What you see in the media is an obsession with the government's budget deficit, and on that criterion the coalition has left the economy in a better state than when it came in. So the only way to explain these poll results is that people have internalised the media's obsession with the deficit.

Now normally you would ask how on earth something like the budget deficit could trump standards of living when judging economic performance. This is where the mediamacro myth of Labour profligacy is so important. One of the lasting images of this election was the man in the recent Leaders *Question Time* who accused Miliband of lying when he said that the global financial crisis rather than Labour profligacy had caused the deficit. He just knew that the last government had bankrupted the economy, and it appears many in the audience did too. And who could blame them: coalition politicians go unchallenged when they say it, and lots of newspapers repeat the line endlessly as fact.

It is a myth, pure and simple, but an important myth, because it places the blame for stagnant or falling living standards during the coalition government on its opponents. They created the mess the coalition had to clear up, and that was bound to be painful for a time. I've watched people who comment on this blog try to twist and turn figures in a desperate attempt to keep the myth alive. I've experienced being rubbished in the partisan media for trying to expose this myth. But in mediamacro this *Question Time* confrontation is described as an awkward moment for Miliband, rather than just the ranting of a bloke who had never looked at the numbers. I cannot recall any major coalition politician being seriously challenged for promulgating this myth.

It is strange watching all this happen. I know that having written one of only two or three academic papers on Labour's fiscal record does not guarantee that what I say is correct, but it certainly gives me confidence that I am not talking rubbish. I write what I can, talk to any journalists who ask, trying to get the facts across. Facts like the deficit before the global financial crisis was only within a typical forecast error of its sustainable level. Facts like the debt to GDP ratio before the Great Recession was below the level Labour inherited.

Yet I know that this message will never be received, however indirectly, by the angry man in that debate, or by most of that audience. Perhaps some do not want to know the facts, but if they did, they are very unlikely to hear them. Instead they will get propaganda from most newspapers, and 'views on the shape of the earth differ' type comments from broadcasters, whose journalists are desperate not to appear to take sides. For that reason, if the coalition government remains in power after this election (or if the Conservatives win outright), then the title of this post will have rather more justification than the *Sun*'s original headline.

4.7
OH WHAT A LUCKY MAN
Friday, 8 May 2015

A few weeks ago I was having dinner with David Cameron. Well, almost: we were at the same restaurant but on tables at the opposite side of the room. He was taking a break from campaigning. I remember thinking he must be one of the luckiest Prime Ministers the UK has ever had. Two strokes of luck in particular stand out: the economy and Scotland. They stand out because between them they enabled him to win an election that he really should have lost.

I've talked at length about mediamacro: a network of myths which enable failure to be turned into success. I've not come across a single non-City, non-partisan economist who does not concur with the view that the performance of the coalition has been pretty poor (or simply terrible), yet polls repeatedly show that people believe managing the economy is the Conservatives' strength. This trick has been accomplished by equating the government's budget with the household, and elevating reducing the deficit as the be all and end all of economic policy.

This allowed Cameron to pass off the impact of bad macro management in delaying the recovery as inevitable pain because they had to 'clear up the mess' left by their predecessor. In a recent poll a third of people blamed Labour for austerity. Yet for that story to work well, the economy had to improve towards the end of the coalition's term in office. The coalition understood this, which was why austerity was put on hold, and everything was thrown at the economy to get a recovery, including pumping up the housing market. In the end the recovery was pretty minimal (no more than average growth), and far from secure (as the 2015Q1 growth figures showed), but it was enough for mediamacro to pretend that earlier austerity had been vindicated. (And, to give them their due, they are very good at pretending.)

So why do I say Cameron is lucky? First, largely by chance (but also because other countries had been undertaking fiscal austerity), UK growth in 2014 was the highest among major economies. This statistic was played for all it was worth. Second, although (in reality) modest growth was not enough to raise real incomes, just in the nick of time oil prices fell, so real wages have now begun to rise. Third, playing the game of shutting down part of the economy so that you can boast when it starts up again is a dangerous game, and you need a bit of fortune to get it right. (Of course if there really was no plan, and the recovery was delayed through incompetence, then he is luckier still.)

The Scottish independence referendum in September last year was close: 45% of Scots voted in September to leave the UK. One of the major push factors was the Conservative-led government. If Scotland had voted for independence in 2014, it would have been a disaster for Cameron: after all, the full title of his party is the Conservative and Unionist Party. That was his first piece of Scottish fortune. The second was that the referendum dealt a huge blow to Labour in Scotland. Labour is far from blameless here, and its support had been gradually declining, but there can be no doubt that the aftermath of the referendum lost the party many Scottish seats, and therefore reduced its seat total in the UK.

Yet that led to a third piece of luck. The SNP tidal wave in Scotland gave him one additional card he could play to his advantage: English nationalism. The wall of sound coming from the right-wing press about how the SNP would hold Miliband to ransom was enough to get potential UKIP supporters to vote Conservative in sufficient numbers for him to win the election.

With the economy you could perhaps argue that there was some judgement as well as luck involved. That is very difficult to believe with Scotland. The man who almost presided over the break-up of the United Kingdom, and had to rely on Labour efforts (including his predecessor Gordon Brown) to avoid that outcome, will continue as Prime Minister as an indirect result. That is why, as I watched David Cameron eat supper at a nearby table, I thought something to the effect of you lucky person.

5

THE
TRANSFORMATION
OF THE LABOUR PARTY

Introduction

*After the election, Labour MPs seemed to collectively decide that
defeat was a result of Miliband moving to the left. Post 5.1 suggests
a very different story. Many Labour MPs also argued that it was time
to embrace austerity: Posts 5.2 and 5.4 argue this was the wrong
thing to do, on political as well as economic grounds. Corbyn's initial
popularity should therefore come as no surprise: while the media
talked about Labour Party members moving to the left, I argue in Post
5.3 that in reality the Parliamentary Labour Party had moved to the
right. Post 5.5 presents a fuller analysis of why Corbyn looked like he
was going to win.*

When he did win, suddenly all this became personal. I was invited onto Labour's newly established Economic Advisory Council (EAC). I explain why I accepted in Post 5.6, and report the stick I got in some quarters for doing so in Post 5.7. One of the arguments suggested for not joining was that it would all be a waste of our time because Corbyn was bound to be a disaster in any general election, which I discuss in Post 5.8. Post 5.9 discusses the stupidity of continuing internal division among Labour MPs. Post 5.10 discusses Labour's alternative fiscal policy rule, and how it was reported in the media.

Labour's fiscal credibility rule, which was part of the party's 2017 manifesto and at the time of writing remains party policy, is for me one of the key achievements of the EAC. The EAC came to an end as a result of Brexit. I have not included any posts from that period because I do not think they are of lasting interest, but it seems appropriate here to explain briefly what happened.

Before the Brexit vote the Council had stressed the serious implications of leaving the EU (discussed in detail in the next chapter). Five days after the vote, around 80% of Labour MPs expressed no confidence in the leadership, which then led to a new leadership contest, where Corbyn was challenged by Owen Smith. One EAC member, Danny Blanchflower, resigned and supported Owen Smith. I also supported Smith, as he opposed Brexit while Corbyn believed (at the time) that the referendum vote meant that we had to leave the Customs Union and Single Market. Otherwise the policy positions of the candidates were almost identical.

I was keen for the EAC to continue if Smith won, so I signed with four other members a statement, published on my blog, expressing support for the concept of the Council but also saying: 'we have felt unhappy that the Labour leadership has not campaigned more strongly to avoid' Brexit. When Corbyn beat Smith, I personally felt that Labour's Brexit position at the time, together with tensions within the party, meant that I could not continue on the EAC. Other members also resigned.

Posts in Chapter 5

5.1
DO POLITICIANS NEED TO PANDER TO MYTHS?
Saturday, 23 May 2015

Paul Bernal has a powerful post where he says Labour lost the election long before 2015, by pandering to three big myths: the myth that Labour created a huge deficit which required austerity in the midst of a recession; the myth of the 'scrounger'; and the myth that Labour made a mistake in allowing excessive immigration.[1] I obviously agree about deficits, I'm appalled at the hostility to welfare recipients stoked by the right-wing tabloids and the harm done by inept reform, and I'm dismayed that politicians shy away from putting the positive case for immigration. For that reason I should agree that in England at least one of the three major parties should be standing up against all these myths. The Conservatives and Liberal Democrats helped manufacture the first myth, and the Conservatives contributed to the second and pander to the third (although some of their supporters would not favour costly immigration controls). Labour failed to combat all three.

The media have, predictably, reached a consensus about why Labour lost: it was too left wing, it was anti-business, it failed to be aspirational (it wanted to raise some taxes on the rich), blah blah blah. But there is no clear evidence for these assertions. Instead, they just happen to represent the things that much of the media dislike about Labour's policies. Watching at least some of Labour's potential future leaders, who the media as a whole describe as 'modernisers', fall in line with the media's diagnosis makes the Parliamentary Labour Party look pathetic. Perhaps it is.

And yet being tough on scroungers and immigration is very popular. And these issues mattered for many voters. In a tweet about Bernal's post, I asked was it better to lose telling the truth than lose being complicit in a lie? But it would be better still if a political party could tell the truth and win! Yet that seems a hopeless task. Jonathan Portes has championed the evidence on immigration, but as the BBC's Nick Robinson put it, he would not get elected in any constituency as a result.

It is tempting at this point to blame the media for this state of affairs. In one sense I agree: I think newspapers should have a responsibility to tell the truth, rather than pander to prejudice when it suits their owners to do so. But in terms of practical politics this does not get you very far. One of the depressing conclusions that will be drawn from the election result is that it is fatal to stand up to Rupert Murdoch.

Is it also true that cutting the deficit is widely popular? Here I think the evidence is less clear. Perceived competence is vitally important, and not only in relation to self-interest. That is why Labour made a strategic mistake in not challenging with more force the coalition's blatant myth making on the deficit issue. It is incredible how the blame for our current problems has so easily been transferred from the finance sector to fiscal profligacy, and not just in the UK. (But not so incredible if you follow the money, and take media power seriously.)

Perhaps I can also make a very personal point here. As one of only a few academics who have written an academic paper on the Labour government's fiscal record[2], which concluded that Labour profligacy was a myth, you might have expected Labour at some stage to have used some of the many words I have written on this to support their case. As far as I know they did not. Perhaps they were put off by some of my criticism of other aspects of Labour's programme. But this didn't put off Alex Salmond, who was happy to quote my support of the SNP's line on austerity, suggesting it had all the more force because I was not an SNP supporter.

Talking of which, I think there is one more piece of received wisdom that needs exposing, and that is Scottish exceptionalism. As I hinted at the beginning, there was one major UK party that did campaign against austerity, was pro-immigration and supportive of welfare. No doubt other factors also led to the huge success of the Scottish National Party, but the party's position on these three issues didn't seem to do it any harm, and in some cases probably helped a lot. This example suggests the answer to the question posed in the title is a clear no.

It is generally presumed by the media, both sides of the border, that this is all because Scots are inherently more left wing than the English. But the evidence suggests differences in social attitudes between Scotland and England are not that great. The question Labour (or at least somebody) should be asking is why the SNP can avoid pandering to these three myths and win decisively, when the consensus is that doing the same in England would be electoral suicide.

5.2
LABOUR AND THE DEFICIT
Wednesday, 15 July 2015

PREAMBLE

This is one of the more restrained posts I wrote during the period between losing the 2015 election and the leadership contest. I had previously written posts attacking articles on the deficit written by senior Labour figures like Chuka Umunna, which sounded far too similar to what George Osborne was saying. In a later post, after a vote abstaining on a bill reducing welfare spending, I said Labour had lost its soul. Of the four prospective Labour leadership candidates, only Corbyn voted against. As I argue here, the irony is that Labour appeared to be adopting austerity macroeconomics at just the point at which public opinion on the issue seemed to be changing. I discuss why it may be changing in Post 5.4. Needless to say, I think the 2017 election, when Labour did campaign on an anti-austerity platform, suggests those who thought 2015 meant Labour had moved too far to the left got it seriously wrong.

A constant refrain from those who help make Labour Party policy goes like this: I know what you economists say makes sense, but we tried that policy at the last election, and failed horribly. We have to listen to what the people are telling us.

So, for example, we cannot oppose George Osborne's deficit plans, because we tried that at the last election and lost. We cannot talk about the problem of rent seeking by the 1%, because we tried that and it was seen by voters as anti-aspiration. We cannot argue for a higher minimum wage because that will be seen as anti-market and anti-business, and then George Osborne does exactly that.

I would draw exactly the opposite conclusion from the election result. On the deficit Labour tried to avoid discussion, and let the Conservatives spin the idea that austerity was the last Labour government's fault. By failing to challenge both this nonsense, and the austerity policy enacted in 2010 and 2011, and the austerity policy proposed after 2015, in terms of perception it adopted the Conservative policy on the deficit. That was why it lost heavily.

Some will say that come the next election the government will be running a budget surplus anyway, so why oppose the process of getting there? The answer to that is aptly illustrated by Labour's decision not to oppose Budget plans to limit child tax credits to the first two children, or plans to reduce the benefit cap. Both are terrible policies, and it is incredible that Labour is not opposing them. But once you concede the need for austerity, it becomes much more difficult to oppose the measures that come with it.

Another argument is that Labour has to accept Osborne's surplus target, because nothing else will stop Labour being accused of being fiscally spendthrift. This just sounds politically naive. George Osborne (as Chancellor or PM) will not suddenly drop the spendthrift argument just because Labour adopts his plans. Instead the argument will change to focus on credibility. He will say: Labour now admits that it was spendthrift in government, and in opposition it has changed its mind so often, you just cannot believe what they say: so any future Labour government will be as spendthrift as the last.

Others will respond to the above by saying, how can you argue Labour lost because it was not left wing enough? But challenging austerity is not 'left wing', it is just good macroeconomics. The idea that opposing austerity, or advocating less inequality, is akin to what Labour did between 1979 and 1983 is absurd.

If there are examples to draw from, it is to see how your opponents succeeded where you failed. The Conservatives did not regain power in 2010 by moving their policies to the left. They did it by changing their image. Until a couple of years before 2010 they had promised to match Labour on spending. But when circumstances changed, they seized their chance to change policy and focus on the deficit. It was a smart move not because of the economics, but because of how it could be spun.

In 2015, the SNP saw that times had changed compared to 2010. The idea that we might become like Greece was no longer credible, and voter attitudes on the deficit were much more divided. So they campaigned against austerity, and partly as a result wiped Labour out. (Their actual policy proposals were not very different from Labour's, but unfortunately few voters look at the numbers: it is perception that matters.)

The lesson is that when the external environment changes, you try to exploit this change in a way that enhances the principles you stand for and gains you votes. As the deficit falls, putting this at the centre of policy will seem less and less relevant. In contrast, the costs of austerity and rising poverty that are the result of 'going for surplus' will become more and more evident. Osborne, by going for an unnecessarily rapid reduction in debt by means of increasing poverty, has thrown a potential lifeline to Labour. Unfortunately, Labour appears to be swimming away from it.

5.3
CORBYN'S POPULARITY AND RELATIVISTIC POLITICS
Friday, 31 July 2015

This is just a short gripe about some of the commentary around the Labour leadership contest. So many who write about this express their puzzlement that someone from the left of the party can suddenly appear to be so popular. This can only mean, they suggest, that the Labour Party membership must have moved to the left.

This mistake reflects something that Paul Krugman has remarked upon in the US: the tendency of commentators to define the centre as simply today's mid-point between the two main parties. So as Labour moves towards the Conservatives, according to this way of looking at it the centre also moves to the right.

Now if that is how you want to define the centre, so be it. Such a relativistic view is very post-modern, I guess. But when that idea is then used to say that Labour Party members must have moved to the left, its limitations become self-evident. In reality all that might be going on is that the views of Labour Party members have not moved at all, but they have been left behind as Labour MPs and other prospective leaders have moved to the right. I think we have clear evidence that this is more likely to be what is happening.

The most obvious example is the welfare bill, and Labour's shameful decision to abstain on this. But another that is close to my heart is austerity. Talk to some, and being anti-austerity has become synonymous with being well to the left. Of course in reality it is just textbook macroeconomics, but if we stick to measuring everything on a left–right axis, then remember that it was only as far back as 2009 that the need for fiscal stimulus rather than deficit reduction was the position advocated by a centre/left Labour Party in the UK, and the Democrats in the US. It cannot be surprising, therefore, that among the relatively well-informed electorate that is the Labour Party membership an anti-austerity position is still seen as a sensible policy. With an extreme relativistic view you could say that by sticking to this position these people have moved to the left, but please don't appear surprised that this has happened.

5.4
IS DEFICIT FETISHISM INNATE OR CONTEXTUAL?
Monday, 3 August 2015

Political scientists Jonathan Hopkin and Ben Rosamond have recently talked about 'political bullshit'.[3] They use 'bullshit' as a technical term due to Princeton philosopher Harry Frankfurt. Unlike lying, bullshit tells false stories that pay no heed to the truth. Their appeal is more to common sense, or what Tyler Cowen calls common sense morality. At a primitive level it is the stuff of political soundbites, but at a slightly more detailed level it is the language of what Krugman ironically calls 'Very Serious People'.

The implication which can then be drawn is that because bullshit does not reside in the 'court of truth', trying to combat it with facts, knowledge or expertise may have limited effectiveness. The conditions under which this might be true, and the extent to which information technology impacts on this, are fascinating issues which the authors briefly discuss. But what makes their discussion even more interesting for me is that they use what they call 'deficit fetishism', and in particular the stories that the UK government told before the last election, as their subject matter.

In the case of fiscal policy, deficit fetishism as bullshit involves appeals to 'common sense' by invoking simple analogies with households, often coupled with an element of morality: it is responsible to pay down debts. The point in calling it bullshit (in this technical sense) is that attempts to counter it by appeals to facts or knowledge (for example, the government is not like a household, as every economist knows) may have limited effectiveness. Instead it might be better to fight bullshit with bullshit, by talking about the need to borrow to invest, or even that it is best to 'grow your way out of debt'. (If you think the latter is nonsense, you are still in the wrong court: the court of truth rather than bullshit. As long as the phrase contains what I have sometimes called a 'half-truth', it has the potential to be effective bullshit.)

If for the sake of argument we accept all this, I want to ask whether deficit fetishism will always be powerful bullshit, or whether its force is a symptom of a particular time, and what is more, a time that may by now have passed. This, rather than discussions of the technical merits of particular fiscal policies, may be the crucial political discussion that needs to take place right now for all those in Europe that want to put an end to needless austerity. (In the US deficit fetishism, and also austerity itself, seems to be taking a breather or having a prolonged rest.) Just to be clear, I'm not discussing bullshit more generally, just the appeal of the particular example of deficit fetishism.

At first sight deficit fetishism seems to be innate, because it appeals to the basic intuition of the household and the morality of good housekeeping. However, households also borrow to invest (such as in a house), and most people understand that this is what firms do as well. The reason why the bullshit involving paying back borrowing may have been particularly powerful over the last five years is that this is exactly what many households have also been doing.

Although the Great Recession may have started with a financial crisis, its persistence despite low real interest rates is often put down to what many economists call a balance sheet recession: individuals and firms cutting back on borrowing (or saving more) over a number of years. That process has been particularly evident in the US and UK, with sustained increases in the aggregate savings ratio. However that process now appears to have come to an end. As individuals start borrowing again (or at least stop running down their debt), perhaps they will become more tolerant of governments doing the same.

To this we could add an obvious external factor. In 2010 and the following two years, deficit fetishism seemed to be validated by a superficial view of external events. The difficulties that some countries were getting into because their governments had 'borrowed too much' was top of the news night after night. In that context, is it any wonder that most people believed the bullshit?

One final indication that the power of deficit fetishism is contextual is what economists call deficit bias. Before the Great Recession, there was a tendency in many countries for government debt as a share of GDP to rise over time for no justifiable reason. Fiscal rules and then fiscal councils were created largely to prevent this. It is difficult to square this phenomenon with the idea that deficit fetishism is always powerful.

Many political parties on the centre-left in Europe (such as the UK) currently seemed resigned to deficit fetishism remaining a powerful force that can sway elections. So, if you cannot beat them, join them (and never mind what is good macroeconomics). This assumption at the very least seems debatable.

5.5
THE CORBYN PHENOMENON
Tuesday, 11 August 2015

For readers not in the UK, some background. When Ed Miliband resigned as Labour leader after the 2015 election defeat, the election process for a new leader went like this. You needed 35 MPs (members of parliament) to nominate potential successors, and there would then be a contest over a few months before party members got to vote to choose one of the nominated candidates as leader. Three people got the required number of MPs to nominate them, but the candidate from the left, Jeremy Corbyn, did not have enough MPs. Some MPs felt it would be good for balance to have someone from the left standing, so they switched their nominations in order that he too got the required 35.

From this you will gather that the left of the Labour Party is pretty weak in parliament. It was also thought to be weak among Labour Party members: the candidate of the left in the elections of 2010, Diane Abbott, received little support from the membership. So the general expectation was that Corbyn would also get little support this time. This expectation has proved completely wrong: polls put him in front, his meetings have been attracting growing audiences, and senior party figures are now panicking that he might actually win (in a similar manner to the reaction of Republican grandees to Trump winning their nomination).

Perhaps as a result, a few people have asked me to write about Corbyn's macroeconomic policies: in some cases in the expectation that I would rubbish them, and in other cases in the hope that I would provide support. But the real question people should ask first is: why is Corbyn proving to be so popular? It is nonsense to suggest that the Labour Party membership has suddenly become markedly more left wing than it used to be. Corbyn's popularity has much more to do with how the party in parliament has responded to both election defeats.

On issues like welfare, immigration, business or inequality, you can see Labour as having two impulses: one to go with its natural inclination, and another to try and woo the floating middle- or working-class voter whose views seem to be nearer those of the *Daily Mail* or *Sun* respectively (that is, much more regressive). In terms of policy, this tended to produce either inoffensive emptiness, focusing on small differences from the government, or simple right-wing appeasement. But perhaps more importantly, in terms of style it produced a kind of defensiveness where the chief goal of their leaders was to avoid anything that could be used against them by the right-wing press. And not without reason: when Miliband gave a thoughtful speech where he talked about how you could have irresponsible capitalism that just went for the quick buck whatever the long-term or social costs, he was forever after dubbed anti-business. This resulted in an opposition seemingly devoid of any clear policy message.

The issue of austerity is indicative. Labour has never adopted a clear anti-austerity line, even during the 2010–11 period of acute cuts. This is because they knew that much of the press would label this as fiscal irresponsibility, and that the BBC follows the lead of the press and the financial markets on these things. Their actual proposals in the 2015 elections involved far fewer cuts than Osborne promised, but because they were desperate to appear to be 'tough on the deficit', they either gave out a confused message or tried to talk about other things. Crucially, they failed to defend their record in government. As a result of their 2015 defeat, many senior party figures are now suggesting it is best for Labour to essentially follow Osborne's macro plans.

The reaction of most of the parliamentary party to the 2015 defeat seems to be that the pre-2015 strategy was right in principle but had just not focused enough in placating the marginal English voter, which they believe means more appeasement and shifting further to the right. The party membership seems to have reacted very differently to the 2015 defeat. The membership appears to believe that the pre-2015 strategy has clearly failed, and it is time to start talking with conviction about the issues you believe in. This is exactly what Jeremy Corbyn does: he is a conviction politician, who is not prepared to try and be someone else to win votes.

Does that mean the choice is between arguing for your convictions and losing or trying to appease the right-wing press and maybe winning? No, there is a way through this dilemma, but it is a way that is alien to most of those in the Labour Party, and that is to spend much more time thinking about political spin. Labour lost the election because it lost the battle of spin. Labour did not lose in 2015 because it was anti-business, but because it was perceived as anti-business. It did not lose in 2015 because it had been fiscally irresponsible in government, but because it was perceived to be. It did not lose Scotland because its policies were damaging to Scotland, but because they were perceived to be.

Again, let's use fiscal policy as an indicative example. Labour lost because it was perceived to have been, and is perceived to continue to be, fiscally irresponsible. That perception did not just arise because of a biased press or bad luck, but also because of good political judgement by Osborne and bad judgement by Miliband and Balls. Before the financial crisis it was generally thought that popular support for a higher level of public spending was too strong, which is why the Conservatives had pledged to match Labour's spending plans. But Osborne was quick to see that the recession changed things, because he could attempt to blame Labour for the deficit that was bound to arise as a result of the recession, and use deficit reduction to achieve the political goal of a smaller state. Labour's counter to this in the first few years of the coalition government was to focus on the stalled recovery, but that in contrast was poor political judgement because eventually the economy was bound to recover, and at that point Labour appeared weak. In addition by failing to effectively challenge the Osborne narrative about the past, Labour lost a crucial battle of political spin.

If Labour is to have any hope in 2020 it has to start attacking Osborne's unnecessary and obsessive austerity, as well as getting the past history straight. There are also reasons for thinking that the power of deficit fetishism for voters will steadily decline. In that sense, on this issue and perhaps others, Corbyn seems to have an advantage.

But, and it is a huge but, you can only successfully run an anti-austerity line if you have a clear and robust counter to the irresponsible borrowing charge. You do have to reassure enough marginal voters, and as a means to that the non-partisan political pundits that determine the political tone in a lot of the media. It is not clear that Corbyn will be able to do this. Firing up the base, as Corbyn clearly does, is only part of a successful winning strategy. There is a strong danger that he will lose credibility on the budget through overoptimistic claims on tax avoidance or misguided ideas about monetary financing. You will not shift the Overton window on austerity and other issues if your position is too easily discredited. Blair and Brown won in 1997 partly by imposing strong discipline on the party, which collectively gave out a clear set of messages to the electorate.

Part of Corbyn's problem is not of his making (unless you take a long historical view), and that is his fellow MPs. It was their majority that chose not to oppose Osborne's welfare bill, which epitomised the disastrous strategy that I have described above. It is very regrettable that two of the three other leadership candidates have refused to serve under him. If, following a Corbyn win, the party united around him in exchange for Corbyn parking some of his less popular policy positions, Labour could once again become an effective opposition. If instead his leadership is accompanied by constant public division within the party, there is a danger that this will overshadow everything else.

It seems very unlikely that Corbyn as leader could win the 2020 election. Perhaps the most optimistic yet still plausible outcome is that the period of a brief Corbyn leadership will be sufficient to shift the centre of political debate (the Overton window) to the left on a sufficient number of issues like austerity. He would then step down to allow a new candidate from the centre-left to take over before 2020, and win enough popular support by appearing to be less of a risk and a more natural leader, while retaining key Corbyn positions like a strong anti-austerity line. Whether that would happen I have no idea.

Whether Corbyn wins or loses, Labour MPs and associated politicos have to recognise that his popularity is not the result of entryism, or some strange flight of fancy by Labour's quarter-of-a-million-plus members, but a consequence of the political strategy and style that lost the 2015 election. They should reflect that if they are so sure they know what will win elections, how come they failed to predict the Corbyn phenomenon? A large proportion of the membership believe that Labour will not win again by accepting the current political narrative on austerity or immigration or welfare or inequality and offering only marginal changes to current government policy. On economic policy in particular they need to offer reasons for voters to believe that there are alternatives to the current status quo of poor-quality jobs, deteriorating public services and infrastructure, and growing poverty alongside gross inequality at the top. That means, whether he wins or loses, working with the Corbyn phenomenon rather than dismissing it.

5.6
ON GIVING ADVICE
Sunday, 27 September 2015

PREAMBLE

Corbyn did win, and I was shortly afterwards asked to be part of an advisory panel for Shadow Chancellor John McDonnell. This post explains why I said yes. The following post talks about some of the reaction I received as a result. The post after that deals with the question of electability.

I was happy to agree to be on an advisory panel for Shadow Chancellor John McDonnell MP. There are only two reasons why I would say no to any major political party that asked me to give it advice. The first is if this restricted what I would otherwise write on this blog or elsewhere. No such request has been made, although if you are hoping that I will reveal in posts accounts of what happens at panel meetings you will also be disappointed.

The second reason why I might have said no is if I thought the advisory panel was for presentation only, and all advice would be ignored. I have no reason for believing that in this case, and some grounds for thinking the opposite, which I discuss in the *Independent*.[4] In particular their position on fiscal policy is similar to the one I suggested, although getting the message clear probably requires some work.

One rather sad comment on the formation of this group is that those joining it will be forever tainted by associating themselves with 'hard left dinosaurs'. Or to put it another way, its members should have said no to the Labour Party leadership because they now have pariah status. As I pointed out in the *Independent* article, the current leadership will have to come to some kind of accommodation with the rest of the parliamentary party, and so Labour policies are unlikely to be the kind of far-left platform that many in the media seem happy to imagine. As Labour is the main opposition to the current government, and I think the government's macro policies are pretty awful, it would have been bizarre indeed if I had said no to this invitation.

5.7
WHEN ECONOMISTS PLAY POLITICAL GAMES
Wednesday, 14 October 2015

I saw you talking to those people the other day. You really should think twice before being seen to talk to people like that.

Similar lines could be taken from countless novels about class, race or some other form of social exclusion. When I agreed to be part of a group that would occasionally advise the new Shadow Chancellor John McDonnell on economic policy, I must admit I hadn't expected something like that to be said to me by economists I respect. Political hacks would say it for sure, but economists interested in promoting good policy?

Just to be clear, McDonnell's group places no restrictions on what its members can say in public about policy. We are not required to support or endorse Labour policy. Indeed, to the extent that Labour does adopt a policy that any of its members disagree with, the group gives those members a slightly higher public profile if we make that disagreement public. As the media generally fails to distinguish good economic advice from political spin, a direct channel like this group seemed like a good idea, with no cost to its members except their time. Except ...

On Monday McDonnell announced a U-turn: he would no longer support Osborne's new fiscal charter. The media focus, as ever, was on the 'political shambles' of a U-turn, with only the occasional suggestion that the charter itself was economic nonsense. A few economists on Twitter, however, suggested that this political shambles somehow reflected badly on the members of the advisory group. One described the members of the group being 'branded' by association. If other economists reading this sympathise with that view, you need to read on.

The new Labour position of not supporting the charter is likely to find general support among the advisory group. (We have not yet met.) Indeed a huge majority of macroeconomists would recommend opposing the charter. I have no idea if the views of any of the group had any influence on this U-turn, but if it did that means the group is having some influence, which has to be a positive thing. Indeed, as I know some of those making this 'guilt by association' charge actually oppose Osborne's charter, they should welcome the fact that we may have helped change Labour's position. Instead they are saying his change of mind reflects badly on us! It makes no logical sense, unless something else is going on here.

I am happy to give advice on macro policy to any of the mainstream political parties, whether I agree with their current macro or other policies or not. Over the past five or more years I have given public and private advice to Treasury officials working for the actual Chancellor. I feel strongly that governments should and can follow good macroeconomics whatever their political persuasion. For me to say I'm not going to talk to you because I do not like your policy on X would be as silly and childish as it sounds.

So what is going on with economists who would not blink an eye at me giving advice to a Chancellor whose policies I often (but not always) oppose, but suggest that when it comes to the Labour Party there is some kind of guilt by association? It seems to me that they are, knowingly or not, part of a political game. The game is to give the current Labour leadership some kind of pariah status. If we were talking about a party like the BNP (British National Party) that might make some sense, but for the main opposition party in which a radical leadership is going to have to reach a consensus with their less radical MPs, it does not. Unless of course your primary interest is to support another party. Which is why the government and many journalists want to foster this pariah status frame of mind. It is a shame that some economists who are parroting this guilt by association line seem not to understand the political game they are inevitably playing.

5.8
WHAT IF LABOUR'S PESSIMISTS ARE RIGHT?
Sunday, 15 November 2015

Want a blow-by-blow account of what happened at the first meeting of Labour's Economic Advisory Council? Before getting on to that, I thought it might be the right time to answer one comment that I have heard a lot since I accepted the invitation. Not the 'it will damage your reputation' line, but this rather more practical one: as the new Labour leadership are almost bound to fail at the polls, why waste your time?

There are two responses which I think are perfectly OK in themselves. First, election forecasting five years out is not a precise science. I do not underestimate the obstacles that the current leadership will have to overcome, but if defeat was certain would newspapers like the *Sun* be wasting front pages with character assassination? If general election defeat were certain under Corbyn they should be quietly hoping that the current leadership survives to fight it.

Second, with so much wrong with current government policy, it is important that the opposition has effective arguments. As we saw with cuts to tax credits, government policy can be changed. The better the arguments of the opposition, the more that might happen.

But neither of these are the best response to the 'why bother' question. Suppose the pessimists are right. What will happen next? There is a danger of lazy thinking here. The thinking goes that (1) the current Labour leadership will adopt a far-left programme, (2) they will fail to deliver in the polls, and (3) the centrists will return in triumph and start afresh with policy. If we accept that (2) is right for the sake of argument, both (1) and (3) are way off.

Corbyn and McDonnell have to compromise with the parliamentary party. Compared to this, confrontation will only reduce what they see as progressive opportunities. Far better to play a longer game, where they seek to gradually shift policy to the left from the top but through consensus. If you think their primary objective involves cementing their position in the party by not compromising on policy, starting an open war with the rest of the parliamentary party and wholesale deselection of MPs, then you still have not got over losing the election. (Of course this may not be true of all their supporters, and one of the tasks they have to deal with is in handling that.)

As a result, the platform they end up adopting will be one that nearly all Labour MPs can sign up to. Just as important, it will be one that most of those who voted for Corbyn can sign up to. The big divide will not be on the merits of the policies but on whether those policies and the leadership can win a general election. So suppose the pessimists are right and they fail at the polls, and Corbyn steps down. Who is more likely to win the subsequent election for leader of the party? Someone who accepts the majority of those policies, but appears to have more charisma and less history? Or someone who has opposed both the leadership and their policies over the previous few years, and wants to shift policy dramatically to the right?

I think the answer is pretty obvious. Public opposition to the current Labour leadership from within will not be forgiven by party members, so it is political suicide. The media will do their level best to hype any hint of division, but for the most part they will find it hard work. That was why the leadership election result was so dramatic a moment. It showed that you cannot lead the Labour Party on a platform which is Conservative-lite when the Conservative programme is well to the right.

Which means, in turn, that a good deal of the policy positions and ideas that the current leadership develops over the next few months and years will survive, even if they personally do not. So for this reason as well, helping to contribute to that platform is not a waste of time, even if the poll pessimists are right.

As for that blow-by-blow account of the first meeting, you didn't really think you were going to get one, did you?

5.9
LABOUR'S NEW MILITANT TENDENCY
Saturday, 27 February 2016

I thought I would write a bit more about the strategy of undermining your own political party's leadership, and why I think it is daft even on its own terms.

One of the characteristics of a few on the far left of politics is a total belief in the ends they strive for, and very little concern about the means used to achieve it. Anything that brings on the revolution is OK. We now seem to have some near the centre of the political spectrum behaving in exactly the same way. Their revolution is deposing Corbyn from the leadership of the Labour Party, and undermining that leadership is their means. For the sake of clarity, let me call this group the anti-Corbynistas.

When someone loses a leadership election, they generally retire gracefully. Sometimes they are offered a senior role under the new leader (Clinton and Obama) and become an active supporter. On other occasions (David and Ed) they would prefer, for whatever reason, to withdraw from the scene. And normally their supporters do the same. The goal of getting the party re-elected overrides any thoughts about who might have been a better leader. Other parties and the media will do their best to exploit these past divisions, but nearly everyone in the party avoids this bait.

As far as the contestants for the 2015 Labour Party leadership are concerned, they have played by these rules. One chose to be in the Shadow Cabinet, and the two that declined have not spent their free time writing critical articles in the media. The majority of Labour MPs have made a similar choice: work with the new leadership or stay quiet. But an important minority, accompanied by a large group of political commentators, have not. They are the anti-Corbynistas.

Their mantra is the impossibility of Labour led by Corbyn winning. This has the same status as a belief in the inevitability of revolution: just as the latter is fed by every injustice, so the former is supported by every opinion poll. For that reason there is no point in trying to contest the certainty of their belief. Instead I want to question the logic of what then follows.

Their reasoning goes like this. Because Corbyn is a barrier to Labour winning, the prime goal must be to hasten his departure by any means. As these individuals have easy access to the media, their main means is to criticise, or even mock, the Labour leadership at every turn. By doing this they ensure that Corbyn's defeat at the polls will be sooner or greater, and thereby they believe will hasten his removal from power.

What I want to argue is that this tactic is counterproductive. Just as the behaviour of the revolutionary makes most sensible people doubt the attraction of any revolution, so the constant sniping at the leadership extends rather than shortens its life.

The reason is straightforward. Corbyn was elected by the membership, and if anything support for him has grown since then. On key issues like Trident this membership shares Corbyn's own views, although it is worth noting that most expect their MP to represent their constituents' views rather than their own. So the question you have to ask is what will persuade Labour members to vote for someone else.

The obvious answer is a gradual realisation that Corbyn cannot win a general election, together with the emergence of someone else who looks like a better bet. The mistake the anti-Corbynistas make is to think that their tactics of open criticism will hasten this process.

In fact the tactic will have the opposite effect. If they kept quiet and Corbyn loses badly in elections, as they are sure he will, then Labour members will see quite clearly the need for change and look elsewhere. By constantly generating bad publicity for the party, they muddy these waters. Corbyn supporters will claim that the bad results are the result of anti-Corbynista activity, and it will not be obvious they are wrong. So if anything the tactic of the anti-Corbynistas will delay, rather than hasten, the day that the membership elects someone else.

If their strategy is so obviously misguided, why do the anti-Corbynistas persist? One reason may be human nature: they hate Corbyn, and find it difficult to bite their tongues. Another is that they are constantly cheered on or goaded by the right, although you might imagine that would worry some people. But there is an alternative and more rational reason. Their real goal may not be the overthrow of Corbyn, but the creation of a new party. That strategy within the UK system is also flawed, but that would have to be the subject of another post.

Why am I, a macroeconomist, writing about such a political issue? I get annoyed by their constant references to me as a Corbyn supporter because I consort with the enemy, but I can live with that. (The same would come from the right anyway.) What annoys me more is that they are playing a large role in depriving the UK of an effective opposition party. Every time the new leadership launches a justified criticism of the current government, there is a fair chance this will turn into a discussion of divisions within Labour.

This is in danger of influencing macro policy. Osborne's fiscal charter, which involves going for a budget surplus, is so isolated in terms of informed opinion and out of tune with current concerns that it deserves to be ridiculed at every turn, so that if nothing else it is not tried again. I think that could happen with concerted pressure, but that pressure needs to include a united opposition. This did not happen before the election because Labour seemed to want to avoid the subject. We then had McDonnell for a moment flirting with the idea of supporting the charter. Now that Labour appears to have decided on a more sensible strategy, it would be tragic if this opposition to Osborne was diluted by some within Labour seeming to support the charter and dishing their own side.

POSTSCRIPT

Unfortunately exactly what I feared transpired, although with the added final twist of the Brexit vote. It was exactly the futile strategy I had predicted, with many members believing that all opposition to Corbyn was just a plot by MPs to take power away from the membership. The post-Brexit revolt against Corbyn, although it included many MPs who were disillusioned by Corbyn's ability to lead, was also the final political misjudgement of Labour's old guard. When Corbyn won again, internal opposition went underground, allowing him to fight a highly successful 2017 election campaign.

5.10
A (MUCH) BETTER FISCAL RULE
Friday, 11 March 2016

PREAMBLE

Labour's new fiscal credibility rules owed a great deal to academic work I did on fiscal rules with Jonathan Portes that we presented at a conference at Manchester University, selected proceedings of which were published in 2015 in the Manchester School.[5] I was asked to present my interpretation of the paper's implications for what a UK fiscal rule should look like to the Economic Advisory Council, and although the need for a rule was questioned by some members, Labour subsequently adopted a modified version of this rule. From a personal point of view, I think it represented one of the main achievements of the Council.

Today the Labour Shadow Chancellor John McDonnell will give a speech where he puts forward an alternative fiscal rule to George Osborne's fiscal charter. It involves a rolling target for the government's current balance: within five years taxes must cover current spending. It leaves the government free to borrow to invest. Investment cannot be unbounded, as there is a commitment to reduce debt relative to trend GDP over the course of a parliament.

No doubt we will hear the usual cries from the opponents of sensible fiscal rules: Labour plans to borrow billions more than George Osborne, and plans to go on borrowing forever. The simple response to that should be that it is right to borrow to invest in the country's future, just as firms borrow to invest in capital and individuals borrow to invest in a house. Indeed, with so many good projects for the government to choose from, and with interest rates at virtually zero, it is absolute madness not to invest substantially in the coming years.

This part of the rule is similar to the main fiscal rule Osborne himself adopted under the coalition, which in turn is not unlike previous rules adopted by Labour. What is new is that McDonnell's rule involves what could be termed a 'zero lower bound knockout': if interest rates hit their lower bound following a recession, the focus of fiscal policy shifts from deficit targets to helping monetary policy support the economy. It reflects the knowledge we have gained since the global financial crisis.

Again critics will claim that the knockout would have meant building up even more debt after the last recession. But what matters with debt is its relationship to GDP, and it is far from clear whether more stimulus in 2009 and 2010 would have increased the debt to GDP ratio, because you are increasing GDP as well as debt. But even if debt to GDP did rise, this reflects the right choice. It means prioritising the real economy, jobs and wages, over an obsession with government debt.

We will no doubt be told by government supporters that this would have led to financial disaster, just as we are also told that the coalition saved us from disaster. We will be told this by some economists working in the financial sector: a sector that created the Great Recession. But there is no evidence for this impending disaster, and plenty of evidence that it is a complete myth. As Paul Krugman might say, in a country with its own central bank the bond vigilantes just keep failing to turn up.

Recessions come and go, you might respond, but higher debt will always be with us. That ignores two key points. First, prolonged and deep recessions cause lasting damage. UK GDP per head is currently over 15% below pre-recession trends. Does none of that have anything to do with the slowest UK recovery from a recession in centuries? Second, using fiscal policy to end recessions quickly does not mean higher debt forever. The key point is that debt can be reduced once the recession is over and interest rates are safely above their lower bound. Doing that will be no cost to the economy as a whole, as monetary policy can offset the impact on demand. Obsessing about debt during a recession, by contrast, costs jobs and reduces incomes, as every economics student knows and as the OBR has shown (see Post 1.9).

The rule happens to mean that pretty well all of the additional austerity Osborne has detailed since the election is unnecessary. But that is a by-product of adopting a sensible rule. If there is any 'reverse engineering' going on, it is with Osborne's fiscal charter, which some argue was adopted with the political purpose of making Labour look less prudent before the election. As McDonnell notes, no economist has attempted to defend Osborne's fiscal charter.

Yet I know this point worries some Labour MPs and commentators. They say, quite rightly, that one of the main reasons the 2015 election was lost was because Labour was not trusted on fiscal policy.

But the basic truth is that you do not enhance your fiscal credibility by signing up to a stupid fiscal rule. Apart from getting attacked for doing so by people like me, your collective heart is not really in it and it shows. You get trapped into proposing to shrink the state as Osborne is doing, or hitting the poor as Osborne is doing, or raising taxes, which makes you unpopular. And if by chance it ever looks like you might be getting that trust back, Osborne or his successor will move the goalposts again.

The far more convincing way to get trust back is to adopt a fiscal rule that makes sense to both economists and the public ('only borrowing to invest'), and actively talking about it. When the Conservatives accuse you of borrowing, you do not try and change the subject, but remind people that is what firms and consumers do. Borrowing is not a dirty word, particularly when it is on vital investment and you can do it for almost nothing! Indeed, borrowing to invest shows you are optimistic about the future and are prepared to do things to make it better. In contrast, those who would turn down these investment projects in order to reduce debt as fast as possible have a negative outlook that fears the future.

The Conservatives know they are vulnerable on public investment. Osborne tries to give the impression that he is doing a lot of it, but the figures do not lie. In the last five years of the Labour government the average share of net public investment in GDP was over 2.5%. During the coalition years it fell to 2.2%, and for the five years from 2015 it is planned to average just 1.6%.[6] That is not building for the future, but putting it in jeopardy, as those whose homes have been flooded have found to their cost.

POSTSCRIPT

The media reception of the fiscal credibility rule was classic mediamacro. The framing was entirely about within-Labour disputes, and how much the rule differed from that proposed by Ed Balls before the 2015 election. Whether the rule was better than Osborne's fiscal charter became the question that no one asked. One BBC journalist described the 'zero lower bound knockout' as a loophole, which I thought was a quintessential expression of mediamacro's deficit obsession.

6

BREXIT

Introduction

Post 6.1 was written on the day the Prime Minister announced that he would hold a referendum on EU membership, and I think its concerns have come to pass. Post 6.2 outlines my concerns about how the media would handle the referendum, all of which came to pass.

The Leave campaign focused on the economy. For my own part I helped organise a letter from academic economists expressing similar economic concerns: as a later poll would confirm, economists were almost unanimous in thinking Brexit would reduce living standards. However the broadcast media, as I had feared they would, treated this view not as an expression of knowledge, but as just another opinion, always to be balanced by an opinion from the other side (Post 6.3). Post 6.4 argues that this failure to get across the overwhelming view of economists might be critical in deciding the result. Equally important, suggests Post 6.6, is the failure to get across economists' equally universal view that immigration improves the public finances.

These failures were critical in part because most of the tabloid press was far from balanced. Indeed it seems fair to argue that the right-wing press had been running the Brexit campaign for years (Post 6.5). On the day after the vote I published Post 6.7, which remains the most widely read post I have ever written. Post 6.8 draws some lessons from what I regard as a disastrous decision. Of course I have continued to write about Brexit as the negotiations unfold, but until we know what Brexit actually means, if anything, it is difficult to know which of those posts will be of any lasting interest.

Posts in Chapter 6

6.1
WHEN NATIONAL INTEREST AND PARTY ADVANTAGE CONFLICT
Wednesday, 23 January 2013

I would not be the first to observe that there is a potential conflict between George Osborne's role as Chancellor and his deep involvement in Conservative Party election strategy. The fact that this is often said does not mean it is real: it could just be a story told by those commentators who are themselves fixated by the battle between political parties. However there are two major areas where the Conservative part of the coalition government seems to be putting perceived election advantage ahead of prospects for the UK economy: immigration and Europe.

Jonathan Portes[1] has clearly described the contradictions between an economic philosophy that stresses the importance of deregulation and a flexible labour market, and tight restrictions on the ability of firms to hire who they want if they happen not to be UK residents. In addition, making it difficult and risky for foreign students to study in the UK directly hits the exports of the education sector. Now perhaps immigration control is so deeply embedded in Conservative philosophy that it trumps economic liberalism, or helping increase UK's exports. Or alternatively, immigration is seen as a vote winner and so any damage that this will do to the UK economy can be set aside.

The Prime Minister has now finally made his commitment to hold a referendum on EU membership in four years' time. This has been widely interpreted as a move to both appease the anti-EU wing of his party, and to stop the drift of voter support to the UK Independence Party. The opposition has claimed that this will create damaging uncertainty, and on this occasion they are almost certainly right. We do not need to just take the word of business leaders on this. A number of studies[2] have recently highlighted the role of uncertainty in influencing the macroeconomy. There can be little doubt that decisions by multinationals or export-orientated domestic firms on where to locate or expand production are heavily influenced by whether countries are inside or outside trading blocs. Given the real risk that a majority in the UK referendum will vote to leave, investment decisions are likely be postponed at best, and diverted elsewhere at worst. Neither is what the economy needs right now. The economic benefits of promising a referendum on EU membership in five years' time are hard to see. It is also hard to imagine why the Prime Minister had to make such a commitment, besides the political imperatives of party unity and keeping votes.

So what is new, the cynic might say. Politicians have always been more concerned with winning elections than the economic health of the country. Well, let's just suppose this is true, for the sake of argument. What is clearly true is that winning elections also depends on the state of the economy. To say the UK economy is not looking too good right now would be an understatement. (Those who point to trends in employment in an attempt to suggest things are not so bad are really deluded. How can the fact that UK labour productivity is still well below levels before the recession, and has hardly increased at all in the last year or two, possibly be good news?)

Which brings me to the potentially conflicted Chancellor. Ministers are meant to represent their portfolio, and most of the time the complaint is that they do this too much, with too little regard to wider interests. Again the cynic might say that is natural enough, because their own personal political capital is bound up with the perceived success of that ministry. So a Chancellor who was totally focused on being a Chancellor, in a situation where the economy was doing badly, would be banging the table against anything that put a recovery at risk. Now perhaps George Osborne has been lobbying hard against immigration controls, and against the referendum commitment, although if he had I suspect we would know about it. A more plausible story is that he shares the Prime Minister's view that on these two issues at least political advantage outweighs economic interests. But in making this judgement, he is acting as Conservative Party strategist and not as the UK Chancellor of the Exchequer.

6.2
CAMERON'S CHICKENS
Thursday, 3 March 2016

Although Donald Trump is despised by the Republican Party establishment, he is an unintended and unfortunate creation of that party. They built up a system where you needed money to enter politics, because they controlled the money. (It is to Bernie Sanders' credit, and the popular will behind his campaign, that he has overcome this hurdle.) But that allowed someone very rich to hijack the system. The Republicans have exploited prejudice to win votes, which allowed someone to throw away the dog whistle and openly attack those from other religions. (Tactics those supporting the Conservative candidate for London mayor, Zac Goldsmith, also seem happy to employ.) In these ways, Trump represents the Republican's chickens coming home to roost. Trump is a rather good con man and so for him the US political system is an easy mark.

Will the EU referendum be the moment David Cameron's chickens come home? Although economic arguments are central, and the case for staying is strong and the case for leaving weak, how much will voters without any economics background be able to come to that conclusion? Most newspapers will push the weak arguments, or more generally just try and muddy the waters as they do all the time on climate change. The visual media's natural format is to set this up as a two-sided debate, and if the Leave campaign can find enough credible advocates to put the economic case for leaving then the main outcome might be confusion.

In contrast, to many voters the other key issue – immigration – looks clear-cut. For the large section of the UK electorate that places migration among their top concerns the logic of the Leave campaign's claim that we will finally 'control our borders' will seem obvious. This will be constantly reinforced by news about refugees and fears about terrorism. Here the Conservative government's focus on the costs of migration (and the pretence that UK benefits are a big draw) may come home to roost. Many in the Conservative Party truly believe large scale migration is a threat to the country, but I suspect Cameron and others running the party are not among them. Until now 'cracking down on immigration' has been a useful ruse for the Conservatives to win votes, but for the Remain campaign it has become a huge liability.

That is one of Cameron's chickens that may come home to roost. Another is his deal. From what I have seen so far, Cameron will not try and counter migration concerns by arguing the benefits of migration, because it runs counter to what he has previously said. For the same reason he will not emphasise that to maintain preferential trade agreements after leaving we would probably have to accept free movement. Instead he will argue that his deal will make all the difference, and in this case he will not impress. His deal will make no tangible difference to migration flows, and for once the right-wing press will go with the evidence.

Nor can Cameron expect that much help from other party leaders. One reason is what happened immediately after the Scottish referendum. Labour, and Gordon Brown in particular, came to Cameron's rescue when it became clear in the final days of the referendum that he could lose Scotland. The thanks they got was a speech from the steps of Downing Street the next day proposing English votes for English laws. In that case it was in Labour's self-interest (in terms of being able to win an election) to be Cameron's chicken, but the political arithmetic is far less clear this time.

The EU referendum is therefore another test of how much economic expertise can influence public opinion. As regular readers will know, we have been here before, and not just on austerity. The overwhelming evidence was that independence would initially leave Scottish people worse off, but for many this evidence was successfully counteracted by the SNP's wishful thinking projections. From recent experience, therefore, I am not too optimistic that the economic evidence will prevail. For a Prime Minister who has preferred the economics of the Swabian housewife to anything taught in universities, this too is a chicken come home to roost.

6.3
MEDIA, ECONOMICS AND BREXIT
Friday, 13 May 2016

PREAMBLE

As the Brexit debate got under way Tony Yates suggested to Paul Levine and myself that we organise a letter on Brexit. We could see that the message that the overwhelming majority of economists thought Brexit would be harmful was not getting across. The letter was published in The Times *on 12 May, signed by nearly 200 economists, most of whom were academics. It spoke of significant long-term costs of leaving the EU, that the costs of uncertainty would 'weigh heavily for many years', and that there was a 'risk of a short-term shock to confidence'.*

Based on our *Times* letter and work by important national and international institutions, the media could say that all the leading economic institutions and the overwhelming majority of academic economists think that Brexit will involve significant short-term and long-term costs. That is now a statement of fact, which readers of some very partisan tabloids may not be aware of. My guess would be that there are at least 25 academic economists who think Brexit will involve significant costs compared to each one who thinks it will bring benefits. That is as close to unanimity among economists as you will ever get. As it is a fact, saying that it appears to be so in no way breaches impartiality.

They could go further. The main response of the Leave campaign has been to say all economic forecasts are hopeless. They are no doubt referring to unconditional macro forecasts of the 'what will growth be next year' type. However, the assessments made by all these economists and economic institutions are not unconditional forecasts, but conditional forecasts: what difference will Brexit make (see Post 8.7)? They are much more reliable than unconditional forecasts. (This point can be got across with simple analogies: a doctor will tell you that being overweight increases the chance of a heart attack, but not when you will have one.)

So trying to discount the near universal assessment of economists by referring to macro forecasts represents either dangerous ignorance or deliberate obfuscation. But for those with little knowledge of these things, it is a deception that could work. Pointing out the difference does not breach impartiality, but informs the debate.

Brexit in the UK, and Trump in the US, represents a critical challenge to the 'shape of the earth: views differ' style of reporting. 'Balance' should never involve ignoring facts that are awkward for one side, or not challenging statements that are false. How many journalists (particularly political journalists) recognise this may determine two critical elections for both the UK and the whole world.

POSTSCRIPT

My guess that for every academic economist who thinks Brexit will not reduce UK prosperity there are 25 who think otherwise was almost right: according to a subsequent Guardian *survey of Royal Economic Society members[3], it is actually 22 to 1. Yet most Leave voters thought that they would be no worse off after Brexit. That could be down to voters not trusting academics, but polls show that voters have a high degree of trust in academics. A simple explanation for these facts is that the media, with its obsession with balance, took the reality of a consensus among academics and turned it into a contested opinion. Another example from Brexit is whether Turkey is likely to join.*

While this is another example where the media, obsessed with balance, ignores the plurality of expert opinion, a still worse case is where facts become politicised. The clear Brexit example of this is the £350 million a week figure. Furthermore it is a clever lie, because it focuses attention on a direct benefit of Brexit, and away from probable costs. (I've no idea if this is true, but I once heard that when Joseph McCarthy claimed there were many communists working in government, he would keep changing the number. As a result, the topic of conversation became how many there actually were, rather than whether there were any at all and whether it mattered.) In both cases, the Leave campaign showed how media practices can be exploited for political ends.

As to the warnings in the original letter, in the short term there was a large depreciation in the exchange rate, and the Bank of England felt it had to cut interest rates and renew Quantitative Easing. Uncertainty has meant that the UK economy has moved from near the top to the bottom of the international growth league. At the time of writing we have yet to leave so we cannot say what the long-term costs will be, but we do know that the government's own post-referendum forecasts show large costs of the size predicted before the referendum.

6.4
BREXIT, IMMIGRATION AND £100
Monday, 16 May 2016

With so many heavyweights, from Barack Obama to Mark Carney, saying that we will be worse off with Brexit, why are the polls still neck and neck? There seem to me two reasonable explanations: that the tabloid media have a strong influence, and that immigration is a big issue among voters. But perhaps the two are connected, for reasons that will become clear.

It is a well-known result that worries about immigration tend to be greatest in areas where there is little immigration. In areas with a high proportion of migrants, like London, UKIP does rather poorly. For most, immigration is not a problem that is facing them directly, but rather an issue they feel is facing the country.

For some this concern about immigration is cultural, while for others it is economic. But if it is economic, on what is this concern based? All too often I come across arguments that make simple economic errors. Like more migrants put greater pressure on public services. Study after study suggests exactly the opposite: because migrants tend to be young adults who work, they pay more in taxes and take less advantage of public services or benefits than the average non-migrant.

Sometimes it is simply false correlations: austerity has put pressure on public services and the recession and productivity slowdown has held back real wages, but both have happened at a time of high immigration. The only area where there might be some negative effect from migration is on the wages of unskilled labour, but even where a negative impact is found it seems to be small. This negative impact could be wiped out by positive effects from higher growth and better public finances.

In some sense what we have is very similar to the austerity problem, with the combination of simplistic ideas and non-causal association. It feels right that governments should tighten their belts when households are doing the same, and the 'clearing up the mess' idea is reinforced because the deficit went up when Labour was in power. With both austerity and immigration we have a visual media that normally makes no attempt to 'educate and inform', and a tabloid media that actively reinforces these mistakes. We have a governing party that does the same, and in the past an opposition that was reluctant to say that immigration benefits the economy as a whole.

So the referendum debate amounts to economics versus immigration. But here is a revealing bit of information from YouGov.

We recently conducted an experiment in which we asked people to imagine how they would vote if they knew Brexit would make them just £100 worse off per year. This instantly changed a neck-and-neck result to a 12 point victory for 'Remain'. The effect is even stronger among undecided voters, who flip 18 points from veering towards 'Leave' to veering strongly towards 'Remain' in this scenario.[4]

It is of course a classic technique economists use to quantify how strongly people feel about an issue, and it suggests the immigration concern is not worth that much to many people. Given that the economic assessments of the costs of Brexit are of the order of at least 10 times £100 a year, the economic argument is key. Which is why it is worrying that the BBC seems to ignore the consensus among academic economists.

6.5
POWER WITHOUT ACCOUNTABILITY IN OUR TABLOID PRESS
Saturday, 18 June 2016

Forget the straw man of newspapers telling readers what to do. The concern is not with which side newspapers formally endorse. It is about how stories are selected and portrayed. Like the recent front-page story from the *Mail* about migrants in a lorry saying 'we're from Europe – let us in'.[5] Except they didn't say that. Incredibly the *Mail* is not the worst offender for putting stories like that on its front page.

Maybe readers of the *Express* want to see countless stories of the migrant 'threat'. But if this is so, you would expect the press as a whole to be balanced in publishing either pro- or anti-Brexit stories, reflecting the balance of the polls. However research finds that, when you weight by circulation, pro-Brexit articles outnumber pro-Remain articles more than 4 to 1.[6]

Even though the 'only reflecting their readers' canard is untrue, there is I think a more important point. I don't just want false or misleading stories about the migrant 'threat' to be balanced by an equal number of misleading stories about how wonderful migration is. I want stories that contain some real facts, so that people who read these stories can be informed. I want a situation where we no longer have nearly 60% of the population believing Turkey will be an EU member within 10 years. (In 2013 the British appeared to be the worst informed about Europe among Europeans. Equally voters appear to be badly informed about key facts like the extent of immigration, and the bias always goes in one direction.)

It is sometimes said that telling facts is the job of the broadcast media, and newspapers are about opinion. Right now I would turn that around. The broadcast media are so frightened of appearing biased that they describe clear falsehoods as simply 'contested'. In the soundbite world they inhabit, that is as far as they go. They set up debates rather than explore issues. They broadcast opinions rather than facts: the opinions of politicians. In print you can go further: you have the space to present the facts and back them up. That is what the broadsheets at their best do.

Why does the *Mail* or the *Sun* not do that? Because their owners have a clear line to push, and all too often the truth gets in the way of that. They will not tell their readers that restricting immigration will make it less easy for them to see their GP or mean a longer wait in A&E. They will not tell their readers this because they would rather their readers believed otherwise.

Facts like these get in the way of the Leave campaign. They would prefer an emotional rather than rational debate. Shamefully, they play on the emotions of nationalism and the threat of others. They will not tell their readers that there is no chance Turkey will join the EU in the near future because they want to use that false threat to generate fear: indeed, Vote Leave leaflets headline with this threat.

And I have to say that those who distort facts to whip up such emotions for political gain have to take some responsibility for the tragic side effects of their actions. When politicians do this we can, in time, hold them to account. When the owners of newspapers do this it appears we have no recourse, and they can go on doing the same again and again. If there is an issue with 'control' in our country, it is not with Brussels bureaucrats but with a small number of press barons that wield such power without a trace of accountability. We need to find a way to 'take back control' of the means of communicating information.

6.6
WHY DO PEOPLE WANT LESS EU IMMIGRATION?
Thursday, 23 June 2016

Why will around half of the UK vote for Brexit? The answer you will hear time and again is EU immigration. But why do people dislike EU immigration? Of course people fear the unfamiliar, and that is a fear that can be played upon, but is that really why people dislike EU immigration? Not according to the IPSOS/MORI poll shown in Figure 6.1.

Figure 6.1: Poll on EU immigration

Overall, would you say that EU immigration has been good or bad, or has had no impact on the following ...

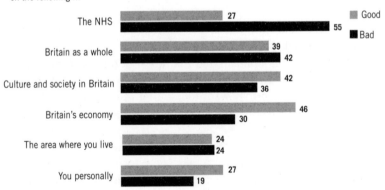

Base: 1,257 GB adults, aged 18+, interviewed by telephone, FW 11-14 June 2016

Source: https://www.ipsos.com/ipsos-mori/en-uk/just-one-five-britons-say-eu-immigration-has-had-negative-effect-them-personally

More people think that EU immigration has been good for them personally than think the opposite. I'll repeat that: more people think that EU immigration has been good for them personally than think the opposite. More people think the culture of Britain has been improved by EU immigration than the opposite.

The reason people think EU migration has been bad for Britain is the impact on the NHS, and therefore by inference other public services. It is common sense to many people that EU immigration increases the pressure on the NHS and public services, and that is confirmed by the newspapers they read.

What people miss is that EU migrants pay tax, which could fund public services. Indeed EU migrants tend to be young, so they are likely to pay more tax in than they are likely to take out from using public services. Which is why the OBR believes that restrictions on immigration would hurt the public finances.

This means that in reality EU migration creates more resources, which allows the government to spend more on the NHS and other public services. Not only do EU migrants pay for themselves in this respect, they also make access easier for natives. Add in the negative impact of making trade with the EU more difficult, and it is clear that Brexit would have a negative impact on public services.

Yet this is an argument David Cameron was reluctant to make, because it raises an obvious question. If EU migration is not the reason why the NHS is in crisis, what is? The answer is that his government has chosen to shrink the share of national income going to the NHS, when there are good reasons why this share should be rising. In other words, the government has taken the taxes EU migrants pay, and used them to cut taxes or cut the deficit. Because Cameron will not make the case for why EU migration helps the NHS, that case is not heard by voters. Instead they are told all the time that the NHS has been 'protected'. Hence the poll result.

Whatever happens today, this point is of vital importance. So many people will be telling both the government and the Labour Party that the EU referendum, whatever the actual result, has shown that to win votes politicians must cut immigration. What the poll shown in Figure 6.2 suggests is that what people really want is a better NHS, and that they incorrectly believe that less EU migration is a way to get it.

6.7
THE TRIUMPH OF THE TABLOIDS
Friday, 24 June 2016

There is a lot of talk right now about an angry, mainly old working class who used Brexit as a way of kicking back at an establishment that had brought them nothing but grief over the last decade. The Leave campaign managed to channel that into anger at the EU, even though it had precious little to do with the EU. The key is to ask how did that happen, and why did it not happen just one year ago?

In the 2015 general election Labour highlighted the decline in UK real wages, and promised more money for public services. They were defeated: no angry electorate wanting to get rid of the establishment then. Did that electorate feel passionate about European migration? UKIP only managed to get one MP elected.

In 2015 the electorate voted Cameron back in because they thought the Conservatives were more competent at running the economy, and that Cameron would be a better leader than Miliband. In the last few hours we can clearly see that both beliefs are incorrect. But that cannot be the whole story because that same leader with the same economic competence has just been heavily defeated.

Did people just vote for the higher food and petrol prices that sterling's depreciation will bring? Of course not. Nor did they vote for a possible recession. They did vote for lower immigration, but only in a small minority of cases because they dislike immigrants. People thought less immigration would lead to a better NHS, more secure jobs and higher real wages. They may get lower immigration, in time, but they will certainly will not get a better NHS and substantially better working conditions as a result.

It is tragic that we have left the EU. But what is equally tragic is that people who voted for that are very quickly going to find out that they were sold a pig in a poke. They have been deceived, and that will only increase the disillusion and disenchantment with the political system. Of course we should blame Johnson and Farage and the rest: the UK has paid a very high price to facilitate political ambition. Of course we should blame Cameron and Osborne for taking the referendum gamble and stoking anger with austerity. But a few politicians alone are not capable of fooling the electorate so consistently. To do that they need to control the means of communicating information.

In 2015 I argued that mediamacro had won it for Cameron and Osborne (see Post 4.6), and pretty well no one took this seriously. Just a year later, the united voice of economists has been successfully dismissed as Project Fear. Not by the people, but by politicians working together with most of the tabloid press, and a broadcast media obsessed with 'balance'. The tabloid press has groomed its readers for Brexit. If any good is to come out of this, it will involve defeating most of the tabloid press, and then forever reducing their influence. And given the power of that media, this can only be done by a united opposition that is prepared to cooperate in an effort to beat Johnson and Farage.

There is also a very big warning here for the US. Clinton may be ahead now, but do not underestimate the power of the media (which is still giving Trump much more coverage) to turn that around.

Brexit is perhaps the first major casualty of the political populism that has followed the financial crisis and austerity. That populism triumphed in the UK because the establishment underestimated its power and did nothing to tackle the resentment on which it feeds and the misinformation on which it thrives. It has been strong enough to turn a traditionally outward-looking nation into one that turns its back on its neighbours. The leaders as well as the people of other countries should not make the same mistake as the UK just made.

6.8
LESSONS FROM BREXIT
Thursday, 30 March 2017

There are precious few opportunities that Brexit will bring, and an awful lot of costs. Those of us of a certain age have got used to losing votes of one kind or another, but in the past you could generally point to some group or class that gained from our loss. What has happened over the last two years, first with austerity in 2015 and now Brexit, has been something quite different: a democracy voting for things that will make almost all of the people worse off, to satisfy the interests or ideology of a minuscule minority. The lessons we should draw from Brexit involve understanding clearly how this could have happened so to ensure it never happens again.

The referendum result went the way it did because of a perfect storm of two groups who had become disenchanted with the way society was going, or the way it had treated them. The first group, often forgotten by the left, were social conservatives who could be quite well off but who had probably not been to university. The kind of people who would react to claims that the Conservatives under Cameron were moving to the right by shouting 'Nonsense. What about gay marriage?' The second group, the 'left behind', were the working class in once-proud industrial areas that had declined steadily for decades. They were people who said before the referendum: 'well it cannot get any worse, can it'.

The first group, because they were social conservatives, were naturally fearful of social change like immigration, although they were likely to live in areas that had seen little of it. The second group were more dependent on the state, and saw in the last few years their access to social provision steadily decline. Yet until recently neither group would have cared much about the EU either way, and certainly would not have been prepared to pay good money to leave it.

In John Major's day the Brexiteers were a very small group who could best be described as an irritant. (John Major had a less kind word for them.) How did this group get to win a referendum? Crucially, they had allies in the owners of two key tabloid newspapers, the *Mail* and the *Sun*. Over a prolonged period these papers pushed two key ideas: that we were in some important sense 'ruled by Brussels bureaucrats', and that immigration was a threat to public services and wages. The first claim resonated with social conservatives, and the second with the left-behind.

After John Major's time in office, this alliance encouraged the opposition to use immigration as a stick with which to beat the Labour government. Not long after Labour was elected in 1997, the Conservatives talked about the UK becoming a 'foreign land'.[7] Concern about immigration started rising well before the arrival of Polish immigrants. This in turn led to growing UKIP support. With the election of Cameron the pressure continued, and being the chancer he was he gave in to the demand for a referendum, thinking both that it wouldn't happen (because he wouldn't win an outright majority in 2015) and that he could win it.

The final part of the strategy was to associate immigration with the EU. The EU was not a major popular concern until 2016. But the tabloids were relentless in their anti-EU, anti-EU-immigrant propaganda before the referendum. The Leave campaign emphasised immigration (Turkey) and the public services (£350 million), and with 'Project Fear' neutralised Remain's strong card. The bias-obsessed broadcast media did nothing to expose these lies, treated academic knowledge on trade as just one opinion, and the polls showed that the lies were believed.

Some have subsequently chosen to focus on the left-behind group, and to suggest that they were hard done by and that their concerns about immigration deserve respect. Authors like Goodhart have suggested that the middle class social liberals that came to dominate the Labour party had little regard for this constituency.[8] We can of course debate the successes and failures of the Labour Party, but it seems this analysis misses the important point.

Those who voted Leave didn't win. If they wanted immigration to quickly fall, it won't. If they 'want their country back', they will find that all the EU interference Brexiteers go on about amounts to little more than a load of bananas. If they think their wages will rise because of Brexit, they will see, are seeing, the opposite: £350 million to the NHS will become £50-odd billion to the EU.

In other words, the big news is that Leave voters were conned. The only people who will gain from Brexit will be the tabloid owners whose power will be enhanced and the ideologues who for some reason think the EU was stopping them reaching their promised land. That, as I suggested at the beginning, is not something I have seen in UK politics in my lifetime. The parallels with Trump's election are in this respect apt. We can no more 'reconcile' ourselves to Brexit than we can think that Trump is in any way presidential. If your takeaway from both events is that Labour should better represent the working class and Clinton was a poor candidate I would politely suggest you are missing something rather important.

If there is a lesson for the left in all this, it is to be smarter about what the hard right is doing, and not to play along by talking about British jobs for British workers. The main lessons are really for those in the centre and the soft right. Don't appease those on the hard right by using migrants as a political weapon (a lesson that was once understood). Don't appease them by offering them referendums. Don't appease the right-wing tabloids by trying to befriend their owners and protecting their backs. Don't appease them by being unbiased between truth and lies. If you continue to do these things, have a look at the Republican Party in the US to see what you and your country will become.

When Donald Tusk received the letter from Theresa May yesterday, he expressed regret that the UK was leaving and said 'we already miss you'. The letter he received made clear threats to end cooperation over security if the UK did not get the deal it wants. This made me rather proud to be European, and rather ashamed at the actions of my country's Prime Minister and her government.

7

THE
MEDIA, ECONOMICS
AND ELECTING DONALD TRUMP

Introduction

I have always believed that the media is much more important in influencing people that many imagine. In Post 7.2 I outline the basis for that view, which is reinforced by some basic ideas in economics. Post 7.10 provides some clear evidence to support that view, surprisingly coming from empirical work by economists. Given the importance of the media, it is necessary to know when and why things go wrong.

Sometimes politicians can put direct pressure on journalists, as Post 7.1 recounts. It also explains why claims that a government has achieved record employment growth when output growth is weak is actually praising failure. Post 7.6 outlines the evidence we have that the majority of economists opposed austerity, and how this majority opinion is seldom heard because the subject is so politically charged. Post 7.4 looks at another potential problem with how journalists report key economic issues, which is their reliance on City economists. Post 7.5 wraps these ideas up in the context of 'mediamacro'.

Unfortunately there are equally serious problems in the way the media reports politics. Post 7.3 discusses how the media, in an attempt to turn voters against leaders whose politics they dislike, may in turn encourage charismatic leaders who are totally unfit for office. This became all too true in the Clinton–Trump election campaign, which I comment on in Posts 7.7 and 7.8. Post 7.9 shows that many of these issues are far from new.

Posts in Chapter 7

7. 1
BEHAVING LIKE LUDDITES
Sunday, 14 July 2013

The Luddites were 19th-century English textile artisans who protested against newly developed labour-saving machinery from 1811 to 1817. Activists smashed Heathcote's lacemaking machine in Loughborough in 1816. At the time, the BBC said that the increase in employment that would result from destroying the machinery 'was of course good news', but there was a concern that output might fall as a result. However, some experts proclaimed that, thanks to the Luddites, we should celebrate that Britain was now leading the way in employment creation. A prominent politician who supported the Luddites accused the BBC of being hopelessly biased, and 'peeing all over British workers'. The BBC Trust subsequently held a seminar on impartiality and economics reporting.

OK, the first two sentences come from Wikipedia, and the rest is nonsense. The idea that the BBC might describe additional employment that resulted from not using labour-saving machinery as good news is surely unthinkable. If a journalist pointed out that these actions were problematic because productivity would fall, it must be inconceivable that any serious politician would accuse that journalist of bias. Unfortunately I made very little of that paragraph up, but just transposed things that happened a year ago back another 200 years. The BBC reporter was Stephanie Flanders and the politician Iain Duncan Smith.

There is one sense in which my transposition may be slightly unfair. In a recession, low productivity growth means that unemployment is lower. So I would have no problem with a line that went:

> Of course the growth in UK employment, given flat output, is bad news. However, if this slowdown in productivity growth is temporary, and we catch up in terms of productivity levels later on, it may have a silver lining. Low productivity growth means that unemployment is lower, so that the pain of the recession is

being more evenly spread by (nearly) everyone receiving lower real wages.

In a car crash, it is good when things like seat belts mean that people escape with minor injuries. But no one should describe the car crash itself as good news.

At the seminar that the BBC Trust did hold in November 2012, there was disagreement over 'whether BBC coverage should reflect a consensus view, in areas where there is one, or whether instead it must reflect the range of opinions even if parts of that range are minority views'. I would suggest that the overwhelming view today is that high productivity growth is beneficial, and that low productivity growth is a serious cause for concern, even if it might in the short term keep unemployment low. Do we really want the media to portray this as just 'one perspective', and then give equal time to the 'opposing view' that strong employment growth and low productivity growth is simply good news? In the case of the BBC and UK productivity, the BBC currently follows the 'opinions on shape of the earth differ' approach, and is then accused of bias for even mentioning that low productivity growth might be a concern.

It is vital that the media does not let politicians dictate how facts are interpreted. In George Osborne's Orwellian nightmare, support for his handling of the economy is growing, and opposition to austerity is crumbling, whereas in the real world the case for austerity has never been weaker. It was always obvious that when the economy started recovering, this would be proclaimed as proof that the government's policies are working, whereas what it really tells us is how used we have become to a no-growth economy.

Now if politicians want to be Luddites that is, of course, their choice. We trust in the system to quickly find them out, so that they do not get to hold positions of responsibility. Yet how is that supposed to happen when the media insists on giving the Luddites equal space? As the opinion poll results presented by Professor Schifferes to the Trust showed, many people follow economics news closely, but remain confused by it.[1] They rely on the media not just to present the news, but to put that news into context. Reporting that says one day 'output growth low: bad' and the next 'employment growth high: good', without putting the two together, is bad reporting.

Polls suggest the UK public has many misperceptions about the real world, such as crime is rising, a third of the population was born overseas, or that teenage pregnancy is widespread. Where do these incorrect perceptions come from? They seem not to come from direct experience of their local area, but instead are misperceptions about the rest of the country. This suggests an obvious source: the misperceptions come from the media.

There is a large part of the media, in the UK and elsewhere, that would regard these mistaken perceptions as a success rather than a failure. It is not a coincidence that these misperceptions all tend to encourage a rather illiberal political agenda. However these perceptions should be a source of deep concern for organisations like the BBC, whose mission is 'To enrich people's lives with programmes and services that inform, educate and entertain'.

Of course the 'two sides' approach has its place. It is not clear, for example, how much of the productivity slowdown in the UK is the government's fault. However, given what we know about output, the strong growth in UK employment is self-evidently bad news. As the coincident slow growth in UK wages shows, we are (nearly) all significantly worse off as a result. It is time the UK media recognised that the Luddites were wrong, and update its reporting accordingly.

POSTSCRIPT

The idea that strong employment when output is weak is a good thing is what I have called a politicised truth: a statement that is true simply because dominant political forces want it to be. Another politicised truth from the same time is that the last Labour government was profligate. The fact that the UK has a serious productivity problem is recognised today, but as I note in Post 7.5 the media in 2013 regarded the deficit as the far more serious problem, simply because the government behaved as if it was.

7.2
RATIONAL EXPECTATIONS, THE MEDIA AND POLITICS
Saturday, 26 October 2013

As those of you who have read a few of my posts will know, on the occasion that I venture into political science I like to push the idea that the attitudes and organisation of the media are an important part of trying to understand the political dynamic today. To put it simply, the media help to cause changes in public opinion, rather than simply reflect that opinion. Yet if you have in your head a certain caricature of what a modern macroeconomist believes, this is a strange argument for one to make. That caricature is that we all believe in rational expectations, which means that people use all readily available information in an efficient way to make decisions. If that was true when people came to form political opinions (on issues like immigration, or crime, for example), then information provided by media organisations on these issues would be irrelevant. In the age of the internet, it is fairly easy to get the true facts.

Some who read my posts will also know that I am a fan of rational expectations. I tend to get irritated with those (for example, some heterodox economists) who pan the idea by talking about superhuman agents who know everything. To engage constructively with how to model expectations, you have to talk about practical alternatives. If we want something simple (and, in particular, if we do not want to complicate by borrowing from the extensive recent literature on learning), we often seem to have to choose between assuming rationality or something naive, like adaptive expectations. For the kind of macroeconomic issues that I am interested in, rational expectations provides a more realistic starting point, although that should never stop us analysing the consequences of expectations errors.

So why do I take a different view when it comes to the role of the media in politics? The answer simply relates to the costs and benefits of obtaining information. If you are trying to think about how consumers will react to a tax cut, or how agents in the foreign exchange market make decisions, you are talking about issues where expectation errors will be costly to the individual agents involved. So there are benefits in trying to gather information to avoid those mistakes. Compare this to political issues, like whether the government should be taking action over climate change. What are the costs for the individual of getting this wrong? Almost negligible: they may cast their vote in the wrong way. Now for society as a whole the costs are huge, but that is not the relevant thought experiment when thinking about individual decisions about whether to be better informed about climate change. Most people will reason that the costs of being better informed are quite high relative to the expected benefit, because the impact of their vote on the actual outcome of an election is negligible.

Which is why most people do not spend much time (on the internet or elsewhere) gathering information about issues like climate change, crime or immigration. That is a rational decision! They do, however, engage with media for other reasons, and are therefore likely to pick up information from there at little cost. So if the media distorts information, it matters.

That is my a priori conjecture, but what about evidence? Take opinions about climate change in the US. A distressingly large proportion of those polled thought that there is 'a lot of disagreement among scientists about whether or not global warming is happening', whereas in fact there is near unanimity among scientists. Now you could I suppose argue that this misperception had nothing to do with Fox News or talk radio, but just reflected the fact that people believe what they want to believe. But that seems unlikely, as you could more easily believe that although climate change was happening, the costs of doing anything about it outweighed the benefits. Certainly those institutions dedicated to climate-change denial think that beliefs about the science are important.

Polls in the UK typically point to large misperceptions. For example, in one poll the public think that £24 out of every £100 spent on benefits is claimed fraudulently, compared with official estimates of £0.70 per £100, and people think that 31% of the population are immigrants, when the official figure is 13%.[2] In contrast, estimates made by people who regularly read a newspaper, or had a Facebook account (where people probably had to draw on their own experience rather than stories in the media), were much more accurate.

These surveys certainly suggest that people's views on at least some key issues are based on perceptions that can be wildly inaccurate. There is an understandable tendency to overestimate things that are 'in the news': in one IPSOS/MORI poll the level of unemployment was overestimated by a factor of 2 or 3, the number of UK Muslims by a factor of 4 or 5, whereas the estimated proportion of those living in poverty was pretty close to the true figure. But it is also striking that the really wild misperceptions were on issues that tend to receive disproportionate tabloid coverage: apart from the benefit fraud example quoted above, we have:

> people are most likely to think that capping benefits at £26,000 per household will save most money from a list provided (33% pick this option), over twice the level that select raising the pension age to 66 for both men and women or stopping child benefit when someone in the household earns £50k+. In fact, capping household benefits is estimated to save £290m, compared with £5bn for raising the pension age and £1.7bn for stopping child benefit for wealthier households.[3]

One final point. Some of the comments on my recent post on this issue said, in effect, how typical of those on the left to think that people who hold views they don't like must have been brainwashed.[4] But of course there are plenty on the right (almost certainly more than on the left) who spend a lot of their time complaining about media bias the other way. The refrain about liberal bias in the US media is ubiquitous, and in the UK it is mainly right-wing think tanks and politicians who go on about BBC bias. And if you think that is because the BBC is biased (towards Labour, Europe and so on), then unfortunately the facts suggest otherwise. In fact, if you are looking for people who honestly believe the media is not that important politically, I suspect you will find more of them on the left than on the right. But wherever they come from, I think they are mistaken.

7.3
DO WE GET THE LEADERS OUR MEDIA DESERVES?
Friday, 28 November 2014

The right-wing press portrays Labour as elitist and/or too intellectual and therefore 'out of touch' with the concerns of ordinary people. Readers from the US will be all too familiar with this tactic, from the Gore–Bush campaign for example. A closely related ploy is to argue that politicians who are not poor who advocate policies to help the poor are somehow hypocrites (which of course tells us a great deal about the ethics of those making that accusation). Of course attempts to use background, income or character as evidence against a politician are not unique to the right. Arguments that because Cameron and much of his circle went to Eton and therefore cannot represent ordinary people are no better.

Or take this quote:

> Miliband is very much an old-style Hampstead socialist. He doesn't really understand the lower middle class or material aspiration. He doesn't understand Essex Man or Woman. Politics for him must seem at times like an extended PPE seminar: elevated talk about political economy and the good society.[5]

This is from an article written by the editor of the *New Statesman*. No evidence is presented that Miliband does not 'really understand the lower middle class or material aspiration'. That can only make sense if it follows from him being 'an old-style Hampstead socialist'.

Of course left and right are not symmetrical in one important sense: power. The right control the media spotlight, and it is focused on Miliband, such that every misfortune becomes a reflection on Miliband's character. So the SNP's popularity, and the likely loss of Labour seats there, is all down to Labour's Westminster elitism, and nothing to do with a resurgence of Scottish nationalism, which in turn is a reaction against the current UK government. Voter defections from Labour to UKIP are put down to an alleged Hampstead/Islington intellectual tone: never mind that we have a governing party actually falling apart over an issue crucial to the future of the country. A tweet of a house festooned with English flags is further evidence of an alleged contempt for the working class, while employing someone at the centre of government who was subsequently jailed for being part of routine phone hacking is apparently not a reflection of anything.

In this situation, is it any wonder Miliband has bad personal poll ratings? When those who voted Labour in 2010 were asked by YouGov whether Miliband would be up to the job of Prime Minister, 54% said yes in early October, but only 34% said so in early November. Did that one month reveal some serious flaw in his abilities as a future Prime Minister, or did his poll ratings fall because the media were incessantly talking about his poor ratings! These ratings are a convenient (because they are endogenous) device to keep the spotlight focused on him.

It has ever been thus. Neil Kinnock, an eloquent and passionate speaker with eminent working-class credentials became at the hands of the media a 'Welsh windbag' who did not have the gravitas of a Prime Minister. The only recent Labour leader not savaged by the press was Tony Blair, but only because Blair deliberately cultivated Murdoch, and had policies that were (designed to be?) not threatening to the establishment of which the press are a part, and who was famously relaxed about inequality and the growing wealth of the 1%. But I digress.

In an *FT* article about a week ago, Bill Emmott, a former *Economist* editor, raised important issues about the role of the media in portraying political leaders. It has a fantastic opening paragraph:

> Look carefully at the photos from Thursday's by-election victory of the UK Independence party in Rochester, or those of last month's Ukip victory in Clacton. Can you see that disembodied smile? No, this is not Lewis Carroll's Cheshire Cat; it is a Milanese mog. That feline grin represents a dangerous trend in British politics, one that goes beyond our arguments about immigration, the EU or globalisation, important though those are. It is the smile of Silvio Berlusconi.[6]

According to polls, our two most popular political leaders at the moment are Boris Johnson and Nigel Farage. Emmott argues that their popularity comes from the same source as with Berlusconi: they raise a smile, and no one looks too deeply at their mistakes, flip flops or even lies. What Emmott does not explore explicitly is why they are able to get away with things that would sink other politicians. With Berlusconi the answer appeared straightforward: he owned a large part of the media. But what Emmott is suggesting is that maybe ownership is not crucial: if the media are prepared to give a leader an easy ride because they are amusing and charming, we may end up with the same result.

You might think this could not happen here: the moment that either Johnson or Farage get close to power the attitude of the media would become more critical. That seems naive: how close do they need to get? The focus of some parts of the media on background and individual character seems to me part of the same trend, and it is not going to change before the election. We already have a media environment where something like a tweet of a house gets more media coverage than the impact of welfare reforms in driving many to rely on food banks to survive, or worse. It is an environment where on the day that Scotland is devolved substantial new powers, Channel

4 News chooses to lead on what an ex-cabinet minister might have said to a policeman in the heat of the moment. Those in the parts of the media that do not have to follow a political line, but who make decisions about what is newsworthy and what is not, need to reflect on what the impact of these decisions might be.

In truth, what a political leader is seen drinking, the quality of their jokes, or even their actions in responding or not to the media, tell us virtually nothing about what they will do if they gain power, and in whose interest they will act. But we are not clueless. As Polly Toynbee says: 'By their policies we know whose sides our politicians are on – whose interests they champion.'[7]

POSTSCRIPT

I had completely forgotten this post until preparing for this book. Little did I know the tendency I was concerned with would manifest itself in a most devastating form not in the UK (yet?) but in the US, with the election of Donald Trump. Since writing this I became aware of a study which showed that the switch of certain newspapers to supporting Blair before the 1997 election might have increased support for him by between 10% and 24% among readers.[8]

7.4
BOND MARKET FAIRY TALES
Thursday and Friday, 11/12 December 2014

I recently argued that the days when budget deficits mattered because of concerns about default are over.[9] In 2010 it briefly looked as if deficits could be so large that default was a real possibility, but we now know that was never true for the US and UK, and within the Eurozone it was only true for Greece, and since then austerity has (unfortunately) brought deficits down substantially. In most countries deficits are now around sustainable levels, by which I mean that they can be financed and sustained at close to current tax rates and spending regimes.

Which raises the question, why isn't this common knowledge? Why in mediamacro do people act as if we were still in 2010? In this respect BBC journalist Robert Peston has an interesting post.[10] Robert Peston is no fool, and his coverage of banking issues in particular is rightly famous in the UK. In his post, he notes correctly that there is a huge gap between the amount of austerity planned by Conservative and Labour after 2015. Let me quote what he says next.

> And here, of course, is where we need to ask Mr Market what he thinks of all this ... The Tory view is that those [low] interest rates can only be locked in if the government continues in remorseless fashion to shrink the state and net debt. What Labour would point out is that countries in a bit of a fiscal and economic mess and currently refusing to wear the hairshirt that the European Commission thinks necessary, such as Italy and France, are also borrowing remarkably cheaply.

So what Mr Market should tell Robert Peston at this point is that France can borrow more cheaply than the UK not because the French government is more credible and less likely to default: these are no longer important issues. The reason is that expected future short rates in France are lower as a result of the Eurozone recession. This means that because the Conservatives will cut back on spending more (than Labour), this will tend to reduce demand and output more, which in turn will mean expected future short rates will be a little lower under the Conservatives than Labour (as monetary policy tries to undo the impact of greater austerity). But what Mr Market actually told Robert Peston is as follows:

> And here is where Mr Market may be capricious, according to my pals in the bond market. They say the UK's creditors would probably be forgiving and tolerant of George Osborne borrowing more than he currently says he wishes to do, in that his record of reducing Whitehall spending by £35bn since taking office

in 2010 has earned him his austerity proficiency badge. But Ed Balls has never been chancellor, although he was the power behind Gordon Brown when he ran the Treasury and much of the country, both in the lean years from 1997 to 2000 and the big spending Labour years thereafter.

So Mr Balls has yet to prove, investors say, that he can shrink as well as grow the apparatus of the state.

What Robert Peston's pals in the bond market seem to be telling him (assuming that nothing was lost in translation) is that it is all about Labour's lack of credibility at being able to shrink the state. My immediate reaction: ?!?!? I have two problems.

- Why the talk about credibility? Talking about credibility makes sense if we are worrying about default, but there is no chance Ed Balls is going to choose to default. You might worry that Labour will not cut the deficit by as much as they plan, which will intensify the mechanism working through monetary policy that I outlined earlier. If that is what his pals meant, why didn't they say this, and why does that involve the markets being capricious?

- What is this about shrinking the apparatus of the state? Shrinking the deficit yes. But in what world does the return on bonds depend on the size of the state?

So it seems that my understanding of how the bond markets work is worlds apart from the understanding of Robert Peston's pals. I suspect that for mediamacro there really is no choice here: why would you believe an academic economist in their little old ivory tower rather than the guys who are directly in touch with the markets you are trying to understand? The fact that the explanation they give you could have been drafted by someone in No. 11 Downing Street (the UK Chancellor's residence) just suggests that George Osborne is in tune with financial realities.

This is a particular example of a more general phenomenon. The macroeconomics coming from economists attached to financial institutions often seems to be rather different to the macroeconomics of academic economists. When it comes to an issue involving financial markets, then it seems obvious who mediamacro should believe. Those close to the markets surely must know more about how those markets work than some unworldly academic. I want to suggest a more nuanced view.

As is often the case in macroeconomics, it all depends on the time horizon. Are we talking about what may happen over the next few days or weeks, or are we talking about what will happen over the next few quarters or years?

In terms of very short-term prediction, financial market economists beat academic economists hands down. The only thing most academic economists can usefully tell you is that it is unlikely you will outsmart market opinion. If you really want to try then you need lots of short-term information and a good nose for how that short-term information is interconnected. Most academics (there are exceptions) just do not have time to do that work. I always remember the reply an academic member of the Bank of England's Monetary Policy Committee gave to some MP who asked him about the implications of some latest data: 'I must have been doing some marking (grading) at the time that came out', was the reply.

Perhaps more surprisingly, those working in the markets are not as concerned about the longer term (what might happen in three or five years' time) as you might expect. That is because money is made in predicting short-term movements, and knowledge of where things are going over the next few years is a relatively weak guide to what might happen over the next few days. When I first started doing work on 'equilibrium exchange rates', I got a lot of queries from those in the markets, but the interest largely disappeared when I told them that 'equilibrium' meant where rates might be in about five years' time.

This may surprise you because economists attached to financial market institutions often tell longer-term stories, and sometimes they even produce detailed numerical forecasts of the type produced by central banks or governments. But macroeconomic forecasts are only slightly better than guesswork. So it is only really worth putting any significant resources into producing a macro forecast if you are taking or seriously influencing decisions, like setting interest rates, where the costs of getting things wrong are extremely large. My suspicion is that financial sector macro forecasts are mainly there to give the impression of expertise to the institution's clients.

I also suspect that economists working for financial institutions spend rather more time talking to their institutions' clients than to market traders. They earn their money by telling stories that interest and impress their clients. To do that it helps if they have the same world view as their clients. Getting things right over the longer term seems less important, as Paul Krugman keeps complaining about in the context of those who have been predicting rapid inflation as a result of Quantitative Easing.

It is also useful if they leave their clients with the impression that they have some unique insight into how the markets work. So instead of suggesting, as an academic would, that markets are governed by basic principles, it is better to suggest that the market is like some capricious god, and they are one of a few high priests who can detect its mood (Post 1.3). Now in the short term the market really can behave in volatile, unexpected and sometimes mysterious ways, but over the longer term there are some basic rules that markets obey.

The incentive system for academics is very different. They are judged by their peers. If they present stories to the media that differ greatly from conventional wisdom about theory or the empirical evidence, they will be given a hard time by their colleagues. They need to have an idea about how markets work to do good macroeconomics. They want to be more like scientists than high priests. (This has an unfortunate by-product. Most academics would rather not lose precious research time talking to journalists, particularly if the quotes they give may fail to contain the caveats normally demanded in academic work. In contrast, talking to the media is part of a city economist's job description.)

So who should journalists trust on the economy? If you want to know about the latest retail sales numbers or where the economy might be heading over the next few months then with a few exceptions financial economists are better bets than academic economists. If you have a more long-term question, like how alternative speeds of deficit reduction will influence interest rates, then perhaps surprisingly you may tend to get a more reliable answer from academics. Like most things in economics, this is a tendency: there are some seasoned City economists who I would trust over many academics.

There is an important implication about political bias as well. Academic economists are no saints on this, but I do not think there is a clear average bias among academic macroeconomists towards the left or right. However, partly because financial economists need to be good at telling stories that their clients find sympathetic their world view tends to be one where a smaller state is good for the economy, higher taxes on top incomes are a bad idea, markets are generally efficient and regulation is harmful.

If you think this is just self-serving conjecture, look at this evidence. The question of whether, in the UK, the 2013 recovery vindicated 2010 austerity was a no-brainer. Anyone who thinks about the logic for a moment will realise the answer is no, even if they think austerity was a good idea. Yet, as Post 1.11 outlines, when the *Financial Times* asked City economists this question around half said yes.

7.5
ON MEDIAMACRO
Friday, 1 May 2015

PREAMBLE

Mediamacro is a term I use to describe macroeconomics as it is understood in the media and which bears little relationship to what is taught to economics students. I first used the term mediamacro in the title of a post in September 2014[11], having watched an interview between Ed Miliband and Channel 4 News presenter Jon Snow. Miliband had just given his speech to the Labour Party conference from memory, and had forgotten a section on the deficit. This omission was pounced upon by the right-wing press. But when Jon Snow, hardly known for his right-wing views, interviewed Miliband shortly after the speech, he asked Miliband what the greatest issue facing the next British government is. Miliband responded that it is getting the country to work for most working people rather than be stuck with a more unequal country. Interesting answer, but inequality is not an issue mediamacro recognises. It was a trick question. Now that is twice that you have forgotten to mention the deficit, responded Snow. How could you not mention paying off this appalling deficit? Surely it is the most important issue of all. It is the essence of our economic crisis, he continued.

This was gotcha journalism for those who get their economics from listening to political commentators. The implication that the deficit is all-important was 'mediamacro' at its worst. Ask most economists what the greatest concern with the current UK economy was and they would probably say flat productivity, and the consequent lack of real wage growth. I conjectured in that post that Cameron in his party conference speech would fail to mention productivity at all, and no one would remark on that. My conjecture proved correct. The following post discusses the concept of mediamacro in more detail.

What do I mean by mediamacro? I realised I had never really defined what I meant by the term, so when some people started implying that it was just a conspiracy theory I thought it was time I should. A formal definition could be a set of ideas about macroeconomics promulgated by the media that seem very different to the macro taught to economic students. A clear example would be the idea that the 2013 UK recovery vindicated 2010 austerity (see Post 1.11).

Although the term mediamacro might have been new, the idea was not. Paul Krugman has for some time talked about VSPs, or Very Serious People, and I think we are talking about much the same thing. In particular, a common feature is to argue in the immediate aftermath of a large recession that reducing the deficit should be the top priority. Why did I use a different term? I think part of the reason was that I felt this was not a problem about individuals, but about a system. Many economic journalists are clever, opinionated and fiercely independent, and are hardly material for a grand conspiracy.

In any case I think mediamacro has much more to do with how political commentators rather than economic journalists interpret macro issues. This is one reason why the mediamacro problem is different from well-known issues about the reporting of scientific questions. Political commentators rarely talk about science, but they are talking about economics all the time, because so much of politics is about economics.

Again, any conspiracy theory would just be silly. If we were only talking about the output of the right-wing press, there would be little to remark upon. However, the idea that reducing the deficit is the overriding priority (and that we were in crisis in 2010 because of it) seems almost universal among political commentators whatever their political leaning, which is why my first post title using mediamacro was about Jon Snow berating Miliband for not mentioning the deficit.

The contrast between political and economic journalists can perhaps best be seen on the issue of Labour profligacy. The idea that fiscal policy under Labour was profligate (as opposed to mildly imprudent) would not be something that most economic journalists would sign up to. They know that the 2007–8 budget deficit of 2.7% of GDP is only about 1% of GDP away from the sustainable deficit with a 40% debt to GDP target, and 1% of GDP is very little given the errors involved in predicting deficits. They also probably recall that in 2007 the consensus view was that the UK economy was pretty close to trend. So the profligacy charge is nonsense. But you would not know that from seeing political commentators routinely allowing charges of profligacy to go unchallenged and asking for apologies from Labour politicians. Partly as a result, many members of the ordinary public just know that Labour was profligate, and accuse either Labour politicians or academic bloggers of lying when they suggest otherwise.

This leads to another point, which is the link between mediamacro and politics in a party political sense. When many people see me make the point above, they assume that I am doing so because I am being politically partisan. The reality is that fiscal policy is probably my main specialism within academic macro, and I have written an academic study of fiscal policy under Labour, so I feel it is almost a duty to point out the truth. If this were not the case, maybe I would just shrug my shoulders and let it pass. But there is a more general issue here: is mediamacro something that could only happen because it supports a particular political point of view?

This raises the issue of why mediamacro exists. I do not have a well worked out theory on this. In the UK it is natural to think the dominance of the right-wing press is important, but that is less of an issue in the US, which suggests it is not a necessary existence condition. I have also talked about the influence of City economists in the reporting of macroeconomic issues, which is obviously true on both sides of the Atlantic. The absence of a clear locus for received academic wisdom on fiscal policy, in contrast to monetary policy and central banks, could be important. Is the fact that all three political parties in the UK are signed up to the unconditional importance of deficit reduction important? That depends a bit on whether you think Labour chose to go that way or was pushed by the media.

How important you think the mediamacro problem is seems to depend on how bad you think the 2010 austerity mistake was. But it should not be like this. Even if you think that 2010 UK austerity was justified because of the particular situation of the time, the mediamacro problem is more generic. In the UK, all the major parties are currently committed to unconditional targets for deficit reduction, even though interest rates remain at their lower bound. That is just dumb macro but it remains unquestioned in the media. In a world where fiscal policy decisions are made by politicians, this matters.

POSTSCRIPT

As I explain in the introduction to this book, I at the time thought that the media had a particular problem with macroeconomics. However I now think it extends to any expertise the subject of which becomes politicised. The problem perhaps became acute with austerity because of the priority the government attached to its policy, and the simple (but inappropriate) household analogies that they could use to justify it. This made it very difficult for even the most intelligent journalists to use expertise to critique a government line. In addition, you can always find some economist who will support austerity, and there is no simple way of knowing what the plurality of opinion is. This is the subject of the following post.

7.6
THE ACADEMIC CONSENSUS ON THE IMPACT OF AUSTERITY
Friday, 5 June 2015

In discussing the forthcoming UK budget, Robert Peston writes:

And before I am savaged (as I always am) by the Krugman crew of Keynesian economists for even allowing George Osborne's argument an airing, I am not saying that the net negative impact on our national income and living standards of cutting the deficit faster is less than their alternative route of slower so-called fiscal consolidation.

I am simply pointing out that there is a debate here (though Krugman, Wren-Lewis and Portes are utterly persuaded they've won this match – and take the somewhat patronising view that voters who think differently are ignorant sheep led astray by a malign or blinkered media).[12]

I do not want to disappoint, and as I was about to write something on the macroeconomic consensus on austerity anyway, let me oblige: not in savaging (I leave that to my American colleague in arms!), but in justifying why I think there is such a consensus in the places that count. By consensus I do not mean that everyone agrees but that a very large majority do, which probably counts as consensus in economics.

Unfortunately we do not have a great deal of information on what academic economists as a whole think about austerity, but we do have two important survey results which are pretty conclusive. In the US, there is the IGM Forum, which regularly asks a group of distinguished economists, including many macroeconomists, their views on key policy issues. The last poll I have seen suggests that 82% of that panel thought the 2009 Obama stimulus had reduced unemployment, while only 2% disagreed. In the UK, the CFM (Centre for Macroeconomics) survey asked a similar question to a smaller group of academic economists, most of whom are macroeconomists. Only 15% agreed that the austerity policies of the coalition government have had a positive effect on aggregate economic activity, while 66% disagreed. That consensus is not universal – it would not apply in Germany, for example – but I doubt if anyone would disagree when I say that US economists call the shots as far as academic macroeconomics is concerned.

This is why economists the world over continue to teach Keynesian macro to undergraduates, and normally not as one 'school of thought' but rather as an initial approximation of how the economy actually works. As Amartya Sen so forcefully reminds us, the experience of the last 100 years has earned Keynesian theory this central role.[13]

However, we have another, more indirect, source of evidence. If you asked whether there was a standard model for analysing the business cycle among economists in academia and in policy making institutions, the answer would have to be the New Keynesian model. I want to include economists in central banks in particular because they have to put theories of the business cycle into practice on a regular basis. The key macromodels that central banks use to forecast and to analyse policy are Keynesian, and many are New Keynesian. Having worked a great deal with New Keynesian models myself, I also know what they imply about temporary changes in government spending in a liquidity trap. It may be possible to adapt these models to give you expansionary austerity, but no such adaptations command general or even partial support.

The models used by pretty well all central banks would therefore imply that temporary cuts in government spending were contractionary, absent any monetary policy offset. The governors of the central banks of the UK and US say this publicly. European central bank governors do not tend to say this, and instead continue to advocate austerity despite deflation. The reason why they might do this despite what their models tell them will be the subject of a later post, but I suspect it has little to do with conventional macroeconomics (but see also the point about German academic views above, and Sen's article). If temporary cuts in government spending are contractionary in a liquidity trap, it follows that it is much better to delay this form of austerity.

I could add repeated arguments from economists at the IMF, and now also the OECD. Of course there are some academic economists who continue to argue that the impact of austerity is expansionary or at least minor: I suspect there always will be, as long as this remains an intense political debate. They would be joined by many City economists, but they are neither unbiased nor the source of any particular expertise on this issue.

This is why, among economists with expertise, there is a clear majority view that fiscal austerity is significantly contractionary in a liquidity trap. That does not automatically mean that the 2010 policy switch was wrong, or that it had a big impact on the UK in 2010–12: there are additional issues here which I have discussed many times. How damaging to the macroeconomy any additional austerity from Osborne will be also depends on whether we are or will be in a liquidity trap. But the fact that we might well be means that additional austerity now is a big mistake, and on this I believe the great majority of academic macroeconomists and those macroeconomists working in policy making institutions would agree.

As far as the media is concerned, I cannot believe that Robert Peston would disagree that a large section are 'malign', given how political this issue is. When I have talked to journalists who have some freedom to report the facts rather than what their editors want them to report, the argument I most often hear is that because this issue is political, they have to report it as a 'debate' come what may. I have never had the pleasure of talking to Robert Peston (he is welcome to email at any time), and I would be very interested in how he would respond to the evidence I have laid out. As for the public, the word 'sheep' is his, not mine. Would he really argue that the public are independently well informed on these matters, or unaffected by the media's presentation of this and similar issues? Which is why I will continue to, as he might say, bang on about this, even though my audience is tiny in comparison to most journalists.

POSTSCRIPT

It is sometimes suggested to me that a way to improve the links between academic economists and the media is for economists to have more media training. In addition, academic economists should invest time in cultivating journalists like Peston rather than waiting to be contacted. (Peston never did take up the invitation made in this post.) But you have to ask yourself, do we really want to be guided by individual economists, or scientists more generally, who happen to have had the best media training and the most charisma? And is it a good use of these scientists' time to engage in media training?

A much better way forward is one implicitly suggested by this post. It took me some time to gather the evidence on what the majority of economists thought about austerity, and even then the evidence is not watertight. Journalists today simply do not have this time. The natural sciences invest considerable effort in establishing institutions that can interact with the media on behalf of all scientists, and perhaps organisations representing economists need to do the same, and put some effort into establishing what the consensus, or plurality of views, are on topical issues.

7.7
NEWS, ENTERTAINMENT AND TRUMP
Wednesday, 19 October 2016

There seem to be two types of media outlet in both the UK and US. There are those who push a clear right-wing political agenda to those who would rather read about celebrities or sport: the *Daily Mail* or *Sun* in the UK and Fox News in the US. As President Obama said, if I watched Fox News even I wouldn't vote for me. And then there is the non-partisan media. What values drive their coverage of political events?

I was thinking about this after reading a comprehensive account by Thomas Patterson of the media's role in the rise of Donald Trump, based on research by the Harvard Kennedy School's Shorenstein Center.[14] The basic story is that the media gave Trump far more coverage than other candidates in the crucial pre-primary period. Furthermore, contrary to popular myth, this was not just the cable news channels, but also papers like the *New York Times* and *Washington Post*. The rise of Donald Trump owes a great deal to this bias in media coverage.

The other remarkable thing about this excess coverage, even among the established newspapers, is that it was favourable. The term 'favourable' needs decoding in this context. What seems to happen involves a two-stage process. First, Trump simply gets attention by saying outrageous things. Once his poll ratings start to rise as a result of this publicity, he is talked about in a positive way because he is gaining popularity.

Journalists in the non-partisan media bend over backwards not to express personal views on policy or character. What they do instead is treat political contests as a horse race. It is all about who is up or down, who is rising and falling. On top of that views are expressed on why some candidates are doing better than others. Those who are winning generally require explanations in terms of positive virtues: hence the favourable treatment of Trump. Few journalists dare say that Trump is gaining popularity because a large section of the population is racist!

In other words, Trump played on conventional, non-partisan news values and won big time. He was great entertainment at first, and after that got him noticed he became the news because the additional news coverage helped increase his poll ratings. That news was favourable because his poll numbers were rising. In case you think this could only happen for someone on the right, according to this research the second part of the dynamic was even more true for Bernie Sanders. The candidate who really suffered was Clinton.

That the media should play such a large role in allowing someone like Donald Trump to get so close to the White House should be a big concern for those working in the media. The free press is supposed to help safeguard democracy from quasi-fascists, not make it easier for them to come to power! I wonder if part of the problem is that the non-partisan media is also mixing politics and entertainment. As talking about policy is not entertaining for most, particularly if it has to be done in a 'balanced' way, it is more attractive to the non-partisan media to treat politics like sport. I cannot help feeling that if in a real horse race it was shown that the commentary on the race had an influence on the outcome, something would be done to change that very quickly indeed.

7.8
CLINTON'S EMAILS AND UK AUSTERITY: A SENSE OF CONTEXT AND CONSEQUENCES

Monday, 31 October 2016

The media obsesses over whether Clinton might have sent an email containing confidential information from her personal account while Secretary of State, and also wonders about whether Trump tells lies, pays any taxes, bribes officials and assaults women. Anyone who reads these stories can see that there is no equivalence here. But anyone who just reads the headlines would be tempted to think otherwise. The very fact that commentators think a renewed focus on these emails is 'bad for Clinton' acknowledges that many people are indeed just reading the headlines. That context matters.

I am constantly surprised by how many on the left parrot the idea that the email affair is potentially serious. No one is suggesting Clinton should have a scrutiny-free march into the White House. But impressions matter, particularly just before an election. If the media spend as much time discussing possible Clinton mistakes as those of Trump, the impression given is that they are of equal importance. By balancing things that are very different, you create an equivalence that is completely misleading. Failure to take that into account still might have disastrous consequences.

I do not think this is just a problem with the media. Whenever I talk about the false accusation that Labour profligacy caused austerity, I get people commenting that it is not really false because Labour did overspend. This is true, and it was for this reason that I originally talked about it as being a myth based on a half-truth. A half-truth is a statement that conveys only part of the truth, especially one used deliberately in order to mislead someone. But in political terms that concedes too much. If there hadn't been a recession and the coalition had had to undo Labour's fiscal excess, I doubt if anyone besides the IFS would have noticed and no one would have called that correction austerity.

Yet even when I make this point, someone still objects that Labour bears some responsibility because they should have seen the recession coming, or that they were responsible for the lack of financial regulation that allowed the global financial crisis to have such a large impact on the UK. While those claims should be discussed in some contexts, they are beside the point when discussing Conservative charges against Labour. When Conservatives claim that Labour profligacy caused austerity, there is an implicit clause that says 'and it would not have happened if we were in charge'. The context is who would be better at managing the economy. If the context was an article about the performance in absolute terms of the Labour government, those caveats would be appropriate (although both can easily be challenged), but when the context is clearly about the relative competence of Labour and Conservatives then they are not.

When a political party makes a claim, or in press coverage during an election period, everything is relative. In a sense it is a bit like voting. Anyone who says they cannot vote for X because X did or will do something does not understand the game they are in. Voting is about comparisons: not whether X is good in some absolute sense, but whether X is better or worse than Y. So to say, as Ed Miliband sometimes did in defending Labour against the profligacy charge, that Labour perhaps was at fault for not regulating enough, he did himself no favours because he was talking out of context. Compared to the Conservatives he has nothing to apologise for on that front.

We can see this clearly if we think about consequences. The consequence of the US media spending so much time on the relatively trivial issue of emails is that, as polls suggest, US voters think they can trust Donald Trump more than Hillary Clinton. The consequence of Ed Miliband apologising about not regulating finance enough when defending Labour against profligacy claims is to appear to concede that in some sense the Conservatives were more competent than Labour. Context matters, and ignoring it has consequences.

7.9
A MISSION TO EXPLAIN
Friday, 18 November 2016

PREAMBLE

I was encouraged and thankful to win the biennial SPERI/New Statesman prize for political economy. My lecture was about the role of the media in misleading people over issues like austerity and Brexit. In doing research for the lecture I came across others who had said some similar things some 40 years ago.

Preparing for my SPERI/NEW Statesman lecture[15] (now sold out I'm afraid), I had a closer look at something that had been in the back of my mind for some time. In the mid-1970s, Peter Jay and John Birt put forward a new philosophy for broadcast journalism. Their first article in *The Times* started: 'There is a bias in television journalism. Not against any particular party or point of view – it is a bias against understanding.'[16]

A lot of the points that I have made in this blog are in their writing: the need to get more economic expertise into reporting, how he said/ she said reporting and panel discussion can reduce rather than increase understanding and knowledge.

What became of their initiative? Both had opportunities to put their ideas into practice, and Birt became Director General (DG) of the BBC in 1987 (in rather unfortunate circumstances, with Alasdair Milne being forced to resign because of conflicts with the Thatcher government, echoes of which are perhaps still with us today). But Birt's period as DG seems to have been associated with more centralisation of news and current affairs, and more 'risk management', which included pulling programmes that were controversial, and might have increased understanding!

It is tempting to draw the conclusion that the mission to explain fell foul of political interference, but that may be too easy on television journalism itself. It may simply be that the mission to explain worked against dominant journalistic values and culture. The need to generate scoops and headlines, for example, which comes from talking to or interviewing politicians rather than explaining economics. The entertainment value that comes from conflict and debate. The idea that it is more exciting television to have a correspondent embedded with troops in a war rather than calmly explaining the roots of the conflict from somewhere less 'dramatic'.

But whatever the reasons for the demise of the 'mission to explain', it is not exactly the same as what I have discussed in the past. Failing to explain does not account for what I call the politicisation of truth: where something becomes true just because one lot of politicians keep saying it and the 'other lot' do not contest it. That comes from insularity, from an excessive focus on the Westminster bubble.

7.10
ECONOMISTS SHOW HOW FOX NEWS CHANGES VOTES
Thursday, 14 September 2017

As I have noted before, economists are getting into media studies (we are natural imperialists) and beginning to provide empirical evidence on an age-old, and critical, debate. Are some media outlets biased simply because their viewers or readers are partisan, or do these media outlets play a causal role in changing political views? And do readers/viewers discount the bias in media outlets, or does this influence how they vote?

We now have clear evidence on this in the case of US news channels, and the answer is that Fox News changes votes in a big way: by magnitudes easily enough to swing elections. Those who argue that partisan right-wing media does not matter very much now need to bring some counterevidence to the table if they want to sustain that position.

The latest piece of evidence has just been published in the *American Economic Review*.[17] Why is the study in a top-rank economics journal? One thing empirical economists are used to doing is looking for good 'instrumental variables', which in this particular case means finding something that influences whether people watch Fox News that has nothing to do with their politics. If you then look at what these 'accidental' viewers do, that gives you a handle on the causal role of watching Fox News.

Let me list four key points from the study:

1 Fox News is the dominant (by primetime viewers) US news channel. A sizeable minority of Fox News viewers are not Republicans.

2 The study's data does not go beyond 2008, but in that year they estimate that if Fox News had not existed, the Republican vote share would have been over 6% points lower.

3 In contrast, the more left-wing MSNBC was far less effective at gaining votes for Democrats.

4 Fox News is not just setting its ideology to maximise viewers: it is much more conservative than that. Instead its choice of ideology maximises its persuasive power.

The 'headline figure' of over 6% points in point (2) is an overestimate because other networks do shift their ideology to gain viewers. So if Fox News disappeared, other networks might have shifted right to capture ex-Fox viewers. But the key point is that Fox is acting in a way to maximise the propaganda power of its extremely right-wing message, and it is successful in changing a significant number of voters' minds. The apologist line that the media is 'just reflecting the views of our readers/viewers' does not hold for Fox News. In short, it is a propaganda organisation, not a 'for profit' news organisation.

During one sample period, a different analysis of the content of Fox suggested that over half the facts it reported were untrue.[18]

One of the nice things about the study is that its results are reasonably consistent with earlier work based on the initial rollout of Fox News in 1996 to 2000. That earlier analysis used a different method to identify the causal impact of Fox on voters' choices, so it is good that two different methods come to similar conclusions.

To some this will be no surprise (except perhaps that the research is in an economics journal). To paraphrase Obama, if he watched Fox News even he wouldn't vote for himself. It helps explain how US politics has shifted so far to the right, and has become so partisan. To UK readers the obvious question is whether we can just substitute *Mail/Sun/Express* for Fox. In my view you can, and Brexit goes a long way to proving that. But explicitly or implicitly, the consensus view appears otherwise. Whether from left, right or centre, analysis of voter behaviour typically ignores or marginalises the role of the press. This and earlier studies suggest that is no longer good science.

Fox and its UK equivalents in the press have an importance way beyond academic studies of popular opinion. The story of Fox News and Trump are inextricably linked, as is Brexit and the right-wing press. When you can serve large sections of the population real fake news, news that denigrates particular minorities or 'outsiders' and pushes the political views of the media owners, then tyranny becomes quite compatible with democracy. Governments wield the 'will of the people' against pluralism and the rule of law, all enabled and even dictated by media as propaganda. We have examples within the EU and on its doorsteps. We are not there yet in the UK and US, but we are getting very close.

POSTSCRIPT

See also the postscript to Post 7.3 for some UK evidence on how strong the impact of the UK right-wing press can be on electoral outcomes, evidence that I was not aware of when I wrote this.

8

ECONOMISTS AND
POLICY MAKING

Introduction

This chapter is about economics and economists, and how both should influence policy. Some may be surprised that I do not talk more about the global financial crisis in this book. This is partly because my blog began some time after that event. Another reason is explained in Post 8.2. I've made a few additions to help with the jargon, but once again understanding the economic terms is not necessary to understand the message. I explore similar themes in Post 8.4, where I suggest that even if macroeconomists had predicted the crisis, they would have been ignored.

Economics is a unique science, but if comparisons have to be made with other sciences I think medicine is the most appropriate. Post 8.10 draws an analogy between the financial crisis and the opioid epidemic in the US, and by implication how crises should be viewed in either discipline. Post 8.5 describes in a light-hearted way why economics, although it has many disadvantages compared to the hard sciences, has one advantage: introspection. Post 8.1 talks about a problem that economics in particular has: ideological influence.

Post 8.7 deals with a major reason why economists get so much stick, macroeconomic forecasting, which ironically hardly any academic economists are involved in. It makes what should be the self-evident point, but one which was ignored in the Brexit debate, that trying to predict the future is very different from trying to assess the impact of, say, changing interest rates or leaving the EU. Post 8.8 argues that delegating decisions like changing interest rates to bankers or economists is making advice more transparent as much as it is about delegating power.

Delegation aside, Post 8.3 looks at an example where economic expertise was fully utilised to good effect: the UK's decision not to join the Eurozone. Post 8.6 is an example of the opposite, where ideas about immigration that economists know to be false are allowed to continue to be regarded as true in public debate. Post 8.9 looks at how the decision to move to austerity was another such failure, and how central banks are important in understanding why this happened.

Posts in Chapter 8

8.1
MISTAKES AND IDEOLOGY IN MACROECONOMICS
Monday, 9 January 2012

PREAMBLE

In early 2012, when this was written, I had just started my blog and there was a heated debate going on between economists in the US about the merits of President Obama's fiscal stimulus package three years earlier, and of fiscal stimulus or austerity more generally. Into this minefield I stepped, a newcomer on the econblog scene but an academic whose recent work was all about fiscal policy. If one post made my name as a blogger it was this, and ever since then my US audience has been equal to that in the UK.

That, however, was not my intention in writing this. I had seen the statements I quote in this post, and was really shocked. I knew what they were saying made no sense, because this was my area of expertise. I wanted to understand how economic 'stars' could make such obvious mistakes. There is some economics jargon in this post, but it is not central to its message and so can be safely ignored.

Imagine a Nobel Prize winner in physics, who in public debate makes elementary errors that would embarrass a good undergraduate. Now imagine other academic colleagues, from one of the best faculties in the world, making the same errors. It could not happen. However, that is exactly what has happened in macro over the last few years.

Where is my evidence for such an outlandish claim? Well here is Nobel Prize winner Robert Lucas:

But, if we do build the bridge by taking tax money away from somebody else, and using that to pay the bridge builder – the

216

guys who work on the bridge – then it's just a wash. It has no
first-starter effect. There's no reason to expect any stimulation.
And, in some sense, there's nothing to apply a multiplier to.
(Laughs.) You apply a multiplier to the bridge builders, then
you've got to apply the same multiplier with a minus sign to the
people you taxed to build the bridge.[1]

And here is John Cochrane, also a professor at Chicago, and someone
who has made important academic contributions to macroeconomic
thinking:

Before we spend a trillion dollars or so, it's important to
understand how it's supposed to work. Spending supported by
taxes pretty obviously won't work: If the government taxes A
by $1 and gives the money to B, B can spend $1 more. But A
spends $1 less and we are not collectively any better off.[2]

Both make the same simple error. If you spend X at time t to build a
bridge, aggregate demand increases by X at time t. If you raise taxes
by X at time t, consumers will smooth this effect over time, so their
spending at time t will fall by much less than X. Put the two together
and aggregate demand rises.

But surely very clever people cannot make simple errors of this kind?
Perhaps there is some way to reinterpret such statements so that
they make sense. They would make sense, for example, if the extra
government spending was permanent. The only trouble is that both
statements were made about a temporary fiscal stimulus package.
Brad DeLong tries very hard along these lines, but just throws up
inconsistencies.[3]

I prefer to just note that if any undergraduate or graduate student
in the UK wrote this in an exam, they would lose marks. The more
interesting question for me is why the errors were made. Of course
everyone is human, including the best economists. (And if they were
not among the very best economists, I would not be talking about
these errors in a blog.) You get to be a brilliant economist or physicist
by having great ideas, not by never making mistakes. But I think

it is still the case that we cannot imagine members of a physics department making such errors. What is different about macro?

I want to suggest two answers. The first is familiarity with models. I cannot imagine anyone who teaches New Keynesian economics, or who talked to people who teach New Keynesian economics, making this mistake. This is because, in these models, we do have to worry about aggregate demand. We focus on consumption smoothing, and Ricardian Equivalence, and teach it from the start. I often tell my first-year undergraduate students that if they write anything like 'Ricardian Equivalence says fiscal stimulus will never work', they are in danger of failing.

Lack of familiarity does not necessarily imply believing something is wrong. In a separate piece, Cochrane writes: '"New-Keynesian" thought is devoted to defending the importance of monetary policy, and incorporating specific frictions in the equilibrium tradition, not to rescuing the ancient view that fiscal stimulus is important and abandoning that tradition.'[4] This is broadly true for New Keynesian theory when monetary policy is unconstrained but not when interest rates are stuck at a lower bound. Cochrane is not saying New Keynesian theory is wrong, but implies incorrectly that it suggests fiscal stimulus will not work.

Lack of familiarity with New Keynesian economics may be partly explained by the history of macroeconomic thought. New Keynesian theory is an 'add-on' to the basic Ramsey/RBC (Real Business Cycle) model, so it is possible to teach macro without getting round to teaching New Keynesian theory. However, what many people find difficult to understand is how monetary policy (or at least monetary policy as seen by pretty much every central bank) could be regarded as an optional add-on in macroeconomics.

The second difference between physics and macro that could lead to more mistakes in the latter is ideology. When you are arguing out of ideological conviction, there is a danger that rhetoric will trump rigour. In the next paragraph Cochrane writes:

These ideas changed because Keynesian economics was a failure in practice, and not just in theory. Keynes left Britain 30 years of miserable growth. Richard Nixon said, 'We are all Keynesians now', just as Keynesian policy led to the inflation and economic dislocation of the 1970s – unexpected by Keynesians but dramatically foretold by Milton Friedman's 1968 AEA address. Keynes disdained investment, where we now all realize that saving and investment are vital to long-run growth. Keynes did not think at all about the incentives effects of taxes. He favored planning, and wrote before Hayek reminded us how modern economies cannot function without price signals. Fiscal stimulus advocates are hanging on to a last little timber from a sunken boat of ideas, ideas that everyone including they abandoned, and from hard experience. If we forget all that, we could repeat the economics of postwar Britain, of spend-and-inflate Latin America, and of bureaucratic, planned India.

Let's not worry about where the idea that Keynes disdained investment comes from, or any of the other questionable statements here. This is just polemic: Keynes = fiscal expansion = planning = macroeconomic failure. It is guilt by association. What on earth does fiscal expansion have to do with planning? Well, they are both undertaken by the state.

The problem too many macroeconomists have with fiscal stimulus lies not in opposing schools of thought, or the validity of particular theories, or the size of particular parameters, but instead with the fact that it represents intervention by the state designed to improve the working of the market economy. They have an ideological problem with countercyclical fiscal policy. But the central bank is part of the state, and it intervenes to improve how the economy works, so this ideological view would also mean that you played down the role of monetary policy in macroeconomics. So ideology may also help explain a lack of familiarity with the models central banks use to think about monetary policy. In short, an ideological view that distorts economic thinking can lead to mistakes.

8.2
CRISIS, WHAT CRISIS? ARROGANCE AND SELF-SATISFACTION AMONG MACROECONOMISTS?
Wednesday, 11 July 2012

In a recent post on economics teaching I upset a number of bloggers. I argued that the recent crisis has not led to a fundamental rethink of macroeconomics. Mainstream macroeconomics has not decided that the Great Recession implies that some chunk of what we used to teach is clearly wrong and should be jettisoned as a result. To some that seems self-satisfied, arrogant and profoundly wrong. Here I want to focus on why I don't think the financial crisis requires a fundamental rethink of macroeconomics, despite articles in the media suggesting it does.

Let me be absolutely clear that I am not saying that macroeconomics has nothing to learn from the financial crisis. What I am suggesting is that when those lessons have been learnt, the basics of the macroeconomics we teach will still be there. For example, it may be that we need to relate the difference between the interest rate set by monetary policy and the interest rate actually paid by firms and consumers to asset prices that move with the cycle. But if that is the case, this will build on our current theories of the business cycle. Concepts like aggregate demand and, within the mainstream, the natural rate, will not disappear. We clearly need to take default risk more seriously, and this may lead to more use of models with multiple equilibria. However, this must surely use the intertemporal optimising framework that is the heart of modern macro.

Why do I want to say this? Because what we already have in macro remains important, valid and useful. What I see happening today is a struggle between those who want to use what we have, and those that want to deny its applicability to the current crisis. What we already have was used (imperfectly, of course) when the financial crisis hit, and analysis clearly suggests this helped mitigate the recession. Since 2010 these positive responses have been reversed, with policymakers around the world using ideas that contradict basic macro theory, like expansionary austerity.

I also think there is a danger in the idea that the financial crisis might have been avoided if only we had better technical tools at our disposal. A couple of years ago I was at a small workshop organised by the Bank of England and Economic and Social Research Council that got together mostly scientists rather than economists to look at alternative techniques of modelling, such as networks. One question is whether finance and macro could learn anything from these other disciplines. I'm sure the answer is yes, and I found the event fascinating, but I made the following observation at the end. The financial crisis itself is not a deeply mysterious event. Look now at the data on bank leverage (the ratio of bank assets like loans to its equity) that we had at the time, but which too few people looked at before the crisis, and the immediate reaction has to be that this cannot go on. Banks were lending too much relative to the equity cushion they had. So the interesting question for me is how those that did look at this data managed to convince themselves that this time was different.

One answer was that they were convinced by economic theory that turned out to be wrong. But it was not traditional macro theory: it was theories from financial economics. And I'm sure many financial economists would argue that those theories were misapplied. Like confusing new techniques for handling idiosyncratic risk, risk that applies to particular assets, with the problem of systemic or global risk. Believing that evidence of arbitrage between assets also meant that fundamentals were correctly perceived. In retrospect, we can see why those ideas were wrong by using the economics toolkit we already have. So why was that not recognised at the time? I think the key to answering that does not lie in any exciting new technique from physics or elsewhere, but in political science.

To understand why regulators and others missed the crisis, I think we need to recognise the political environment at the time, which includes the influence of the financial sector itself. And I fear that the academic sector was not exactly innocent in this either. A simplistic take on economic theory (mostly micro theory rather than macro) became an excuse for rent seeking. The really big question of the day is not what is wrong with macro, but why the financial sector has grown so rapidly over the last decade or so. Did innovation and deregulation in that sector add to social welfare, or make it easier for that sector to extract surplus from the rest of the economy? This is what economists need to investigate, and in some cases they are.

8.3
HOW KNOWLEDGE TRANSMISSION SHOULD WORK
Friday, 5 July 2013

The tenth anniversary of the UK's 2003 decision not to join the Eurozone has just passed. With all my complaints about how bad macroeconomic policy making has been recently, and how austerity is ignoring basic academic macroeconomics, I thought it was worth analysing an example of a good decision. Good not just because it was the right decision given the events of the last few years, but good also because of how it was done, and the way academic knowledge was used.

Here is just a short summary. The UK opted out of being one of the founding members of the Eurozone, but the possibility of us joining shortly afterwards was always taken seriously. The Chancellor Gordon Brown announced five tests that would need to be passed if this were to happen, and the Treasury spent a couple of years doing extensive work on these five tests. It eventually published 18 studies.[5] Although there is some original work there (of which more later), they were mainly very good summaries of the relevant academic literature, and various academics were consulted to help ensure this was the case.

I should declare an interest here. I wrote one of those studies, which tried to assess what exchange rate the UK should join at, if the decision was yes. However, I do not think this has any influence on what I have to say below, because in an important sense my study was secondary to the question of whether we should join.[6] In contrast, much more critical was modelling work done by Peter Westaway, at the time a Bank of England economist who had previously built the Bank's core macromodel.

Now some will argue that these 18 studies, and the years of work that went into them, were window dressing for a decision that had already been made. I think that is simply incorrect. Some of the reasons I think that are described by Dave Ramsden,[7] who masterminded the analysis and who recently gave a lecture on the subject. In essence if the politicians involved had already made up their mind, they went to quite elaborate lengths to conceal the fact from those that worked for them. (Compare this to the Iraq war, for example, where a dodgy dossier sufficed.) Furthermore, the studies themselves contain some very strong arguments (probably too strong) why joining the Eurozone could be very beneficial, which is not the kind of thing you do if you want the analysis to back up a foregone conclusion.

As a result, I think the exercise was what it purported to be: an attempt by civil servants to give the best advice they could to politicians. What marks it out for me was the extent to which those civil servants involved academics, and placed academic work at the centre of their analysis. The merits or otherwise of the euro did divide macroeconomists, but there was no attempt to just consult those who agreed with some predefined view.

So why did this particular process turn out to be close to what I consider an ideal of how academic knowledge should be used? Here are three reasons. The first is that the decision, although it generated strong opinions on either side, was not fundamentally ideological. There was no existing political apparatus that was clearly aligned with potential winners and losers. The second is that you had a Chancellor who had a very strong respect for economic ideas, whatever else you may think of him as a politician. Third, the Chancellor had to convince the Prime Minister, Tony Blair, and so whatever decision he came to needed to be backed up as strongly as possible.

Most people would now agree that the 2003 decision (only one of the five tests were passed) was the correct one. While the analysis, and particularly the work by Westaway, contained some of the elements that came to the fore in the Eurozone crisis, I think Ramsden in his lecture is clear that the 18 studies also failed to foresee other elements of the crisis, perhaps not surprisingly, as most macroeconomists missed these too. Yet the deeper point is this. The decision was based on the best analysis that macroeconomics at the time could provide. It is a shame that this way of making economic decisions now looks like the exception rather than the rule.

8.4
BANKS, ECONOMISTS AND POLITICIANS: JUST FOLLOW THE MONEY
Monday, 26 August 2013

Economics rightly comes in for a lot of stick for failing to appreciate the possibility of a financial crash before 2007/8. However, it is important to ask whether things would have been very different if it had. What has happened to financial regulation after the crash is a clear indication that it would have made very little difference.

There is one simple and straightforward measure that would go a long way to avoiding another global financial crisis, and that is to substantially increase the proportion of bank equity that banks are obliged to hold. This point is put forcibly, and in plain language, in Admati and Hellwig (2013).[8] They suggest the proportion of the balance sheet that is backed by equity should be something like 25%, and other estimates for the optimal amount of bank equity come up with similar numbers. The numbers that regulators are intending to impose post-crisis are tiny in comparison.

It is worth quoting the first paragraph of a *Financial Times* review of their book by Martin Wolf:

The UK's Independent Commission on Banking, of which I was a member, made a modest proposal: the proportion of the balance sheet of UK retail banks that has to be funded by equity, instead of debt, should be raised to 4 per cent. This would be just a percentage point above the figure suggested by the Basel Committee on Banking Supervision. The government rejected this, because of lobbying by the banks.[9]

Why are banks so reluctant to raise more equity capital? One reason is tax breaks that make finance through borrowing cheaper. But non-financial companies, which also have a choice between raising equity and borrowing to finance investment, typically use much more equity capital and less borrowing. If things go wrong, you can reduce dividends, but you still have to pay interest, so companies limit the amount of borrowing they do to reduce the risk of bankruptcy. But large banks are famously too big to fail. So someone else takes care of the bankruptcy risk: you and me. We effectively guarantee the borrowing that banks do. Admati and Hellwig make a nice analogy with a rich aunt who offers to always guarantee your mortgage.

The state guarantee is a huge, and ongoing, public subsidy to the banking sector. For large banks, it is of the same order of magnitude as the profits they make. We know where a large proportion of the profits go: into bonuses for those who work in those banks. The larger is the amount of equity capital that banks are forced to hold, the more the holders of that equity bear the cost of bank failure, and the less is the public subsidy. Seen in this way, it becomes obvious why banks do not want to hold more equity capital: they rather like being subsidised by the state, so that the state can contribute to their bonuses.

This is why the argument is largely a no-brainer for economists. Most economists are instinctively against state subsidies, unless there are obvious externalities which they are countering. With banks the subsidy is not just an unwarranted transfer of resources, but it is also distorting the incentives for bankers to take risk, as we found out in 2007/8. Bankers make money when the risk pays off, and get bailed out by governments when it does not.

So why are economists being ignored by politicians? It is hardly because banks are popular with the public. The scale of the banking sector's misdemeanours is incredible. I suspect many will think that banks are being treated lightly because politicians are concerned about choking off the recovery. Yet the argument that banks often make, which is that holding equity capital represents money that is 'tied up' and so cannot be lent to firms and consumers, is simply nonsense. This is about how bank loans are financed, and not about not lending money. A more respectable argument is that holding much more equity capital would translate into greater costs for bank borrowers, but economists suggest this effect would not be large. In any case, public subsidies are bound to be passed on to some extent, but that does not justify them. Politicians are busy trying to phase out public subsidies elsewhere, so why are banks so different?

There is one simple explanation. The power of the banking lobby (and the financial industry more generally) is immense, from campaign contributions to regulatory capture of various kinds. It would be nice to imagine that the UK was less vulnerable than the US in this respect, but there are good reasons, based on party funding and lobbying, to think otherwise. In Europe, where bank lobbying is also intense, we had what Mark Blyth describes as the biggest bait-and-switch operation in modern history, where a banking crisis involving private-sector debts was turned into a public-sector debt crisis.[10] As a result, the power and influence of banks and bankers within government has hardly suffered as a result of the Great Recession that they played a large part in creating.

So to return to my original question, would it really have made much difference if more mainstream economists had been fretting about the position of the financial sector before the crisis? I think they would have been ignored then even more than they are being ignored now. The single most effective way of avoiding another financial crisis is to reduce the political influence of the banking sector.

8.5
BERTRAND RUSSELL'S CHICKEN (AND WHY IT WAS NOT AN ECONOMIST)
Wednesday, 27 November 2013

When that pioneering economist David Hume wrote about the problem of induction, he talked about the possibility that the sun would not rise one morning. There is no way we can know 'for sure' that it will rise. Just because the theories we have suggest it will rise each morning, and those theories have been right so far, does nothing to ensure they will continue to be right. In contrast, we know for sure that $1 + 1 = 2$.

The problem with this example is that it is very difficult to imagine the sun not rising every morning. Bertrand Russell had perhaps a better example. The chicken that is fed by the farmer each morning may well have a theory that it will always be fed each morning: it becomes a 'law'. And it works every day, until the day the chicken is instead slaughtered.

When I used to lecture about economic methodology, I liked to say that this chicken was not an economist. Now you might say that no chicken is an economist, but suppose that chickens were as intelligent as the farmer who keeps them, so they could be economists. Economics is at a disadvantage compared to the physical sciences because we cannot do so many types of experiments (although we are doing more and more), but we have another source of evidence: introspection. To understand how people in general behave, we can ask how we personally behave.

So if Bertrand Russell's chicken had been an economist, they would not simply have observed that every morning the farmer brought them food, and therefore concluded that this must happen forever. Instead they would have asked a crucial additional question: why is the farmer doing this? What is in it for him? If I was the farmer, why would I do this? And of course trying to answer that question might have led them to the unfortunate truth.

THE LIES WE WERE TOLD

I thought of this when reading through the fascinating comments on my post on rational expectations, and posts that others had written in response.[11] Rational expectations is the idea that people use all the available information (assuming it is not too costly to obtain it) to efficiently formulate their expectations. You can see why the habit of introspection would make economists predisposed to assume rationality generally, and rational expectations in particular. (I think it also helps explain economists' aversion to paternalism.) It only works to use your own thought processes as a guide to how people in general might behave if you think other people are essentially like yourself. So if your own thoughts lead you to postulate some theory about how the economy behaves, then others similar to yourself might be able to do something like the same thing.

But of course this line of reasoning could also be misleading. An economist who introspects does so with the help of the economic theory they already have, so their introspection is not representative. A psychologist or behavioural economist might come to very different conclusions from introspection, they may ask: 'what biases do I bring to this problem?' Economists may also be fooled into thinking their introspection is representative, because they are surrounded by other economists. So this conjecture about introspection does little to show that assuming agents have rational expectations is right (or wrong), but it may be one reason why most economists find the concept of rational expectations so attractive.

8.6
ECONOMICS AND THE IMMIGRATION DEBATE
Wednesday, 1 January 2014

As the storm force winds blew, I wondered to what extent the debates on immigration and austerity shared a common feature. In both cases economists might feel like someone trying to walk against high winds: it is hard, perhaps painful, and you seem to be getting nowhere fast.

To be less metaphorical, in both cases the economic arguments seem to be irrelevant to the public debate, and the politicians want to go in the opposite direction to the one suggested by the economics.

I have talked a great deal about austerity before, but not about immigration. Typical complaints about immigration are that it reduces real wages, and reduces access to public services. Econometric studies are mixed, but they tend to find little or no evidence of any impact on real wages, even for unskilled workers. Economists are however quite clear about the impact of immigration on public services. As migrants tend to be younger, more immigration raises GDP per capita, because there are more workers for each pensioner. For this and other reasons, migrants make fewer demands on the state, so more immigration reduces government spending per person (for example, the elderly use the NHS more) which leads to lower taxes. This beneficial tax effect could easily offset any small negative impact on real wages.

In short, migration is beneficial for the economy as a whole, and for households as a whole. The economist who has done most to bring these results into the UK public domain is Jonathan Portes. Yet the political debate presumes the opposite. It is taken as read that migration causes all kinds of harmful effects, and the debate revolves around measures to prevent these. It is summed up by this quote from BBC political journalist Nick Robinson. 'What Jonathan Portes has helped us do is define the difference between an economist and a politician', said Robinson. 'A fine economist he might be, but I suggest he would not have a chance of getting elected in a single constituency in the country. It is a widespread view that there is exploitation of the benefits system by migrants.'

So you see why I think there is a potential parallel with the austerity debate. The evidence suggests that migrants make a net fiscal contribution relative to natives, just as all the evidence suggests that austerity is harmful in a liquidity trap. However, the 'public' believes otherwise, and (by implication) economists should get real and stop going on about evidence so much.

THE LIES WE WERE TOLD

There is a difference, however. Government debt is not a 'doorstep issue', whereas immigration is. In 2010 the Eurozone crisis brought the issue of debt to the fore, but since then in most countries it has been the politicians and sections of the elite that have kept the debt problem alive (to justify austerity). The 'need' for austerity is accepted by the public because it is portrayed as governments doing what households do in bad times: tighten their belts. I do not think excessive government debt is an issue that many politicians encounter when they go canvassing for votes, but migration certainly is. Equally I doubt that the current UK government would have made migration such a big issue if it wasn't perceived as a vote winner, and if it was not for UKIP.

Does this make a difference to how economists react in each case? We plug away at the economics of course, but how do we explain why the economics seems to be ignored? With austerity most explanations involve thinking about how politicians and sections of the elite think: why they may be irrationally worried about market panics, or why debt may be a cover for other agendas. With migration the focus has to be about why large sections of the electorate believe that migration harms them.

I see three strands of thought here, although none are mutually exclusive. The first is to acknowledge that there is a natural tendency for communities to be concerned about outsiders, but blame the media and some politicians for playing on this concern. This can explain why popular concern about immigration can be so high in areas where there is very little. The second is to grant that migration may be beneficial for the economy as a whole, but acknowledge that for some the immediate (and therefore personally verifiable) impact is negative (for example, fewer unskilled vacancies, lower wages, higher rents). A third takes the concern about outsiders more seriously, and talks about the benefits and costs of social diversity.

A second difference involves politics. To the extent that austerity is a cover for sections of the elite to push for a smaller state, then austerity morphs into a standard debate between right and left. This helps explain why what on the surface should be a technical macroeconomic discussion about multipliers and the effectiveness of unconventional monetary policy is in reality so politically polarised. This is not the case with migration. Restricting migration generally runs counter to the neoliberal agenda. Others argue that public concern about migration reflects the failure of the left to oppose (or worse, pursue) this agenda.

Perhaps I can sum things up this way. While I find the macroeconomics of austerity interesting (it's my field), I believe the reasons why the economics is ignored are fairly straightforward and much less interesting. In the case of migration, I think understanding why the economics is ignored is much more of an intellectual challenge.

POSTSCRIPT

I wrote this at the beginning of 2014, which is before Brexit. Immigration played a central role in the Brexit vote, and this forced me to sharpen my thinking on the issue. One consequence is to see more links between immigration and austerity than I set out above. It is likely (see Post 6.6) that many voted to leave because they believed lower immigration would improve access to public services. This idea does not just come from the media, but also reflects 'common sense' that sees the immigrant as a consumer of public services but not as a producer of the taxes that fund them. There is therefore a parallel with the 'common sense' idea that the government is like a household and should tighten its belt in a recession.

I have also explored further the idea that right-wing governments exploit immigration to attract votes in Posts 9.8 and 9.9. The reason why this is so attractive is fairly straightforward, if we think about politics as two-dimensional: augmenting the traditional right/left economic axis with a socially liberal or conservative axis. Many voters who would normally vote left on economic grounds are also socially conservative. An anti-immigration agenda can attract these voters away from left-wing

THE LIES WE WERE TOLD

parties, particularly if they can be convinced that immigration is also detrimental to them economically.

8.7
CONDITIONAL AND UNCONDITIONAL FORECASTING
Friday, 15 August 2014

Sometimes I wonder how others manage to write short posts. In my earlier post about forecasting, I used an analogy with medicine to make the point that an inability to predict the future does not invalidate a science. This was not the focus of the post, so it was a single sentence, but some comments suggest I should have said more. So here is an extended version.

The level of output depends on a huge number of things: demand in the rest of the world, fiscal policy, oil prices and so on. It also depends on interest rates. We can distinguish between a conditional and an unconditional forecast. An unconditional forecast says what output will be at some date. A conditional forecast says what will happen to output if interest rates, and only interest rates, change. An unconditional forecast is clearly much more difficult, because you need to get a whole host of things right. A conditional forecast is easier to get right.

Paul Krugman is rightly fond of saying that Keynesian economists got a number of things right following the recession: additional debt did not lead to higher interest rates, Quantitative Easing did not lead to hyperinflation, and austerity did reduce output. These are all conditional forecasts. If X changes, how will Y change? An unconditional forecast says what Y will be, which depends on forecasts of all the X variables that can influence Y.

We can immediately see why the failure of unconditional forecasts tells us very little about how good a model is at conditional forecasting. A macroeconomic model may be reasonably good at saying how a change in interest rates will influence output, but it can still be pretty poor at predicting what output growth will be next year because it is bad at predicting oil prices, technological progress or whatever.

This is why I use the analogy with medicine. Medicine can tell us that if we eat our five (or seven) a day our health will tend to be better, just as macroeconomists now believe explicit inflation targets (or something similar) help stabilise the economy. Medicine can in many cases tell us what we can do to recover more quickly from illness, just as macroeconomics can tell us we need to cut interest rates in a recession. Medicine is not a precise enough science to tell each of us how our health will change year to year, yet no one says that because it cannot make these unconditional predictions it is not a science.

8.8
SHOULD ECONOMISTS RULE?
Saturday, 18 April 2015

Tim Harford in the *Financial Times* talks to seven random mainstream economists about their radical ideas for economic policy.[12] Nick Stern wants green cities (with much greater economic autonomy), Jonathan Haskel wants more spent on research (because the returns are very high), Gemma Tetlow wants to merge income tax with national insurance, Diane Coyle wants to reduce boardroom pay, John van Reenen wants new institutions to promote infrastructure, Kate Barker wants changes to how housing is taxed, including capital gains on main residences, and Simon Wren-Lewis wants 'democratic helicopter money'.

Helicopter money is the idea that, to stimulate the economy, the central bank should create more money directly and give it to people. My democratic bit is that the central bank gives the created money to the government on condition that it is used for a stimulus package, but the form of the stimulus package would be the government's choosing. I was impressed that Tim managed to turn a very pleasant chat over coffee (while taking few notes) into a coherent account of my argument. The only point I might have added is that my suggestion of turning helicopter money democratic is in part to avoid some of the political difficulties he alluded to.

The common strand in many of these suggestions, which Tim draws out, is a desire to replace direct political control by something more technocratic. Now you could say that this is simply a power grab by economists. However, if you think about the examples here, they represent important and widely recognised policy mistakes which tend to be universal and persistent: failure to deal with climate change; failure to invest enough in R&D; unnecessary complications in the tax system; runaway boardroom pay; failure to invest in infrastructure even when borrowing is ultra-cheap; a broken housing sector; and pro-cyclical fiscal policy. It is not as if the status quo is doing just fine.

I would add just two observations. First, the argument is often not about 'losing democratic control', but instead about advice being open and transparent. The alternative to some advisory body, whose deliberations should be publicly available and subject to scrutiny, is often secret advice from the civil service, or worse still from what Paul Krugman calls policy entrepreneurs or partisan think tanks. Second, what is thought politically infeasible today may relatively quickly become commonly accepted.

I was quite surprised that Tim thought democratic helicopter money was particularly radical and politically infeasible. But then I remembered fiscal councils. My first published piece advocating (advisory) fiscal councils was in 1996, and for more than a decade this was considered the impractical idea of a few 'out of touch' economists, who were obviously anti-democratic. Then, little more than a decade later, the idea very quickly became acceptable. Nowadays, it seems like fiscal councils are everywhere. So the one part of Tim's piece that I would not take too seriously are his scores for political feasibility and radicalism. Today's supposedly radical idea can quite quickly become received wisdom.

8.9
THE KNOWLEDGE TRANSMISSION MECHANISM AND MACROECONOMIC CRISES
Wednesday, 3 June 2015

PREAMBLE

In many posts I have used the phrase 'knowledge transmission mechanism' to denote how academic knowledge either does or does not find its way into economic policy. Even when I do not use this phrase, much of this book is about understanding why policymakers sometimes undertake policies, like austerity, that most academics know to be bad. What follows is in fact a combination of two posts, the second of which is called 'Austerity as a knowledge transmission mechanism failure', and each is based on a more comprehensive paper.[13]

Sometimes when people talk about the influence of macroeconomic ideas on policy they seem to have a very simple framework in mind. Policymakers need to understand how the economy works, so they go to academics to find out what the current received wisdom is. In this framework, when things go wrong, in the extreme if there is a macroeconomic crisis, we need to ask why the received wisdom was wrong. In short, to understand macroeconomic crises you need to understand the bad or inadequate theory that generated it.

The archetypal example of this would be the Great Depression of the 1930s. Policymakers had a classical view of macro, which had no room for recessions caused by demand deficiency. Friedman has attempted to propagate a similar story for the failure to control inflation in the 1970s, but it is far less convincing, as the work of James Forder shows.[14]

A simple story about the financial crisis is that policymakers were too dependent on macro models that ignored finance, models which therefore implicitly assumed a financial crisis could not happen. As a result, macroeconomists failed to predict the crisis. This story can be often found in heterodox accounts, but some eminent policymakers have said similar things. The bit about macro models neglecting finance is true, but as an account of why the financial crisis happened it is also probably wrong, as I argue in Post 8.4.

Where the simple idea that crises reflect bad theory comes completely unstuck is for the Eurozone crisis of 2010. Here the crisis owed a good deal to policymakers ignoring the received wisdom. This happened on two occasions. The first time was in the fiscal architecture of the Eurozone, where the problem of competitiveness imbalances caused by asymmetric shocks was wished away, and therefore the potential for national countercyclical fiscal policy to moderate these imbalances was ignored. I would never claim that had macroeconomic received wisdom been incorporated into Eurozone fiscal rules from the start the 2010 crisis would not have happened, but it certainly would have been more manageable.

The second time that the macroeconomic received wisdom was ignored by policymakers was in the reaction to the 2010 crisis: the subsequent austerity which was the major factor behind the second Eurozone recession. So in both cases policymakers did not act on the prevailing macro theories, but ignored them, and in doing so helped create a crisis.

One way of explaining how this could happen is that policymakers were well aware of the macroeconomic received wisdom, but chose to ignore it. In some cases that may be what happened. However, another possibility is that what I call the knowledge transmission mechanism between academics and policymakers broke down. To explore that possibility you need to think seriously about what could be called 'policy intermediaries' (see Figure 8.1).

Figure 8.1: Policy intermediaries

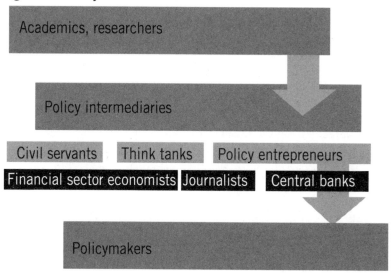

I want to cast the net of potential policy intermediaries pretty wide. Obvious candidates are the civil service and policy think tanks, or the policy entrepreneurs that Paul Krugman has talked about. However, to get a full picture of what went on in 2010, I think you need to also think about economists in the financial sector, the media and especially central banks. Of course central banks are policymakers when it comes to monetary policy, but on fiscal policy issues they can advise governments.

It is easy to understand how partisan policy entrepreneurs or think tanks can distort the transmission process. They will choose the policies that favour those interests, and will neglect to inform politicians that these ideas do not represent any kind of consensus. Indeed politicians may not even ask. A classic example is the Laffer curve. Hardly any economists believe that tax cuts increase tax revenues, yet the Republican Party looked to the few who did, and it became a party line.

In the Great Recession, the obvious sources of received wisdom were central banks. Their job, after all, was to stabilise the economy. As they all tended to use Keynesian models to forecast and evaluate policy, they should have been shouting loudest (privately and publicly) that austerity would reduce output, and with interest rates stuck at the zero lower bound, central banks could do little to offset that.

Of course this does not happen. The extent to which it does not happen varies among the major banks. In the US Bernanke did occasionally (and somewhat discreetly) say things along these lines. In the UK Mervyn King is believed to have actively pushed for greater austerity, and the Bank of England has never to my knowledge suggested that austerity might compromise its control of inflation. The ECB, of course, always argues for austerity. It is one of the great paradoxes of our time how the ECB can continue to encourage governments to take fiscal or other actions that their own models tell them will reduce output and inflation at a time when the ECB is failing so miserably to control both.

So what is going on here? I think there are two classes of explanation, related to the distinction between the roles of interests and ideas in political economy. The first class talks about why the interests of the elite might favour austerity, and how these interests could be easily mediated through senior central bankers. It could also explore the interests of finance, and their close connections to central banks.

The second class might focus on ideas involving perceived threats to central bank independence. In the US, this might be nothing more than a desired quid pro quo whereby central bankers avoid mentioning fiscal policy so that politicians steer clear of comments on monetary policy. More seriously, among other central bankers it may represent a primal (and in the current context quite unjustified) fear of fiscal dominance: being forced to monetise debt and as a result losing both independence and control of inflation. In this context I often quote Mervyn King, who said, 'Central banks are often accused of being obsessed with inflation. This is untrue. If they are obsessed with anything, it is with fiscal policy'.[15] Of course no central bank governor seriously thought they were about to lose control of inflation, but there is always the fear that at some future date they might do if government debt is too high.

The story I like to use about the Great Recession is that it exposed an Achilles' heel with the what I call the consensus assignment that helped give us the decade or two of stability before the crisis. Yes, it was best to leave monetary policy to independent central banks, but the Achilles' heel is that this would not work if interest rates hit their lower bound. Fiscal policy, in that situation, had to come in as a backup for monetary policy. But if the analysis above is right, the creation of independent central banks may have helped make that backup process much more difficult to achieve. By concentrating macroeconomic received wisdom in institutions that were predisposed to worry far too much about budget deficits, a huge spanner was thrown into the (socially efficient) working of the knowledge transmission mechanism.

8.10
ECONOMISTS AS MEDICS
Thursday, 6 April 2017

I got some stick on Twitter the other day for my longstanding view that economics is in many respects like medicine. It is of course not exactly like medicine: as the title to Daniel Hausman's great book on economic methodology[16] says, economics is an inexact and separate science. But think about what most doctors spend their time doing. They are in the business of problem solving in a highly uncertain environment in which they only have a limited number of clues to go on. They have solutions to a subset of problems that work with varying degrees of reliability.

If you read Dani Rodrik's book *Economics Rules*,[17] you will see that economists have a large number of distinct models, and the problem that many economists spend their time solving is which model is most applicable to the problem they have been asked to solve. Where doctors have biology as the underlying science behind what they do, they also rely on historical correlations to see if the science is appropriate. Think about solving the problem of why there had been an increase in lung cancer in the middle of the last century.

The science for economists is microeconomic theory, now enriched by behavioural economics. Most of the models economists use are derived from this theory. But as Rodrik emphasises, the trick is to know which model is applicable to the problem you have been asked to solve. To help solve that problem, economists, like doctors, want data. Many have observed how journal articles are now more likely to be about investigating data than establishing theoretical results. Economists have recently started adopting the terminology of medicine in economic studies, talking about treatment effects for example. We both do controlled trials (for economists, mainly in development economics).

Sometimes the paths of the two disciplines cross (as they do all the time, of course, in health economics). One of the big empirical discoveries of recent years has been by Case and Deaton, looking at mortality rates of the US white population. Figure 8.2 shows a key chart from their 2015 study.[18]

Mortality has been falling steadily almost everywhere, except since just before 2000 among US whites. Focusing just on the US, the problem seems to be mainly for non-college-educated whites.

Case and Deaton have a new study which tries to understand why this is happening.[19] They describe it as evidence of 'deaths of despair'. In each age cohort among this group, deaths from suicide, drug overdose or alcohol have been steadily rising. The interpretation that the authors give for the despair is the decline in economic circumstances and status of the white working class in the US.

Figure 8.2: All-cause mortality, ages 45–54 comparison

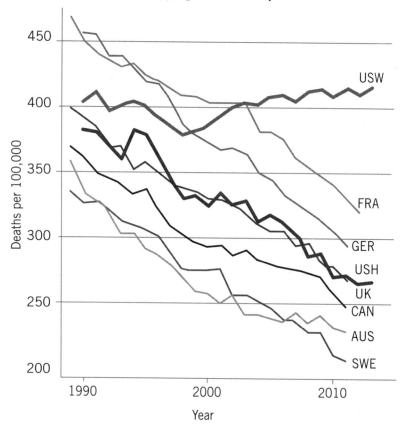

Notes: All-cause mortality, ages 45–54 for US White non-Hispanics (USW), US Hispanics (USH), and six comparison countries: France (FRA), Germany (GER), the United Kingdom (UK), Canada (CAN), Australia (AUS), and Sweden (SWE).

Source: Anne Case and Angus Deaton (2015) 'Rising morbidity and mortality in midlife among white non-Hispanic Americans in the 21st century', *Proceedings of the National Academy of Science*, 112, pp 15078–15083.

One of the factors that they describe as an 'accelerant' in this development has been the overprescription of opioid drugs that provide short-term pain relief, but which have negative consequences in the longer term. US policy over the last 20 years has led to what some describe as the worst drug epidemic in US history. Enough opioids are prescribed in the United States each year to keep every man, woman and child on them around the clock for one month. Could medicine, which prides itself on empiricism, have taken such a wrong turn?

Of course individual doctors make mistakes all the time, but the profession as a whole can make major mistakes. It is of course subject to pressures from individuals and large organisations (drug companies). In this, again, it is like economics.

Consider Figure 8.3, taken from Alan M. Taylor, 'The great leveraging'. The solid line shows the percentage of high income countries experiencing a financial crisis each year. Crises were endemic until after World War II, when it appeared for two decades or more that they were a thing of the past. In the 1980s they returned, but without any major impact on high income countries. Then there was Japan's lost decade, and plenty of papers were written about how that was a particularly Japanese problem. The 2000s seemed quiet, and some called it the Great Moderation, until the global financial crisis arrived.

Looking at Figure 8.3, it is hard to believe that economics, which prides itself on its empiricism, could have made the mistake of believing that now things were different. But economics, like medicine, can make big as well as small mistakes. The point I want to make here is the different nature of the response to these mistakes from outside these disciplines. No one says that medicine has failed us, and we need to find fresh voices. No one will say that 'mainstream medicine' is in crisis, and we need to look at alternatives.

They do not say that because it would be stupid to do so. With the opioid epidemic something has gone very wrong and it needs to be corrected, and the same is true for economics and the financial crisis.

Figure 8.3: The frequency of banking crises

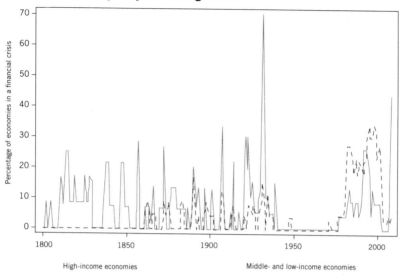

High-income economies   Middle- and low-income economies

Source: Alan M. Taylor, 'The great leveraging', National Bureau of Economic Research, Working Paper, No 18290.

So why the overreaction when it comes to academic economics? One reason is that doctors are not generally asked how long people will live, and even when they do their forecasts are not published almost every day in the press. Most economists are as honest as doctors would be about that kind of unconditional forecasting (see Post 8.7), but it suits the media to appear shocked and surprised when things go wrong. Another reason is that ordinary people can see doctors doing good things all the time to themselves, their friends and families, but the work of economists is felt less directly. It also seems intuitive that medics are in some sense better than economists, although how you could measure that I do not know. Both factors may explain why medicine is internally policed to a large degree (doctors can be stopped from practising), whereas economics is not.

Another big difference involves politics. Economists bring unwelcome news to both left and right, so it suits both sides to occasionally bash the discipline that brings the message. We have seen a great deal of that from the right over Brexit. For the left more than the right there are also non-mainstream economists who have an interest in arguing that the mainstream has been corrupted by ideology. Quite why so many on the left choose to attack mainstream economics rather than use the mainstream to attack the right I do not know. All I do know is that they have been doing it for 40+ years, as I remember being told by many economists that the mainstream was fatally flawed back in Cambridge in the early 1970s, which was before Thatcher and Reagan.

But these differences should not obscure the similarities between economics and medicine. We both deal with people, and their minds and bodies can be pretty complicated whether as individuals, or as a society. In some areas we have developed quite detailed degrees of quantitative understanding that allow us to make successful interventions (more so than in other social sciences I suspect). In other areas we do things that work most of the time but sometimes fail, but there are many important areas where if we are honest we do not have any real idea of what is going on. So we make mistakes, which can sometimes be extremely costly for huge numbers of people, but we also learn from these mistakes.

FROM
NEOLIBERALISM
TO PLUTOCRACY

Introduction

When I started this blog I didn't expect to be writing about neoliberalism. In my brief account of Mrs Thatcher's macroeconomic failures and successes in Post 9.2, written shortly after her death, I did not mention the term. I first had to think about it when trying to understand its German variety (Post 9.3) when puzzling over German attitudes to Keynesian economics. I think part of my initial reluctance to mention the term was that I found popular usage confusing, and political economy was not my field.

By 2016 I felt it necessary to write about neoliberalism and its relationship to economics, in Post 9.7. A key issue is whether neoliberalism has become embedded in economic theory, or whether, as I suggest, economics is essential to critique neoliberal ideas. Posts 9.4, 9.5 and 9.6 are specific examples where economic theory is used to critique three neoliberal ideas: that high executive pay just reflects performance, that choice over pensions has to be good, and that the growing incomes of the 1% do not matter to ordinary people.

Posts 9.8 and 9.9 are some of the most recent posts I've included, and both attempt to make sense of recent events as part of the history of neoliberalism. Post 9.8 talks about both austerity and Brexit as neoliberal overreach, by which I mean extending neoliberal ideas way beyond anything that is sustainable. But if neoliberalism has become unstable, what are we heading towards? The answer given for the US and UK in Post 9.9 is a form of plutocracy, which critically can be consistent (at least initially) with democracy because of the influence of the media. I only became aware in putting together this book that some of the ideas in Post 9.9 I had anticipated far earlier in Post 9.1.

Posts in Chapter 9

9.1
INFORMATION, MONEY AND POLITICS
Wednesday, 28 March 2012

A post that helps put the mainly in mainly macro

A Conservative Party Treasurer is caught on camera trying to solicit £250,000 from businessmen by offering to, among other things, feed their suggestions into the policy process at No. 10. Having just passed NHS Reform that will greatly increase the involvement of the private sector, David Cameron suggests privatising parts of the road network. Are we seeing either end of a single process here?

To which one might respond, *plus ça change*. Others take a less sanguine view. Let us look to the US, which we often need to do to see what happens next in the UK. Here we find Paul Krugman helping to uncover the activities of the American Legislative Exchange Council (ALEC). According to Krugman, the ALEC drafts legislation which is often adopted word for word by US states, is funded by the usual right-wing billionaires and corporations, and which has a particular interest in privatisation. It or associated organisations may as a result see advantage in having laws passed that increase business for some of those privatisations, like prisons for example.

But what exactly is wrong with all this? Presumably it is legitimate for a lobbying organisation to draft legislation that furthers its interest. The organisation does not force legislators to pass it. And what is wrong with people with lots of money using it to fund such organisations? Of course corporations have interests, but it is up to politicians whether they are listened to or not.

One thing we can object to is secrecy. It is generally regarded as good practice to declare personal interests where appropriate. For similar reasons it seems appropriate that organisations and think tanks disclose the source of their funding. In the UK at least that is quite hard to persuade some think tanks to do. I cannot see any justification for keeping this information secret. The default position is that we should be automatically suspicious of any organisation that allows its benefactors anonymity, and discount its output accordingly.

Why does disclosure matter? The media tends to have two ways of framing issues: either there is general consensus, or there are two sides to every question. With that two category model, it is quite important which category the media decides to put a particular issue into. Moneyed interests can manufacture controversy through think tanks, as has happened with aspects of the climate change debate. It is therefore important that everyone, including the media, knows where organisations get their finance. More generally, the media needs to be a little braver in going beyond the spin and 'following the money', as Aeron Davis argues.[1]

There are also limits on what money should be allowed to do in the political process. If some organisation or individual offered to directly buy your vote, this would be illegal in most places. Where it becomes less clear is when we move to political advertising. Now, of course if we try and pretend that advertising is just about providing information, and that there are adequate safeguards to ensure that advertised information is always 'true', then we might believe the more information people have the better. However, that would be a foolish thing to believe.

In a previous post I wrote 'money buys votes'. Immediately on writing that my academic self thought, hold on, should I not qualify that a bit, but then I thought, don't be silly. Of course advertising in elections does not guarantee that votes will follow, just as advertising a commodity can be more or less successful. But the correlation is surely positive. If advertising is about persuasion, or more pejoratively manipulating minds, then should we allow one political party a greater opportunity to do this than another? If the answer is even a qualified no, then I think we are entitled to put limits on how much money political parties or their supporters can spend. (In the UK this is done at election time, but the logic implies limits should operate at all times.) It also suggests that there should be limits on how much individuals are allowed to contribute to political parties.

9.2
ON THE ECONOMIC ACHIEVEMENTS AND FAILURES OF MARGARET THATCHER
Wednesday, 10 April 2013

I was not going to write anything on Mrs T, but then I just happened to read yesterday a journal article that says something important about her legacy today. I also decided to write something to challenge some of the myths and taboos created by the political right and left. The right in the UK tends to mythologise Margaret Thatcher, in a similar way I think the right in the US does with Ronald Reagan. So it's worth pointing out two major macroeconomic errors that were made while she was Prime Minister. The left is less inclined to hero worship its own Prime Ministers (generally it does the opposite), but it has its own taboos when it comes to macroeconomic history.

What was the journal article? It is a paper that looks at the causal impact of fathers' job loss on their children's educational attainment and later economic outcomes. The place and time is the UK recession of the early 1980s. The study concludes: 'Children with fathers who were identified as being displaced did significantly worse in terms of their GCSE attainment than those with non-displaced fathers.'[2] Not a very surprising result, but further evidence of the long-term damage done by high and prolonged unemployment (what macroeconomists call hysteresis effects).

The UK recession at the beginning of the 1980s was the worst since World War II. UK unemployment increased dramatically, from below 6% to nearly 12%, and stayed high until the end of the decade. Figure 9.1 boxes the Thatcher years. (Unemployment would have been higher still if the government had not encouraged the unemployed to register as disabled.)

Figure 9.1: UK unemployment

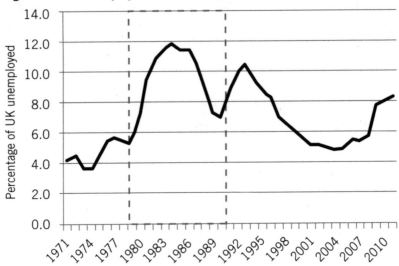

Source: ONS

Did the government led by Margaret Thatcher intend for this to happen? Almost certainly not. Their plan involved replacing traditional macroeconomic policy by monetarism, which meant gradually declining targets for the growth of a particular monetary aggregate. They expected this would lead to a steady decline in inflation, with a minor and temporary dislocation in terms of output.

Many thought at the time that was a foolish thing to believe, but in macroeconomic terms Mrs Thatcher's administration were revolutionaries who despised conventional wisdom. I remember well (I was working as a Treasury economist) that when presented with Treasury forecasts telling them with unusual accuracy what would happen, they rubbished the Treasury advice. As unemployment rose rapidly, and many in her party urged her to change course, she gave her famous 'this lady's not for turning' speech that is so eulogised by some Conservatives today.

The attempt to hit their monetary targets failed dismally: 81/80 target money growth 7–11%, actual 19.1%; 82/81 target growth 6–10%, actual 13.7%. After that monetary targets were effectively abandoned. One of the biggest experiments in UK macroeconomic policy turned out to be a disastrous failure. As GDP fell by over 2% in 1980, and remained flat in 1981, and manufacturing output fell by 15% in two years, it is not surprising that inflation fell rapidly, although too many on the left believed it would not.

Yet this period is regarded by many as Mrs Thatcher triumphing over doubters, including most academic economists. This myth may be partly responsible for the current government's obstinacy about austerity. So how can it be regarded as a triumph? Output did recover: well, of course it did, but as Figure 9.1 shows, unemployment stayed persistently high, with the long-run costs that I noted above. Inflation came down rapidly, but far more rapidly than was intended.

Was this unintended cold turkey cure in any sense optimal? I think that is highly unlikely for many reasons. One is that the traded sector bore the main cost of the recession. The period coincided with North Sea oil coming on stream, which in itself would have led to an appreciation in sterling and a movement of resources away from the traded sector. In these circumstances, embarking on a policy that produced a further appreciation (in what economists would call Dornbusch overshooting) led to the very uneven recession. Now the Dornbusch analysis was fairly new, so perhaps the government can be forgiven for not anticipating that this would happen, but by 1980 it was all pretty clear what was going on, and that was the point at which the lady refused to turn.

But the key point remains that this skewed, cold turkey policy to reduce inflation was never part of the plan. The plan itself was a complete failure, and if you think the outcome was optimal (which I do not) then that is down to luck rather than judgement.

The second failure involved North Sea oil. In Norway the government created a sovereign wealth fund, so that the gains from North Sea oil could be enjoyed by future generations. The UK government thought the people should make that choice, and so cut taxes. The people, for one reason or another, do not appear to have invested that money to replicate what a sovereign wealth fund would do. So Mrs Thatcher made the wrong choice, and whether it was for ideological reasons or more base electoral considerations is secondary. It was a major mistake that current and future generations will pay for.

Those are two major failures, but what about the successes? The Thatcher era saw the implementation of supply side reforms that ended and then reversed the relative decline of UK productivity. The lags here need to be long, but I think we have good reason to believe that they are. This improvement came about partly through increased goods market competition, but of course it also reflected a reduction in union power that was one of the major aims of government policy. The taboo on the left is not to admit (at least publicly) that UK trade unions had grown too powerful in the 1970s, and that any benefits this had were outweighed by inefficiency and often severe dislocation.

The battles of the 1980s, and the path Mrs Thatcher took, were not inevitable, and it is possible that the UK could have moved to something like the German model, where unions retain a strong presence. However, the path followed by the UK is at least partly the responsibility of the left as well as the right: some of the proposals later introduced by Mrs Thatcher were first tabled by the 1969 Labour government and Barbara Castle, and were defeated by the Trade Union Congress and the later Labour Prime Minister Jim Callaghan.

This post is not meant to be comprehensive: I have said nothing about the rise in poverty under Mrs Thatcher, inequality more generally and the role that taxation had in increasing that (of which the poll tax was just one example), selling off state assets or underinvesting in what was left. A second major UK macroeconomic disaster also occurred right at the end of her premiership. The UK entered into the European Exchange Rate Mechanism at an overvalued exchange rate, which led to another major recession. That story, and my own very small part in it, will have to wait for another time.

9.3
ORDOLIBERALISM, NEOLIBERALISM AND ECONOMICS
Wednesday, 22 January 2014

Everyone has heard of neoliberalism, but not many outside Germany have heard of ordoliberalism. I'm hardly an expert on it either, and in particular I know very little about the particular thinkers involved and the many varieties of each concept. However, as an economist it seems to me that ordoliberalism is much closer to economics than neoliberalism is.

The clear difference between the two ideologies involves the role of the state. Neoliberalism wants to minimise all forms of state interference in markets. Its attitude to markets is essentially laissez-faire: leave market participants alone. In contrast, ordoliberalism sees a vital role for the state, in ensuring that markets stay close to some notion of an ideal market. In particular, ordoliberals believe that without a strong government powerful private interests would undermine competition. This view is often credited with inspiring strong competition laws in Germany, and perhaps also in the European Union.

Ordoliberalism therefore seems much closer to the attitude an economist would naturally take. There is a clear sense in which perfect competition is an ideal in certain situations, but no clear reason why this ideal should obtain naturally. There are plenty of reasons why imperfect competition may persist, and only a few may be the consequence of government 'interference'. There is therefore an obvious role for government to counteract anti-competitive behaviour by 'big business'.

From this economics perspective, there is no reason to limit the role of the state to preventing anti-competitive behaviour. There are many other market imperfections that can be eliminated or reduced through government action. For example, externalities can be tackled using particular types of taxation. The very use of the term 'market imperfection' seems to match the ordoliberal perspective. Whether this broader view of market failure and a role for state intervention is taken on board in ordoliberal thought is less clear. This is rather important, for reasons that I'll come to.

Once you see the state as necessary to achieve a market ideal, you need to worry about how you get the right sort of state. Ordoliberal thought sees the same danger of vested interests subverting the 'proper' functioning of the state just as they see in big business subverting perfect competition. There seems to be limited faith in democracy ensuring this does not happen (perhaps for obvious historical reasons), and instead a focus on rules and independent institutions. This would include, for example, an independent central bank: again there are parallels with current economic ideas. You can perhaps also see this focus on rules in the Eurozone's fiscal compact.

There are, of course, many respects in which ordoliberal and neoliberal views are similar. One is an antagonism to Keynesian ideas. Yet even here I think there is a potential difference. The neoliberal rejection of Keynesian demand management, even at the zero lower bound (or within a monetary union), is straightforward: it is a form of government intervention in the market. However, it is less clear whether the rather limited Keynesian policies advocated by New Keynesians have to be incompatible with basic ordoliberal ideology. If you see the friction generated by sticky prices as something that generates externalities, then you can see a role for the state in limiting the impact of these externalities. Most of the time (or at the level of the monetary union), this intervention could be handled by monetary policy, but at the zero lower bound or within a monetary union countercyclical fiscal policy could play a role. In other words, while it is clear to me why a neoliberal would be anti-Keynesian, it is not so clear why an ordoliberal has to be.

So to summarise, I think any economist, if they are open-minded, can see the problems with neoliberalism. You might say that neoliberalism borrows from economics only in the sense that astrology borrows from astronomy. Ordoliberalism, because it admits the possibility of market imperfections and a role for the state in correcting them, seems, to adapt a phrase from Margaret Thatcher, more like an ideology that economists can do business with.

9.4
UNDERSTANDING EVER-INCREASING EXECUTIVE PAY
Wednesday, 29 January 2014

Ed Balls announces that, if Labour wins the next election, he will reintroduce a 50p top tax rate (reduced to 45p by Osborne). Assorted captains of industry say that this would be disastrous for the UK economy. In this situation we need economists to provide a narrative of why the pay of the top 1% has surged ahead in the US and UK since the 1980s, a narrative to counter the claims from the 1% themselves that it just represents the market rewarding skill and productivity. This post talks about one narrative that I think has great power, and also has important implications for that top tax rate.

This narrative matters because change has to be mediated through politics. Although restoring the 50p rate in itself is popular in the UK, in the end voters may be more swayed by business leaders saying that it (or a Labour victory more generally) will damage the economy. Labour under Blair, Brown and, to an extent, Balls went out of their way to be business friendly and woo the business sector, because they thought this was essential to electoral success. Most of the reasons why they thought this have not gone away.

There is a widespread belief that there is too much inequality in the UK and US, while at the same time the public underestimate the degree of inequality that actually exists. Yet arguably elections get won or lost on who the electorate believes is competent to 'manage' the economy. If political parties that aim to do something about growing inequality also appear not to enjoy 'the confidence of business', then they may not get elected. We need people who have some knowledge and objectivity about the economy and markets to argue that those that speak for business are actually just speaking for their own personal interests.

So what is the alternative story to the argument that executive pay reflects the market rewarding the rising productivity of chief executives? The first obvious point is that executive pay is not determined in anything that approximates an idealised market where prices are set to balance supply and demand. Instead it is set within a bargaining framework between employer (the firm) and employee (the CEO). Even if we imagine the employer in this case to be someone who genuinely reflects the interests of shareholders, the costs associated with losing your CEO, together with informational problems in assessing their true worth (which can lead to the age-old problem of judging quality by price), mean that the CEO potentially has substantial bargaining power.

Yet this situation did not suddenly arise in the 1980s, and it will be true in most countries, and not just in the US and UK. So why did executive pay start taking off in the 1980s in these two countries? Well, something else happened at the same time: tax rates on top incomes were also substantially reduced. Why does reducing the tax rate on top incomes lead to a rise in those incomes pre-tax? With lower tax rates, the CEO has a much greater incentive to put lots of effort into the bargaining process with the company. They, rather than the tax man, will receive the rewards from being successful.

This is the idea set out in a paper by Piketty, Saez and Stantcheva.[3] They call this a 'compensation bargaining' model. The paper backs up this theoretical model with evidence that there is a 'clear correlation between the drop in top marginal tax rates and the surge in top income shares'. In addition, they present microeconomic evidence that CEO pay for a firm's performance that is outside the CEO's control (that is industry-wide, and so does not reflect personal performance) is more important when tax rates are low. (Things like stock options.)

Now, one reaction to this model is that it ignores many other social/ economic factors that may also have been important. Things like changing social norms and political changes (loosely, the rise of neoliberalism), reduced union power, changes in financial regulations, growing financialisation and so on. I think this reaction is correct, but as the authors themselves say, such explanations are 'multi-dimensional and it is difficult to estimate compellingly the contribution of each specific factor'. Economists like simple models that can be tested against the data. That is what the compensation bargaining model set out by Piketty and his colleagues does. I don't think it is too much of a stretch to think about bargaining effort as a proxy for all these other factors.

There is a nice parallel between the compensation bargaining model and the union bargaining model popular outside the US in the 1970s/80s, which made many economists somewhat antagonistic to growing union power. There is a difference. There union power distorted the economy by raising the real wage, and generating involuntary unemployment. In the compensation bargaining model, increasing executive pay is just a rent-seeking redistribution, and is socially costly only because effort is wasted on bargaining. However, as it involves redistribution to the 1% from the 99%, I don't think many besides economists will worry about that too much. (Economists and others have begun to discuss some of the indirect costs of this inequality. Besides social costs there is also the distortion of representative democracy or encouraging the portrayal of poverty as self-induced.)

The compensation bargaining model has a clear policy implication. The problem with lowering the top rate of income tax is that it encourages the executive class to engage in efforts to raise their pay at the expense of everyone else. We need a high top rate of tax to discourage this, even if this rate might not actually bring in more income. Perhaps most importantly, it provides a plausible alternative

9.5
PENSIONS AND NEOLIBERAL FANTASIES
Saturday, 29 March 2014

As those in the UK will know, one of the major changes announced in the recent budget was to 'free up' defined contribution pension schemes so that recipients were no longer forced to buy an annuity with their pension, but could instead take the cash sum and spend or save it how they liked. This has been generally praised by our predominantly neoliberal press. The government's line that this was a budget for savers and pensioners has been accepted uncritically. Giving people the choice of what to do with their money: what could be wrong with that? After the budget the UK press was full of stories of new pensioners trying to cancel their annuity contracts.

So if I suggest that those who are due to receive a defined contribution pension in the next few years and who want to invest their money prudently are likely to be worse off as a result of this budget, that might come as a bit of a surprise. The reason is because of three things that economists (who are not automatically neoliberal) worry about: adverse selection; moral hazard; and myopia. I will translate these in turn, in ascending order of importance. But before I do, a very simple point. Annuities are a good idea, because they insure against uncertain lifetimes. So unless you know that your date of death will be earlier than for your age group, you should invest a large part of your pension in some form of annuity.

Moral hazard. Pensioners can now take the risk that they will not live for long and blow their pension on expensive holidays, knowing that if they are wrong and live longer they can always fall back on the welfare state.

Myopia. There is abundant evidence from the experimental and other empirical literature that we are poor at providing for the future and also poor at responding rationally to risk. We also know that people underestimate the life expectancy of their age group.

Adverse selection. If everyone has to take out an annuity, annuity providers can make a reasonable guess at how long people on average will live. If instead people can choose then annuity providers face an additional uncertainty: are those not choosing to take out an annuity doing so because they believe they will not live as long as the average for their age group? If that is true, which it almost certainly is, then annuity rates will fall, because those still taking out annuities will live on average for longer. A greater concern is that this additional uncertainty will reduce annuity rates still further, as annuity providers require an additional margin to compensate them for the extra risk they face. In theory, the market could collapse completely.

I do not mean to imply that any of these, or even all three combined, are sufficient to justify compulsory annuitisation. What they do show is that the naive 'choice must be good' line may be neoliberal, but it is not economics. What does seem pretty clear is that the budget will lead to a reduction in annuity rates, so a perfectly reasonable headline after the budget would have been 'Chancellor cuts incomes for new prudent pensioners'. If you do not remember that headline in your newspaper, perhaps you should change newspaper.

There is another neoliberal fantasy, and that is that private provision must be better than public provision. Yet pensions illustrate one area where this can be the opposite of the truth. Defined contribution pension schemes suffer from intergenerational risk. Suppose that those arguing real interest rates will stay low for a long time are right (secular stagnation). That means that the generation receiving their pension during this period will end up with a lower pension income than those who go before or after them. Indeed, it is just this effect which has made annuities unpopular and which the government is playing to. People would like to insure against this kind of risk, but the problem in this case is that we need an insurer who in effect lives forever, so they can smooth out these good and bad times.

There is just one economic actor that could do this, and that is the state. The state could do this in many ways, ranging from some form of unfunded government pension scheme to providing insurance to annuity providers.

This post was inspired by a post by Tony Yates, and also drew heavily on this post-budget briefing by IFS economist Carl Emmerson.[4]

9.6
INEQUALITY AND THE COMMON POOL PROBLEM
Wednesday, 13 August 2014

The classic common pool problem in economics is about how the impact of just one fisherman extracting more fish on the amount of fish in the lake is small, but if there are lots of fishermen doing the same we have a problem. Those thinking about fiscal policy use it to describe the temptation a politician has to give tax breaks to specific groups. Those groups are very grateful, but these tax breaks are paid for (either immediately or eventually) by everyone else paying more tax. However, the impact of any specific tax break on the tax of other people is generally so small that it is ignored by these people. As a result, a politician can win votes by giving lots of individual tax breaks, as long as each one is considered in isolation.

The same logic can be applied to high executive pay, but it is often ignored. Here is part of one comment on an earlier post that was left at the FT: 'the rise in incomes at the very top ... may be a worry in the dining halls of Oxford but in many decades not one person has mentioned such a worry to me. What worries people here, especially those at the bottom of the income distribution, is the decline in real wages.' But if higher executive pay has not led to higher aggregate GDP that pay has to come from somewhere.

Perhaps there is a tendency to think about this in a common pool-type way. The impact of high wages for any particular CEO on my own wage is negligible. But that is not true for the pay of the top 1% as a whole. Pessoa and Van Reenen look at the gap between median real wages and productivity growth over the last 40 years in the US and UK.[5] They have a simple chart for the UK (Figure 9.2). (The legend goes in the opposite direction to the blocks.) I'll explain this first and then how the US differs.

In the UK over this period median real wages grew by 42% less than productivity. None of that was due to a fall in labour's share compared to profits, called net decoupling in Figure 9.2. Most of it was due to higher non-wage benefits (mainly pension contributions) and rising inequality. There are two obvious differences in explaining

Figure 9.2: Decoupling decomposition in the UK, 1972–2010

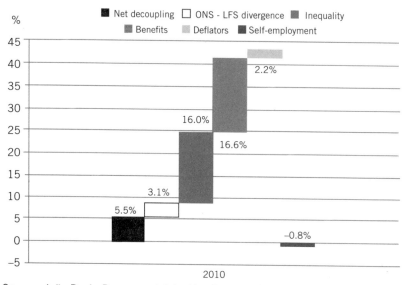

Source: João Paulo Pessoa and John Van Reenen (2013) 'Decoupling of wage growth and productivity growth? Myth and reality', CEP Discussion Paper No 1246, published by the Centre for Economic Performance, p. 5.

the larger (63%) gap between median real wages and productivity in the US: the non-wage benefits were mainly health insurance, and in the US there is some decline in the labour share. However, in both countries rising inequality explains a large part of the failure of median real wages to track productivity gains.

Unfortunately the paper does not tell us how much of this increase in inequality is down to the increasing share of the 1%, but a good proportion is likely to be. In a separate paper, Bell and Van Reenen find that, in the 2000s in the UK, increases in inequality were primarily driven by pay increases (including bonus payments) for the top few per cent. 'By the end of the decade to 2008, the top tenth of earners received £20bn more purely due to the increase in their share ... and £12bn of this went to workers in the financial sector (almost all of which was bonus payments).'[6] If that £20bn had been equally redistributed to every UK household, they would have each received a cheque for around £750.

More generally, we can do some simple maths. In the US the share of the 1% has increased from about 8% at the end of the 1970s to nearly 20% today. If that has had no impact on aggregate GDP but is just a pure redistribution, this means that the average incomes of the 99% are 15% lower as a result. The equivalent 1% numbers for the UK are 6% and 13%, implying a 7.5% decline in the average income of the remaining 99%.

So there is a clear connection between the rise in incomes at the very top and lower real wages for everyone else. Arguments that try and suggest that any particular CEO's pay increase does no one any harm may be appealing to a common pool type of logic, and are just as fallacious as arguments that some tax break does not leave anyone else worse off. It is an indication of the scale of the rise in incomes of the 1% over the last few decades that this has had a significant effect on the incomes of the remaining 99%.

9.7
NEOLIBERALISM

The term 'neoliberalism' has become so ubiquitous that some might think it has lost all meaning, beyond being a useful catch-all for everything some people on the left dislike about current social and economic trends, or, more specifically, for those on the left to be rude about those on the centre-left. That is in my view far too dismissive, but the reasons for both the use of the term and confusion over its meaning have real historic and cultural roots.

I know what I mean when I (occasionally) use the term neoliberal. Neoliberalism is a political movement or ideology that hates 'big' government, dislikes any form of market interference by the state, favours business interests and opposes organised labour. The obvious response to this is, why 'neo'? In the European tradition we could perhaps define that collection as being the beliefs of a (market) liberal (although that would be misleading for reasons I give below). The main problem here is that in US discourse in particular the word 'liberal' has a very different meaning. As Corey Robin writes, neoliberals

> would recoil in horror at the policies and programs of mid-century liberals like Walter Reuther or John Kenneth Galbraith or even Arthur Schlesinger, who claimed that 'class conflict is essential if freedom is to be preserved, because it is the only barrier against class domination'.[7]

So in this US line of thought, neoliberalism is an adaptation of a position on the left towards the ideas of the right.

Contrary to some perceptions, the term neoliberal was not a US invention, but was first used by Rüstow. It was designed to be a 'third way' between socialism and a German version of capitalism. It was adopted by a group that later became the Mont Pèlerin Society, which included Mises and Hayek and Milton Friedman, but it would be a great error to view that group as some kind of united intellectual conspiracy. As Hartwich and Sally remark, it is 'named after the location as the participants could not agree on anything else'.[8] It was sufficiently diverse that the idea of what we now call a social market economy can also trace some of its roots to this group.

One of the disagreements in the group was over the problem of what we might call 'corporatism': the domination of markets by a small number of large firms or cartels that is a long way from the ideal of a perfectly competitive market. Rüstow saw that as a problem that was inherent to capitalism and required a strong state to prevent it (an idea that is central to what we now call ordoliberalism), whereas Mises thought corporatism is the result of state intervention. (Economists would just say that both are potentially true and it all depends, which is one reason why many economists find it hard to talk about ideologies that involve their own discipline.)

From this group we have the term neoliberal being adopted as a modification of European liberalism and (for some at least) it involved a move from the right to the left. I think the clearest way of thinking about the Mont Pèlerin group is that it had in common a dislike of communism, but out of that different ideologies emerged, including ordoliberalism and neoliberalism as we understand these terms today. I am tempted to argue that what we now call the neoliberal element of the Mont Pèlerin discussions placed such an emphasis on their dislike of the state that they were prepared to ignore the market imperfections that a state could correct.

I think this alone would be a good reason for the use of the term neoliberal rather than, say, market liberal. Neoliberalism, as most people use the term, seems quite relaxed about departures from the ideal of a market as seen by economists. A clear example is CEO pay. When people argue that CEO pay 'should be left to the market', they mean something very different from 'be determined by the market'. The role of any market in determining CEO pay is marginal compared to most ordinary workers: pay is set by remuneration committees who reference the pay of other CEOs. What 'left to the market' actually means here is 'no state or union interference'.

Yet this example also tells us that dismissing neoliberalism as a non-existent ideology is wrong. How often have you heard people arguing that CEO pay should be left to the market, and this assertion has gone unchallenged? This common acceptance of 'left to the market' really meaning 'no state or union interference' suggests something like an ideology at work. Other commonly used language, like taxpayers' money (by which is normally meant income tax payers) rather than public money, or wealth creators for the 1%, does the same.

Attitudes to the state, on both the right and centre of politics, are very different to those I (distantly!) remember from the 1960s. The ability of the state to achieve economic goals is today routinely denigrated. Part of the reason for the success of Mazzucato's *The Entrepreneurial State*[9] (apart from it being a very good book) is that it points out how creative and wealth creating the state can be. What would have seemed obvious in the days when we put a man on the moon now needs to be argued case by case.

This is why I do not think it is a problem that few today would describe themselves as neoliberal. Indeed that may be part of the greater problem as perceived on the left: neoliberal ideas have become so commonplace, not just on the right but also the centre of politics, that no self-identification by label is required. But there may be another reason why few call themselves neoliberal, and that is because if we try and regard it as a coherent and consistent set of beliefs it can very quickly be shown to be inadequate and confused. Commonly held beliefs do not have to be coherent and consistent.

This is where many accounts on the left go wrong. Rather than seeing 'left to the market' as a deliberately misleading shorthand for no state or union interference, they think neoliberalism involves a devotion to free markets, or, worse still, they equate neoliberalism with unbridled competition. While that might have been true for some of those at Mont Pèlerin, it is no longer true of neoliberalism today.

The reason is obvious enough. Neoliberalism has been adopted and promoted by moneyed interests on the right, and that money often resulted from what we might call today crony capitalism. So, for example, there is a big difference between promoting competition within the NHS (which some research suggests works if done in the right context, such as fixed prices), and the privatisation of health contracts. Privatisation is neither necessary nor sufficient for competition. To describe the promotion of competition within the NHS as neoliberalism is confusing and alienating.

More generally, it is a huge error to think that because neoliberalism invokes a highly selective and distorted view of basic economics, the left must therefore oppose mainstream economics. It is a huge error because using mainstream economics is an excellent way of challenging neoliberal ideas. Take the example of banking. At first sight the financial crisis was simply a failure to regulate a free market. But it was a market that included what is to all intents and purposes a huge state subsidy, which is that if the market goes wrong the state (either directly or through its central bank) will come to the rescue. Here state interference in the market encourages lack of competition: only those too big to fail could be sure of support.

For this and other reasons (natural monopolies and other forms of rent seeking), the financial sector embodies many of the things that those who first used the term neoliberalism were opposed to. It is important that those who use the term neoliberalism today recognise this contradiction. It does not mean that using the term neoliberalism to describe the dominant ideology is wrong, but it is a mistake to assume the ideology has not been moulded/adapted/distorted by those in whose interest it works. These changes have made it intellectually weak at the same time as making it politically strong.

POSTSCRIPT

I had been reluctant to write much about neoliberalism before this, partly because it is an emotive term for many, and also because many people have written at great length on the subject. These fears proved justified, as a few weeks later one of those people, Philip Mirowski, wrote in rather negative terms about what I had written in this post.[10] He had two problems. One is that my definition of neoliberalism was 'untutored'. I have no problem with that, as I was not trying to give a precise definition. One of the reasons I did not follows from my point about how the ideology had been adapted by moneyed interests.

His second criticism is that he did not like my point that economics can and should be used as a means of critiquing the whole concept of neoliberalism. On this I think he is quite wrong, and if anyone is interested I wrote what I hope was a robust response on 28 May 2016. I was later to review a book by Colin Crouch on neoliberalism which did in part critique neoliberal ideas using ideas from economics.[11]

9.8
WAS NEOLIBERAL OVERREACH INEVITABLE?
Monday, 3 July 2017

In June 2017 a member of the hard left of the Labour Party, reviled by the right and centre for his association with left-wing leaders and movements around the world and for his anti-nuclear views, in a few short weeks went from being one of the most unpopular party leaders ever to achieving the highest vote share for his party since Tony Blair was leader. While this unexpected turn of events was in part the result of mistakes by, and inadequacies of, the Conservative Prime Minister, there is no doubt that many Labour voters were attracted by a programme that unashamedly increased the size of the state.

Contrast this with the United States. A Republican congress seems intent on passing into law a bill that combines taking away health insurance from a large number of citizens with tax cuts for the very rich. Let me quote a series of tweets from Paul Krugman:

The thing I keep returning to on the Senate bill is the contrast between the intense hardship it imposes and the triviality of the gains. Losing health insurance – especially if you're older, low-income, and unhealthy, which are precisely the people hit – is a nightmare. And more than 20 million would face that nightmare. Meanwhile, the top 1% gets a tax cut. That cut is a lot of money, but because the 1% are already rich, it raises their after-tax income only 2 percent – hardly life-changing. So vast suffering imposed to hand the rich a favor they'll barely even notice. How do we make sense of this, politically or morally?[12]

Or to put it another way, an estimated 200,000 more deaths over the next 10 years for a marginal increase in the after-tax income of the 1%. This is no anachronism created by a Trump presidency, but an inevitable consequence of Republican control of Congress and the White House.

Although these two events appear to be in complete contrast, I think they are part of (in the US) and a consequence of (in the UK) a common process, which I will call neoliberal overreach. Why neoliberal? Why overreach? Neoliberal is the easy part. Although some people get hung up on the word, I use it simply to refer to the set of ideas associated with Ronald Reagan and Margaret Thatcher in the 1980s. That includes the goal of reducing the role of the state in many areas of society, including its role in either replacing or regulating markets and taxing individuals, particularly reducing taxes for the well-off.

Overreach is more contentious. I use the term because I think, in the UK at least, the period from the 1990s until the global financial crisis could be described as a stable neoliberal hegemony. By this I mean that governments largely accepted the transformations that took place in the 1980s, even when Labour or Democrats were in power. Of course changes did occur. In the UK Labour were prepared to involve the state in alleviating poverty in ways that Thatcher never contemplated, but Labour's concern did not extend to the other end of the income distribution, and the income share of the 1% continued to rise. They were prepared to see an expansion in the size of the state to meet a natural increase in the demand for health, but they also experimented with bringing in market elements into state provision. However, none of these changes compared in scale to what went before or came afterwards. (As Tom Clark argues, Labour did not change the [essentially neoliberal] political discourse.)[13]

This period was also characterised in the UK and US by macroeconomic stability: inflation had been contained, perhaps through the delegation of monetary policy to central banks, and growth remained strong such that the high levels of unemployment seen in the 1980s gradually disappeared. This was the 'great moderation'.

It was undone by a major flaw in the neoliberal project: the self-destructive nature of an unregulated financial sector. The reaction to that, if the left had remained in power, might have been greater controls on finance and perhaps some attempt to reduce inequality (as the two are related). But the left lost power, and we got what I call neoliberal overreach.

Neoliberal deceit in the UK

By 2008 the conversion of the right in the UK to neoliberal ideas was largely complete. This meant that they were determined to continue where Thatcher had left off. But they faced what appeared to be an insurmountable problem: voters wanted the NHS (and other public services) and they wanted more of it partly because they were getting older and wealthier. The recession gave the right the opportunity to continue the neoliberal project by deceit, using two mechanisms.

The first was austerity, which I have talked about many times, but alas what I and other macroeconomists say has so far reached only a small minority (a minority which, importantly, includes the Labour Party). What I call deficit deceit was the pretence that we needed above all else to cut spending (which would reduce the size of the state) because otherwise the markets would not buy the government's debt. There was never any real evidence to back this story up, and plenty to suggest it was nonsense. The fevered imagination of some market participants who turned out to be wrong does not count as evidence. But the politics to make deficit deceit possible was all there: a recent financial crisis, consumers cutting back on debt themselves, a Treasury worried as Treasuries do, a central bank head who acted as central bank heads often do, and a Eurozone crisis that mediamacro made no attempt to understand.

The second deceit was immigration. Elements in society are apt to blame immigrants at a time of rising unemployment and falling real wages, and terrorism gave this an extra twist. The right and their supporters in the press had decided before the crisis that they could exploit fears over immigration to their advantage, and after the recession this became a more powerful weapon. They talked about how immigration was responsible for reduced access to public services and falling real wages, and they promised to bring levels of immigration down. It was deceit because those in charge knew full well that immigration benefited the economy in various ways and as a result they had no intention of really controlling it. But, as with austerity, the deceit worked: so much so that an already weak opposition appeared not to know how to respond.

Some may disapprove of the language I use here. Should a normally sober Oxford macroeconomist talk about political parties deliberately deceiving the electorate? It is not a view I have adopted lightly, but when a Chancellor repeatedly argues that public spending must be cut to meet deficit targets at the same time as reducing inheritance or corporation tax, or a Prime Minister continually repeats the lie that immigration reduces access to public services, what other conclusion can you come to? They could get away with this deceit because academic economists (the majority of whom know that austerity would reduce output, and that immigration improves the public finances) are largely ignored by the media.

Austerity and the deceit required to achieve it was neoliberal overreach in the UK. Austerity quickly became a disaster because it was done at just the wrong time, when monetary policy was unable to offset its effects. That hurt the economy a lot. Whether GDP was reduced by a few percentage points temporarily or permanently we may never know for sure. But for the political reasons I have already outlined, combined with feeble opposition, the Conservatives got away with it sufficiently to win a general election in 2015.

Populism and anti-neoliberalism

The deceit over immigration was also key to a second disaster: the vote to leave the EU. Although the case to remain in the EU was led by the Prime Minister and Chancellor, neither could combat anti-immigration rhetoric with a positive case because of their earlier deception. For this reason alone you could also label Brexit as a consequence of neoliberal overreach. More importantly, factions on the right that actively campaigned for Brexit did so in part because they believed they could only achieve their regulation-free neoliberal nirvana by doing so.

As Jan-Werner Müller writes

> The image of an irresistible populist 'wave' was always misleading. Farage did not bring about Brexit all by himself. He needed the help of established Conservatives such as Boris Johnson and Michael Gove (both now serve in Prime Minister Theresa May's post-election cabinet). Likewise Trump was not elected as the candidate of a grassroots protest movement of the white working class; he represented a very established party and received the blessing of Republican heavyweights such as Rudy Giuliani and Newt Gingrich.[14]

It would be wrong to say that Brexit or Trump represent an evolution of neoliberalism. Both promote strong restrictions to trade, and so it would be more accurate to view the leadership and money behind Brexit (not the voters) as a split within neoliberalism. What is clearer to me is that populism is a consequence of neoliberalism as reflected in the policies of the political right. In the UK immigration was used as a scapegoat for the impact of austerity, which fuelled the Brexit vote. In the US one of the first acts of Reagan was to repeal the Fairness Doctrine, which led eventually to the precursor and cheerleaders for Trump: talk radio and Fox News. In addition, neoliberalism demonises any kind of regional or industrial strategy designed to alleviate the impact of globalisation.

Why was it Corbyn who led the revolt against austerity in 2017 rather than Miliband in 2015? One obvious explanation is that the more 'moderate' left in both the UK, much of Europe and the Democratic establishment in the US had become compromised by neoliberal hegemony. Instead it required those who had stayed faithful to socialist ideas, together with the young who had not witnessed the defeats of the 1980s, to mount an effective opposition to austerity and perhaps neoliberalism more generally. William Davis expresses a similar view.[15]

I am less familiar with the details of US politics, which are clearly different in some ways from the UK. The way the Republican Party has co-opted both race and culture to its cause is different and clearly crucial. But there are plenty of similarities as well. Both countries have had austerity combined with tax cuts for the rich. Both countries have a right-wing media which politicians can no longer control, leading to Brexit and Trump respectively. Bernie Sanders, like Corbyn, came from nowhere preaching socialism, but unlike in the UK the established Democratic Party halted his rise to power.

Was overreach inevitable?

I'm not going to speculate whether and by how much this neoliberal overreach will prove fatal: whether Corbyn's 'glorious defeat' marks the 'death throes of neoliberalism' or something more modest. Instead I want to ask whether overreach was inevitable, and if so, why? Many in the centre ground of politics would argue that it would have been perfectly feasible, after the financial crisis, to change neoliberalism in some areas but maintain it in others. It is conceivable that this is where we will end up. But when you add up what 'some areas' would amount to, it becomes clear that it would be hard to label the subsequent regime neoliberal.

I think it is quite possible to imagine reforming finance in a way that allows neoliberalism to function elsewhere. I will come to whether it is politically possible without additional reforms. If we think about populism, one key economic force behind its rise has been globalisation. If we want to retain the benefits of globalisation, then counteracting its negative impact on some groups or communities becomes essential. Whether that involves the state directly, or indirectly through an industrial strategy, neither of those solutions is neoliberal.

Then consider inequality. I would argue that inequality, and more specifically the extreme wealth of a small number of individuals, has played an important role in both neoliberal overreach (in the US, the obsession within the Republican Party with tax cuts for the wealthy) and populism (the financing of the Brexit campaign, Trump himself). More generally, extreme wealth disparities fuel political corruption. Yet 'freeing' 'wealth creators' of the 'burden' of taxation is central to neoliberalism: just look at how the loaded language in this sentence has become commonplace.

Indeed, it could well be that gross inequality at the very top is an important dynamic created by neoliberalism. Piketty, Saez and Stantcheva have shown (Post 9.4) how reductions in top rates of tax, a hallmark of neoliberalism in the 1980s, may itself have encouraged rent seeking by CEOs, which makes inequality even worse. Rent extractors naturally seek political defences to preserve their wealth, and the mechanisms which that sets in place may not embody any sense of morality, leading to the grotesque spectacle of Republican lawmakers depriving huge numbers of people of health insurance to be able to cut taxes for those at the top. It may also explain why the controls on finance actually implemented have been so modest, and in the US so fragile.

The other key dynamic in neoliberal overreach has to be the ideology itself. In the UK surveys suggest that less than 10% of the population favour cutting taxes and government spending to achieve a smaller state (see Post 1.10). There is equally no appetite to privatise key state functions: indeed renationalisation of some industries is quite popular. Yet the need to reduce the size and scope of the state has become embedded in the political right. Given that, it is not hard to understand the motivation behind the twin deceits of austerity and immigration control by Conservative-led governments.

The dynamic consequences of extreme inequality and an unpopular ideology both suggest that neoliberal overreach may not be a bug but a feature.

9.9
IF WE TREAT PLUTOCRACY AS DEMOCRACY, DEMOCRACY DIES
Saturday, 2 December 2017

The snake-oil salesmen

There are many similarities between Brexit and Trump. They are both authoritarian movements, where authority lies with either a single individual or a single vote. This authority expresses the movement's identity. They are irrational movements, by which I mean that they cast aside expertise where that conflicts with the movements' wishes. As a result, you will find their base of supporters among the less well educated, and that they see universities as an enemy. Both groups are intensely nationalistic: both want to make America or England great again.

It is easy to relate each group to familiar concepts: class, race or whatever. But I think this classification misses something important. It misses what sustains these groups in their beliefs, allows them to maintain their world view which is so often contradicted by reality. Both groups get their information about the world from a section of the media that has turned news into propaganda. In the US this is Fox, and in the UK the right-wing tabloids and the *Telegraph*.

A profound mistake is to see this media as a symptom rather than a cause. As Post 7.10 demonstrates, the output of Fox News is not designed to maximise its readership, but to maximise the impact of its propaganda on its readership. I think you could say exactly the same about the *Sun* and the *Mail* in the UK. Fox and the *Sun* are owned by the same man.

Even those who manage to cast off the idea that this unregulated media just reflects the attitude of its readers generally think of this media as supportive of political parties. There is the Conservative and Labour supporting press in the UK, and similarly for the US. In my view that idea is 10 or 20 years out of date, and even then it underestimates the independence of the media organisations. (The *Sun* famously supported Blair in 1997). More and more, it is the media that calls the shots and the political parties follow.

Brexit would not have happened if it had remained the wish of a minority of Conservative MPs. It happened because of the right-wing UK press. Brexit happened because this right-wing press recognised that a large section of their readership were disaffected with conventional politics, and began grooming them with stories of EU immigrants taking jobs, lowering wages and taking benefits (and sometimes much worse). These stories were not (always) false, but like all good propaganda they elevated a half-truth into a firm belief. Of course this grooming played on age-old insecurities, but it magnified them into a political movement. Nationalism does the same. It did not just reflect readers' existing views, but rather played on their doubts and fears and hopes and turned this into votes.

This is not to discount some of the very real grievances that led to the Brexit vote, or the racism that led to the election of Trump. This analysis of today's populism is important, as long as it does not get side-tracked into debates over identity versus economics. Stressing economic causes of populism does not devalue identity issues (like race or immigration), but it is the economics that causes the swings that help put populists in power. It was crucial, for example, to the trick that the media played to convince many to vote for Brexit: that EU immigrants and payments were reducing access to public services, whereas in reality the opposite is true.

Yet while economic issues may have created a winning majority for both Brexit and Trump, the identity issues sustained by the media make support for both hard to diminish. Brexit and Trump are expressions of identity, and often of what has been lost, which are very difficult to break down when sustained by the group's media. In addition, both Trump and Brexit maintain, because their proponents want it to be maintained, the idea that it represents the normally ignored, striking back against the government machine in the capital city with all its experts.

But to focus on what some call the 'demand' for populism is in danger of missing at least half the story. Whatever legitimate grievances Brexit and Trump supporters may have had, they were used and will be betrayed. There is nothing in leaving the EU that will help the forgotten towns of England and Wales. Although he may try, Trump will not bring many manufacturing jobs back to the rust belt, and his antics with NAFTA (North American Free Trade Agreement) may make things worse. Identifying the left-behind is only half the story, because it does not tell you why they fell for the remedies of snake-oil salesmen.

As I wrote immediately after the vote in Post 6.7, Brexit was first and foremost a triumph for the UK right-wing press. That press first fostered a party, UKIP, that embodied the views the press pushed. The threat of that party and defections to it then forced the Prime Minister to offer the referendum the press wanted. It was a right-wing press that sold a huge lie about the UK economy, a lie the broadcast media bought, to ensure the Conservatives won the next election (Chapter 4). When the referendum came, it was this right-wing press that ensured enough votes were won and thereby overturned the government.

Equally Donald Trump was first and foremost the candidate of Fox News. As Bruce Bartlett has so eloquently written, Fox may have started off as a network that just supported Republicans, but its power steadily grew.[16] Being partisan at Fox became misinforming its viewers, such that Fox viewers are clearly less well informed than viewers of other news providers. UK readers may remember Fox reporting that Birmingham was a no-go area for non-Muslims.

Fox became a machine for keeping the base angry and fired up, believing that nothing could be worse than voting for a Democrat. It was Fox News that stopped Republican voters seeing that they were voting for a demagogue, concealed that he lied openly all the time, that incites hatred against other religions and ethnic groups, and makes its viewers believe that Clinton deserves to be locked up. It is not reflecting the views of its viewers, but moulding them. As economists have shown, the output of Fox does not optimise their readership, but optimises the propaganda power of its output. Despite occasional tiffs, Trump was the candidate of Fox in the primaries.

We have a right-wing media organisation that has overthrown the Republican political establishment, and a right-wing press that has overthrown a right-wing government. How some political scientists can continue to analyse this as if the media is simply passive, supportive or even invisible when it brings down governments or subverts political parties I do not know.

The plutocracy

Trump and Brexit are the creations of a kind of plutocracy. Politics in the US has had strong plutocratic elements for some time, because of the way that money can sway elections. That gave finance a powerful influence in the Democratic Party, and made the Republicans obsessive about cutting higher tax rates. In the UK plutocracy has been almost non-existent by comparison, and operated mainly through party funding and seats in the House of Lords, although we are still finding out where the money behind the Brexit campaign came from.

By focusing on what some call the demand side of populism rather than the supply side, we fail to see both Trump and Brexit as primarily expressions of plutocratic power. Trump's administration is plutocracy personified, and its substantive agenda constitutes a full-throated endorsement of the GOP economic elite's longstanding agenda. The Brexiteers want to turn the UK into their vision of Singapore, a kind of neoliberalism which stresses that markets should be free from government interference, rather than free to work for everyone, and that trade should be free from regulations, rather than regulations being harmonised so that business is free to trade.

It is also a mistake to see this plutocracy as designed to support capital. This should again be obvious from Brexit and Trump. It is in capital's interest to have borders open to goods and people rather than creating barriers and erecting walls. What a plutocracy will do is ensure that high inequality, in terms of the 1% or 0.1% and so on, is maintained or even increased. Indeed many plutocrats amassed their wealth by extracting large sums from the firms for which they worked, wealth that might otherwise have gone to investors in the form of dividends. In this sense they are parasitic to capital. And this plutocracy will also ensure that social mobility is kept low so the membership of the plutocracy is sustained: social mobility goes with equality.

It is also a mistake to see what is happening as somehow the result of some kind of invisible committee of the 1% (or 0.1% and so on). The interests of the Koch brothers are not necessarily the interests of Trump. The interests of Arron Banks are not those of Lloyd Blankfein. Instead we are finding individual media moguls forming partnerships with particular politicians to press not only their business interests, but their individual political views as well. And in this partnership it is often clear who is dependent on whom. After all, media competition is slim while there are plenty of politicians.

What has this got to do with neoliberalism, which is supposed to be the dominant culture of the political right? It is a mistake to see neoliberalism as some kind of unified ideology. It may have a common core in terms of the primacy of the market, but how that is interpreted is not uniform. Are neoliberals in favour of free trade, or against it? It appears that they can be both. Instead neoliberalism is a set of ideas based around a common belief in the market that different groups have used and interpreted to their advantage, while at the same time also being influenced by the ideology. Both interests and ideas matter. While some neoliberals see competition as the most valuable feature of capitalism, others will seek to stifle competition to preserve monopoly power. Brexiteers and their press backers are neoliberals, just as the Cameron government they brought down were neoliberals.

I think there is some truth in the argument, made by Philip Mirowski among others, that a belief in neoliberalism can easily involve an anti-enlightenment belief that people need to be persuaded to subject themselves fully to the market. Certainly those on the neoliberal right are more easily persuaded to invest time and effort in the dark arts of spin than those on the left. But it would be going too far to suggest that all neoliberals are anti-democratic: as I have said, neoliberalism is diverse and divided. What I argued in Post 9.8 was that neoliberalism as formulated in the UK and US had made it possible for the plutocracy we now see to become dominant.

By the nature of an unorganised plutocracy, what types of neoliberalism hold sway may be largely random, and depend a lot on who owns media organisations. It leads to a form of politics which is in many ways unpredictable and irrational, with an ever-present tendency to autocracy. This is what we are witnessing, right now, in the UK and US. It is not the normal politics that either of these countries are used to, although it may be more familiar to those in quasi-dictatorships. We all know about how the Republican's tax-cutting bill just happens to favour real-estate moguls who inherit their money as Trump did. This is simple corruption, enacted in a corrupt way. That the President of the United States retweeted a British far-right group that inspired an individual to murder a British MP is not normal. When Brexit-supporting MPs respond to the Irish border problem by saying, 'we are not going to put one up', this should not pass as an acceptable response: it should be laughed at as the nonsense it is.

When politics becomes the whims and mad schemes of a small minority that only listen to themselves, unmodified by the normal checks and balances of a functioning democracy, it should be treated by the non-partisan media for what it is, not normalised as just more of the same. If we treat a plutocracy as a democracy, democracy dies. We should not be fooled that this plutocracy looks like normal politics just because the plutocrats have taken over the main party of the right.

A dividing point

We are very close to a point where neoliberalism becomes something much worse. The POTUS is following a fascist strategy of demonising a religious minority. If Mueller's investigations proceed as expected, but he is sacked and/or the Republicans block any attempt at impeachment, we may have passed that critical point. If the Brexiteers succeed in breaking away from the EU's customs union and single market, the UK may have nowhere else to go but the arms of a permanently Republican US.

If there is a way of escaping this fate, and rescuing democracy in both the UK and US, it has to involve a democratic defeat of the right-wing parties that allowed this plutocracy to emerge, and indeed encouraged it and then made bargains with it when it believed it was still in control. The defeat has to be overwhelming and total. Those who brought us Brexit and backed or tolerated Trump have to be disgraced as the harbingers of disaster. Their control of the Republican and Conservative parties must end.

Only that will allow the left, and I think it has to be the left, to end a system by which elements of the plutocracy can control so much of the means of information. In the UK that means extending rules that apply to broadcasters, suitably adapted, to the press. In the US it means not just bringing back the Fairness Doctrine repealed under Reagan, but also bringing controls on election spending similar to those in the UK (and the UK controls need to be strengthened). In short, we need to take money out of politics to ensure democracy survives. Give journalists the freedom to write about or broadcast the news as they see it, rather than as their employer want it to be seen.

Why the left rather than the centre? The centre will agonise over what this means for freedom of expression or freedom of the press and therefore nothing much will happen (see Leveson), as nothing happened under Clinton or Blair. That may be a little unfair to both leaders, because the danger of plutocracy may have been less obvious back then, and the media was more restrained. But with Brexit and Trump no further evidence is needed. The left should see more clearly how in practice this freedom is in reality just a freedom to sustain a plutocracy. Only it will have the courage to radically reverse the power and wealth of the 1%. I fear the centre will not have the will to do it. In discussing his book *The Lure of Greatness* (2017, Unbound), Anthony Barnett puts this point very well: if all you want to do is stop Brexit and Trump and go back to what you regard as normal, you miss that what was normal led to Brexit and Trump.

That will have many wise and sensible people shaking their heads, but the alternative does not work. Defeating or impeaching Trump and letting the Republican Party survive in its current form achieves little, because they will go on gerrymandering and Fox News will go on poisoning minds. The energy of Democrats will be spent on trying to clear up the damage Trump has caused, and the next autocrat from Republican ranks who wins power because they will 'clear the swamp' will be smarter than Trump. In the UK, if the Conservatives survive in their current form, their ageing membership is in danger of selecting more Brexit nutters who will overwhelm the dwindling number of reasonable Conservative MPs. We will find the BBC, if it survives at all, will become more and more like the mouthpiece of a press dominated by plutocrats. (This is why arguments that say the UK press are becoming less powerful because of its falling readership fail. If this press dominate the news agenda of the broadcasters, they do not need many readers.) In either case a critical point will have passed.

I know from many conversations I have had that there is a deep fear among many of leadership from the left. Here the UK is ahead of the

US. The story in the UK used to be that the left could never win, and it was a plausible story, but recent events have cast great doubt on it. That remains the story in the US, but there are good reasons for doubting it there too. There is no reason why all of the disenchanted who fell for the lies of the snake-oil salesmen could not support radical remedies from the left: identity and the media are strong but it is economics that dictates the swings.

In the UK now the story seems much more elemental: that somehow the left threatens the existence of capitalism and democracy. In truth there is no way Corbyn could persuade the Labour Party to abandon democratic capitalism, just as there is no way Sanders or Warren could do the same in the US. All we are talking about is rolling back many of the results of neoliberalism. But it is difficult to logically convince someone the ghosts they see do not exist. In contrast to these ghosts on the left, the dynamic of plutocracy that I have described here is very real, and it requires radical change to bring an end to this dynamic.

CONCLUSIONS

I wanted to tell the story of austerity, the Eurozone crisis, the 2015 UK election and its aftermath, and Brexit and Donald Trump as I saw it at the time to emphasise that these were no accidents that we only understand in hindsight, but disasters that were obvious as they were happening. I wanted to call the book *The Lies We Were Told* because I became increasingly aware that expertise and knowledge that could have told us what was happening as it happened was being ignored or diluted.

During the period covered with these posts I increasingly saw the media as a kind of filter that distorted reality to suit a political received wisdom at the time. The coalition government in the UK wanted to tell stories of 'maxed out credit cards' and 'clearing up the mess Labour left', and both the partisan and broadcast media largely obliged, despite both stories being untrue and the majority of experts knowing them to be untrue. We would probably have had UK austerity whatever the media had done, but the same cannot be said of the 2015 UK general election. Mediamacro talked about a strong economy, when by any historical standards the economy was exceptionally weak, and it focused on the deficit rather than living standards, both of which were probably enough to swing that election to the Conservatives. With Brexit expertise was diluted and the lies told by the partisan media were not challenged by the broadcast media. That could well have been worth the 2% required to change the outcome of that vote. Someone totally unsuited to the White House became President in part because the non-partisan media wanted to talk about Clinton's emails.

One of my great regrets is that, because this view of the power of the media appeared to be a minority view, I failed to be brave when it came to the UK general election in 2017. I have not included any posts on this period in the book because its importance is as yet unclear, but you will probably recall that since Corbyn's election as leader Labour's poll ratings had been very poor. As the election began they were even worse, and May was predicted to win by a landslide. But in the following three weeks we saw the most remarkable swing to Labour.

As I wrote five days before the poll, and wished I had predicted earlier, the reason for this unprecedented surge was that general election rules meant both parties were now speaking directly to voters instead of information being filtered by the media. In that three weeks politicians had much more power in choosing the agenda and getting their message across than at any other time. The filter the media used to select and package the news had been largely turned off, and the results were dramatic.

The conventional story of that election focuses on the poor judgement of May's team in writing their manifesto and Corbyn's abilities at campaigning. This is unconvincing as a complete explanation for two reasons. First, the received wisdom had been that election campaigns make little difference. Second, the qualities in each leader and their teams that this three weeks had exposed were clear before the election. They were clear but largely hidden from the public.

What we saw during that election campaign was the power of the media's filter through what happened in its absence. The normal filter was not just anti-Corbyn or pro-government bias. Political commentators talk positively about who they think are winners and vice versa. The polls before the election, coupled with received wisdom that no one from the 'radical left' could be popular, generated self-fulfilling negative political commentary.

There are many people who would dearly wish we could go back to a time before Brexit and Donald Trump. One of the other things I hope I have shown in this book is that both events are not some kind of freak event that will never occur again. They are instead very much the product of recent history, and we have to recognise this if we want to stop either happening again or happening elsewhere. I start with austerity because that is when this blog began, but I also think austerity is an essential part of the Brexit and Trump story, much more so than the global financial crisis.

The global financial crisis was obviously a very important event in itself, but it certainly need not have led to austerity. In 2009 governments around the world put together fiscal stimulus packages which helped prevent a rerun of the 1930s depression. It was the election of a right-wing government in the UK that gave us front-loaded austerity that delayed the recovery for three years. It was the Republican Party in the US that blocked larger stimulus packages. It was the Eurozone crisis that allowed ordoliberal German influence on the Eurozone to impose widespread austerity and a second recession.

Without austerity in the UK we could have had a recovery that was strong and long. Instead the political right used immigration as a scapegoat for the impact of austerity, which in turn was the means by which Brexiteers and the right-wing press were able to win the EU referendum vote. The essential question to ask, therefore, is not why do some on the right support Brexit, but why did the Conservatives (in 2008) and Liberal Democrats (in 2010) embrace austerity? Equally in the US, although Trump has given us the quintessential plutocratic authoritarian administration, the Republican Party has for many years become more polarised, moving further to the right and putting a greater emphasis on tax cuts for the rich. In Europe austerity has helped accelerate the decline of centre-left parties, and has provided a gift to the far right in various countries.

A lot of the discussion about Brexit and Trump look at them as populist movements, and focus on both as a kind of revolt by those left behind by globalisation. I think neoliberalism does encourage a lack of concern for those whose lives are fundamentally changed by globalisation or technical progress. However, I believe neoliberalism is implicated in both Brexit and Trump in many more ways: through austerity, encouraging anti-immigration and racist rhetoric, and in creating a degree of inequality at the top that is damaging in both economic and political terms. Even if Trump and the Republicans are ejected by the electorate, and Brexit self-destructs or becomes softer than soft, we need to explore why they and austerity happened in order to ensure they do not happen again.

When I started writing my blog, I thought I would probably run out of ideas within a few months, in part because I thought I would be largely talking to myself. Instead I found myself part of an international conversation among economists who knew austerity was wrong and dangerous, and that knowledge and sometimes even basic facts were being excluded from their national debate. It seemed both natural and important to move beyond the specifics of the macroeconomics of austerity to explore issues to do with the media and Brexit. Having written over a thousand posts, many repetitive and many of the moment, it seemed the right time to gather what still seemed important into this book. I hope you have found it of interest.

NOTES

Introduction
1   IPSOS/MORI poll of Royal Economic Society economists commissioned by the *Observer* and published on 28 May 2016.

Chapter 1
1   Paul Krugman (2013) 'How the case for austerity has crumbled', *New York Review of Books*, 6 June.

2   See S. Wren-Lewis (2011) 'Lessons from failure: fiscal policy, indulgence and ideology', *National Institute Economic Review*, 217, no 1, pp R31–R46. For those who like their theory state of the art, see M. Woodford (2011) 'Simple analytics of the government expenditure multiplier', *American Economic Journal of Macroeconomics*, 3, pp 1–35.

3   Jonathan Portes (2012) 'Moody's downgrade: both Osborne and Balls get it wrong', NIESR blog, 14 February, https://www.niesr.ac.uk/blog/moodys-downgrade-both-osborne-and-balls-get-it-wrong

4   'United Kingdom: 2010 Article IV consultation—staff report; staff supplement; public information notice on the Executive Board discussion; and statement by the Executive Director for the United

Kingdom' (2010), International Monetary Fund, November, www.imf. org/external/pubs/ft/scr/2010/cr10338.pdf

5   Mark Thoma (2018) 'The purpose of macroeconomic policy?' Economist's View blog post, 28 January.

6   P. De Grauwe (2011) 'The European Central Bank: lender of last resort in government debt markets?', CESifo Working Paper 3569.

7   Jonathan Portes (2012) 'It's not too late to change course: Macbeth and fiscal policy', NIESR blog, 27 March, www.niesr.ac.uk/blog/its-not-too-late-change-course-macbeth-and-fiscal-policy

8   Jeremy Warner (2013) 'Oh boy! There was nothing wrong with fiscal policy under Labour, says top economics prof', *Daily Telegraph,* 19 June.

9   Bovine TB: The scientific evidence (2007) 'Final report of the Independent Scientific Group on Cattle TB', June.

10   P. Bateson et al (2012) 'Culling badgers could increase the problem of TB in cattle',*Guardian*, 14 October, https://www.theguardian.com/theobserver/2012/oct/14/letters-observer

11   Damian Carrington and Jamie Doward (2012) 'Badger cull "mindless", say scientists', *Guardian*, 13 October, https://www.theguardian.com/environment/2012/oct/13/badger-cull-mindless

12   'Badger culls "could increase TB levels"' (2012) *BBC News*, 14 October, https://www.bbc.co.uk/news/uk-19939393

13   Jill Treanor and Rajeev Syal (2013) 'George Osborne under pressure as Britain loses AAA rating for first time', *Guardian*, 23 February, https://www.theguardian.com/business/2013/feb/23/george-osborne-britain-aaa

14   'Clegg says Coalition was wrong to cut capital spending' (2013) *BBC News*, 25 January, https://www.bbc.co.uk/news/uk-politics-21190108

15   'David Cameron's economy speech in full' (2013), politics.co.uk, 7 March, http://www.politics.co.uk/comment-analysis/2013/03/07/david-cameron-s-economy-speech-in-full

16   B.J. DeLong and L.H. Summers (2012) 'Fiscal policy in a depressed economy', Brookings Papers, Spring.

17   Jeremy Warner (2013) *Daily Telegraph*, 11 September.

18   Chris Dillow (2014) 'The outcome bias', 2 January, http://stumblingandmumbling.typepad.com/stumbling_and_mumbling/2014/01/the-outcome-bias-.html

19 S. Wren-Lewis, P. Westaway, S. Soteri and R. Barrell (1991) 'Evaluating the UK's choice of entry rate into the ERM', Manchester School, 59, no S1, pp 1–22. Although this paper was published after we entered the ERM, the analysis was first published and publicised before we entered.

20 George Osborne: Policy making after the crash (2009) 'Conservative Party Speeches', 8 April, https://conservative-speeches.sayit.mysociety. org/speech/601376

21 S. Wren-Lewis (2017) 'A general theory of austerity' in *Debating austerity in Ireland: crisis, experience and recovery*, ed Emma Heffernan, John McHale and Niamh Moore-Cherry, Royal Irish Academy. See also Blavatnik School of Government Working Paper 2016/14.

Chapter 2

1 Benjamin Fox (2013) 'French tax hikes would "destroy" growth, EU says', euobserver, 26 August, https://euobserver.com/news/121205

2 Jan in't Veld (2013) 'Fiscal consolidations and spillovers in the euro area periphery and core', *European Economy Economic Papers* 506.

3 Dawn Holland and Jonathan Portes (2012) 'Self defeating austerity?', *National Institute Economic Review*, no 222, pp F4–10.

4 Philippe Martin and Thomas Philippon (2014) 'What caused the great recession in the Eurozone? What could have avoided it?', *VoxEU*, 11 November.

5 A. Kentikelenis, M. Karanikolos, A. Reeves, M. McKee and David Stuckler (2014) 'Greece's health crisis: from austerity to denialism', *The Lancet*, 383, pp 748–753.

6 Jim Donnelly (2011) 'The Irish Famine', BBC History website, http://www.bbc.co.uk/history/british/victorians/famine_01.shtml

7 'Genocide and the famine' (2011) *The Irish Times*, 7 September, https://www.irishtimes.com/opinion/letters/genocide-and-the-famine-1.592889

8 Peter Doyle (2015) 'The euro and the IMF now', *FT Alphaville*, 17 April.

9 Thomas Piketty, Jeffrey D. Sachs, Heiner Flassbeck, Dani Rodrik and Simon Wren-Lewis (2015) 'Austerity has failed: An open letter from Thomas Piketty to Angela Merkel', *The Nation*, 7 July, https://www.

thenation.com/article/austerity-has-failed-an-open-letter-from-thomas-piketty-to-angela-merkel/

10   Peter Bofinger (2015) 'German wage moderation and the EZ Crisis', *VoxEU*, 30 November.

Chapter 3

1   D.K. (2013) 'Breeding discontent', *The Economist,* 4 April.
2   Nicholas Watt (2013) 'George Osborne "playing politics" with Philpott deaths', *Guardian*, 5 April, https://www.theguardian.com/politics/2013/apr/05/george-osborne-playing-politics-philpott; Patrick Wintour (2013), 'George Osborne "cynical" to link Philpott case with welfare cuts, says Ed Balls', *Guardian*, 5 April, https://www.theguardian.com/politics/2013/apr/04/balls-osborne-philpott-welfare-attack . See also Peter Walker (2013) 'Ed Miliband attacks Tories' "divisive politics" in Philpott benefits row', *Guardian*, 8 April, https://www.theguardian.com/politics/2013/apr/08/ed-miliband-divisive-politics-benefits
3   OECD Economic Outlook Statistical Appendix and James Cusick (2013) 'Fall in wages puts Britain in Europe's bottom four', *The Independent*, 11 August, https://www.independent.co.uk/news/uk/politics/fall-in-wages-puts-britain-in-europes-bottom-four-8755957.html
4   'Introduction to IFS's assessment of the 2013 Autumn Statement' (2013) 6 December; Andy McSmith (2013) 'PM denies two child limit for benefits is part of Tory welfare policy', *The Independent*, 15 December, https://www.independent.co.uk/news/uk/politics/pm-denies-two-child-limit-for-benefits-is-part-of-tory-welfare-policy-9006056.html
5   Trussell Trust data can be found here: https://www.trusselltrust.org/news-and-blog/latest-stats/.
6   http://webarchive.nationalarchives.gov.uk/20100702215619/http://archive.cabinetoffice.gov.uk/pittreview/thepittreview/final_report.html
7   Michael Amior, Rowena Crawford and Gemma Tetlow (2013) 'Fiscal sustainability for an independent Scotland, Institute for Fiscal Studies, https://www.ifs.org.uk/comms/r88.pdf, 35.
8   Rev. Stuart Campbell (2014) 'The wee blue book', Wings over Scotland, 11 August, https://wingsoverscotland.com/weebluebook/
9   Simon Wren-Lewis (2015) 'Autumn Statement: Forget the idea that parts of the public sector will be protected', *The Independent*, 25 November, https://www.independent.co.uk/voices/autumn-

statement-forget-the-idea-that-parts-of-the-public-sector-will-be-protected-a6749096.html

10   John Appleby (2015) 'NHS spending: squeezed as never before', The King's Fund, 20 October.

11   See Sarah Bloch (2016) 'Hunt "misrepresented" data on 7-day NHS', *BBC News*, 24 February, https://www.bbc.co.uk/news/health-35597243

12   See note 9 above.

Chapter 4

1   George Parker and Emily Cadman (2015) 'Osborne claims high ground as GDP rises' *Financial Times*, 27 January, https://www.ft.com/content/49f26424-a64a-11e4-9bd3-00144feab7de#axzz3QOvhmikN

2   Graham Ruddick (2015) 'Labour government will be catastrophic for Britain, warns Boots boss', *The Telegraph*, 31 January, https://www.telegraph.co.uk/finance/newsbysector/retailandconsumer/11382145/Labour-government-will-be-catastrophic-for-Britain-warns-Boots-boss.html

3   'The importance of elections for UK economic activity' (2015) The CFM Surveys, 28 March, http://cfmsurvey.org/surveys/importance-elections-uk-economic-activity

Chapter 5

1   Paul Bernal (2015) 'Labour didn't lose the election in 2015', Paul Bernal's blog, 18 May, https://paulbernal.wordpress.com/2015/05/18/labour-didnt-lose-the-election-in-2015/

2   Simon Wren-Lewis (2013) 'Aggregate fiscal policy under the Labour government, 1997–2010', *Oxford Review of Economic Policy*, 29, 1, pp 25–46.

3   Jonathan Hopkin and Ben Rosamond (2015) 'Deficit fetishism and the art of political bullshit', SPERI Comment, 15 July.

4   Simon Wren-Lewis (2015) 'Forget "Corbynomics": Labour's leadership can win over the party and the voters by smart politics', *The Independent*, 27 September, https://www.independent.co.uk/news/business/comment/forget-corbynomics-labour-s-leadership-can-win-over-the-party-and-the-voters-by-smart-politics-a6669691.html

5   Jonathan Portes and Simon Wren-Lewis (2015) 'Issues in the design of fiscal rules', *Manchester School*, 83, pp 56–86.

6   OBR Public Finance Databank, http://obr.uk/data/

Chapter 6
1   Jonathan Portes (2013) 'Immigration as a growth strategy', NIESR
       blog, 9 January, https://www.niesr.ac.uk/blog/immigration-growth-
       strategy
2   See M. Ayhan Kose and Marco Terrones (2012) 'Uncertainty weighing
       on the global recovery', Vox, 18 October, https://voxeu.org/article/
       uncertainty-weighing-global-recovery; Scott Baker, Nicholas Bloom,
       Steven Davis, and John Van Reenen (2012) 'Economic recovery and
       policy uncertainty in the US', Vox, 29 October, https://voxeu.org/article/
       economic-recovery-and-policy-uncertainty-us
3   See Sonia Sodha, Toby Helm and Phillip Inman (2016) 'Economists
       overwhelmingly reject Brexit in boost for Cameron', *Guardian*, 28 May,
       https://www.theguardian.com/politics/2016/may/28/economists-reject-
       brexit-boost-cameron
4   Freddie Sayers (2016) 'Campaign memo: It's the economy
       versus immigration', YouGovUK, 28 April, https://yougov.co.uk/
       news/2016/04/28/campaign-memo-its-economy-versus-immigration/
5   Nadia Khomami (2016) 'Daily Mail publishes correction to story about
       "migrants from Europe"', *Guardian*, 17 June, https://www.theguardian.
       com/media/2016/jun/17/daily-mail-publishes-correction-story-migrants-
       from-europe?CMP=share_btn_tw
6   David Deacon, Dominic Wring, Emily Harmer, James Stanyer and John
       Downey (2016) 'Hard evidence: analysis shows extent of press bias
       towards Brexit', *The Conversation*, 16 June, https://theconversation.
       com/hard-evidence-analysis-shows-extent-of-press-bias-towards-
       brexit-61106
7   Tim Bale (2017) 'Truth to tell: populism and the immigration debate',
       LSE, 1 March, http://blogs.lse.ac.uk/politicsandpolicy/truth-to-tell-
       brexit-will-not-reduce-migration/
8   David Goodhart (2017) *The road to somewhere: The populist revolt and
       the future of politics*, C.Hurst and Co.

Chapter 7
1   Steve Schifferes (2012) 'Fair and balanced? The audience view of
       media coverage of the financial crisis', Presentation to the BBC Trust, 6

November, https://www.slideshare.net/cityjournalism/fair-and-balanced-the-audience-view-of-media-coverage-of-the-crisis

2 'Perceptions are not reality' (2013) IPSOS/MORI, 9 July, https://www.ipsos.com/ipsos-mori/en-uk/perceptions-are-not-reality

3 See note 2 above.

4 Simon Wren-Lewis (2013) 'What is wrong with the USA?' *mainly macro*, 23 October, https://mainlymacro.blogspot.com/2013/10/what-is-wrong-with-usa.html

5 Jason Cowley (2014) 'Ed Miliband's problem is not policy but tone – and increasingly he seems trapped', *New Statesman*, 5 November, https://www.newstatesman.com/politics/2014/11/ed-miliband-s-problem-not-policy-tone-and-increasingly-he-seems-trapped

6 Bill Emmott (2014) 'Cheshire Cat smiles mask danger in UK politics', *Financial Times*, 21 November.

7 Polly Toynbee (2014) 'Labour must fight off these bogus Tory attacks on class', *Guardian*, 25 November, https://www.theguardian.com/commentisfree/2014/nov/25/labour-tory-class-right-emily-thornberry-left-inequality

8 Jonathan McDonald Ladd and Gabriel Lenz (2009) 'Exploiting a rare communication shift to document the persuasive power of the news media', *American Journal of Political Science*, 53, pp 394–410.

9 Simon Wren-Lewis (2014) 'Government debt, financial markets and dead parrots', *mainly macro*, 4 December, https://mainlymacro.blogspot.com/2014/12/government-debt-financial-markets-and.html

10 Robert Peston (2014) 'The £50 billion gap between Tories and Labour', 4 December, BBC website.

11 Simon Wren-Lewis (2014) 'More mediamacro', *mainly macro*, 25 September, https://mainlymacro.blogspot.com/2014/09/more-mediamacro.html

12 Robert Peston (2015) 'A budget that will define this government', *BBC News*, 4 June, https://www.bbc.co.uk/news/business-33003955

13 A. Sen (2015) 'The economic consequences of austerity', *New Statesman*, 4 June.

14 Thomas E. Patterson (2016) 'Pre-primary news coverage of the 2016 presidential race: Trump's rise, Sanders' emergence, Clinton's struggle', Shorenstein Centre, 13 June.

15   S. Wren-Lewis (2016) 'What Brexit and austerity tell us about economics, policy and the media', SPERI Paper 36, University of Sheffield.

16   'Mission to explain', powerbase, http://powerbase.info/index.php/Mission_to_explain

17   Gregory J. Martin and Ali Yurukoglu (2017) 'Bias in cable news: persuasion and polarization', *American Economic Review*, 107, pp 2565–99.

18   Aaron Sharockman (2015) 'MSNBC, Fox, CNN move the needle on our Truth-O-Meter scorecards', PUNDITFACT, https://www.politifact.com/punditfact/article/2015/jan/27/msnbc-fox-cnn-move-needle-our-truth-o-meter-scorec/

Chapter 8

1   Paul Krugman (2011) 'A note on the Ricardian equivalence argument against stimulus (slightly wonkish)', *The New York Times*, 26 December, https://krugman.blogs.nytimes.com/2011/12/26/a-note-on-the-ricardian-equivalence-argument-against-stimulus-slightly-wonkish/

2   John H. Cochrane (2010) 'Fiscal stimulus, RIP,' 9 November, http://faculty.chicagobooth.edu/john.cochrane/research/papers/stimulus_rip.html

3   Grasping reality with both hands: Bradford-delong.com (2012) 'Understanding the Chicago anti-stimulus arguments: A response to Kantoos', 4 January, http://delong.typepad.com/sdj/2012/01/understanding-the-chicago-anti-stimulus-arguments-a-response-to-kantoos.html

4   John H. Cochrane (2009) 'Fiscal stimulus, fiscal inflation, or fiscal fallacies?', 27 February, http://faculty.chicagobooth.edu/john.cochrane/research/papers/fiscal2.htm

5   See 'EMU studies on membership of the single currency', http://webarchive.nationalarchives.gov.uk/20081230225657/http://www.hm-treasury.gov.uk/euro_assess03_studindex.htm

6   If anyone ever asks whether I can keep a secret, I always give this as evidence that I can. The original work I did for the study was done and written up in 2002. At the time the euro/sterling rate was at or near 1.6 €/£, and my analysis suggested something closer to 1.4 €/£ was sustainable. So for nearly a year I sat on information that was extremely market sensitive, and I received plenty of phone calls trying to extract

any hint at what my analysis would be, and I'm glad to say no one got anything out of those calls. Alas, I also felt it would be improper for me to bet on my own analysis, which had been funded by the Treasury: perhaps that just makes me an honest fool.

7   MEG98 Dave Ramsden, 'The euro: 10th anniversary of the assessment of the five economic tests' (2013), YouTube, https://www.youtube.com/watch?v=sB2IZObvaUU

8   A. Admati and M. Hellwig (2013) *The bankers' new clothes: what's wrong with banking and what to do about it*, Princeton, NJ: Princeton University Press.

9   Martin Wolf (2013) 'Why bankers are intellectually naked', *Financial Times*, 17 March, https://www.ft.com/content/39c38b74-715d-11e2-9b5c-00144feab49a#axzz2PCSpoST7

10   M. Blyth (2013) *Austerity: the history of a dangerous idea*, Oxford: Oxford University Press.

11   Simon Wren-Lewis (2013) 'Defending rational expectations', *mainly macro*, 7 November, https://mainlymacro.blogspot.com/2013/11/defending-rational-expectations.html

12   Tim Harford (2015) 'The economists' manifesto', *Financial Times*, 17 April.

13   S. Wren-Lewis (2015) 'The knowledge transmission mechanism and austerity', Social Europe (with Hans Böckler Stiftung), https://www.socialeurope.eu/book/re-no-7-the-knowledge-transmission-mechanism-and-austerity

14   James Forder (2014) *Macroeconomics and the Philips curve myth*, Oxford: Oxford University Press.

15   Commentary: 'Monetary policy implications of greater fiscal discipline' (1995) from Symposium Proceedings, Budget Deficits and Debt: Issues and Options, Federal Reserve Bank of Kansas City.

16   Daniel Hausman (1992) *The inexact and separate science of economics,* Cambridge: Cambridge University Press.

17   Dani Rodrik (2015) *Economics Rules*, New York: Norton.

18   Anne Case and Angus Deaton (2015) 'Rising morbidity and mortality in midlife among white non-Hispanic Americans in the 21st century', *Proceedings of the National Academy of Science*, 112, pp 15078–15083.

19   Anne Case and Angus Deaton (2017) 'Mortality and morbidity in the 21st century', Brookings Papers, Spring.

Chapter 9

1   Aeron Davis (2012) 'Lamentable media coverage and state deception, the scandal of NHS legislation', *Open Democracy*, 24 March.

2   P. Gregg, L. Macmillan and B. Nasim (2012) 'The impact of fathers' job loss during the recession of the 1980s on their children's educational attainment and labour market outcomes', *Fiscal Studies*, 33, pp 237–264.

3   Thomas Piketty, Emmanuel Saez and Stefanie Stantcheva (2014) 'Optimal taxation of top labor incomes: a tale of three elasticities', *American Economic Journal: Economic Policy*, 6, pp 230–271.

4   Tony Yates (2014) 'Pensions reform: adverse selection, our future selves, and intergenerational risk sharing', longandvariable, 26 March, https://longandvariable.wordpress.com/2014/03/26/pensions-reform-adverse-selection-our-future-selves-and-intergenerational-risk-sharing/ ; Carl Emmerson (2014) 'Budget 2014: Pensions and saving policies', Institute for Fiscal Studies, https://www.ifs.org.uk/budgets/budget2014/pensions_saving.pdf

5   João Paulo Pessoa and John Van Reenen (2013) 'Decoupling of wage growth and productivity growth? Myth and reality', CEP Discussion Paper No 1246.

6   Brian Bell and John Van Reenen (2010) 'Bankers' pay and extreme wage inequality in the UK', CEP Special Papers 21, Centre for Economic Performance, LSE.

7   Corey Robin (2016) 'The first neoliberals', Jacobin, 28 April, https://www.jacobinmag.com/2016/04/chait-neoliberal-new-inquiry-democrats-socialism/

8   Oliver Hartwich and Razeen Sally (2009) 'Neoliberalism: The genesis of a political swearword', Centre for Independent Studies, 21 May.

9   Mariana Mazzucato (2013) *The Entrepreneurial State*, London: Anthem Press. Revised edition published in 2018 by Penguin.

10   Philip Mirowski (2016) 'This is water (or is it neoliberalism?)', Institute for New Economic Thinking, 25 May.

11   Colin Crouch (2017) 'Can neoliberalism be saved from itself?', *Social Europe* Edition, https://www.socialeurope.eu/book/can-neoliberalism-saved

12   https://twitter.com/paulkrugman/status/880035577764229120

13 Tom Clark (2015) 'Blair's frail legacy shows why Labour must win arguments as well as votes', *Guardian*, https://www.theguardian.com/commentisfree/2015/dec/11/blair-frail-legacy-labour-corbynistas

14 Jan-Werner Muller (2017) 'How populists win when they lose', *Social Europe*, 29 June, https://www.socialeurope.eu/populists-win-lose

15 William Davies (2017) 'Reasons for Corbyn', *London Review of Books*, 13 July.

16 Bruce Bartlett (2015) 'How Fox News changed American media and political dynamics', *The Big Picture*, 21 May.

INDEX